Flexible Families

Flexible Families

Nicaraguan Transnational Families in Costa Rica

CAITLIN E. FOURATT

Vanderbilt University Press
Nashville, Tennessee

Parts of Chapter Two appeared in Caitlin E. Fouratt, "Temporary Measures: The Production of Illegality in Costa Rican Immigration Law," *PoLAR: Political and Legal Anthropology Review* 39, no. 1 (2016): 144–60.

Map shape files source: Humanitarian Data Exchange (data.humdata.org), contributed by UNFIS and UNROLAC under (CC BY-IGO). https://data.humdata.org/dataset/costa-rica-subnational-administrative-boundaries and https://data.humdata.org/dataset/nicaragua-administrative-level-0.

Library of Congress Cataloging-in-Publication Data
Names: Fouratt, Caitlin E., 1982– author.
Title: Flexible families : Nicaraguan transnational families in Costa Rica
  / Caitlin E. Fouratt.
Description: Nashville : Vanderbilt University Press, [2022] | Includes
  bibliographical references and index.
Identifiers: LCCN 2021047923 (print) | LCCN 2021047924 (ebook) | ISBN
  9780826504364 (Paperback) | ISBN 9780826504371 (Hardcover) | ISBN
  9780826504388 (ePub) | ISBN 9780826504395 (PDF)
Subjects: LCSH: Immigrant families—Nicaragua. | Nicaragua—Emigration and
  immigration—Social aspects. | Nicaragua—Emigration and
  immigration—Economic aspects. | Women immigrants—Family
  relationships—Nicaragua. | Grandmothers—Family
  relationships—Nicaragua. | Children of immigrants—Family
  relationships—Nicaragua. | Fatherless families—Nicaragua. |
  Grandparents as parents—Nicaragua. | Intergenerational
  relations—Nicaragua. | Transnationalism—Social aspects—Nicaragua.
Classification: LCC JV7426 .F68 2022 (print) | LCC JV7426 (ebook) | DDC
  305.8959/72077285—dc23/eng/20220111
LC record available at https://lccn.loc.gov/2021047923
LC ebook record available at https://lccn.loc.gov/2021047924

To Magda and Arlo. To family, near and far.

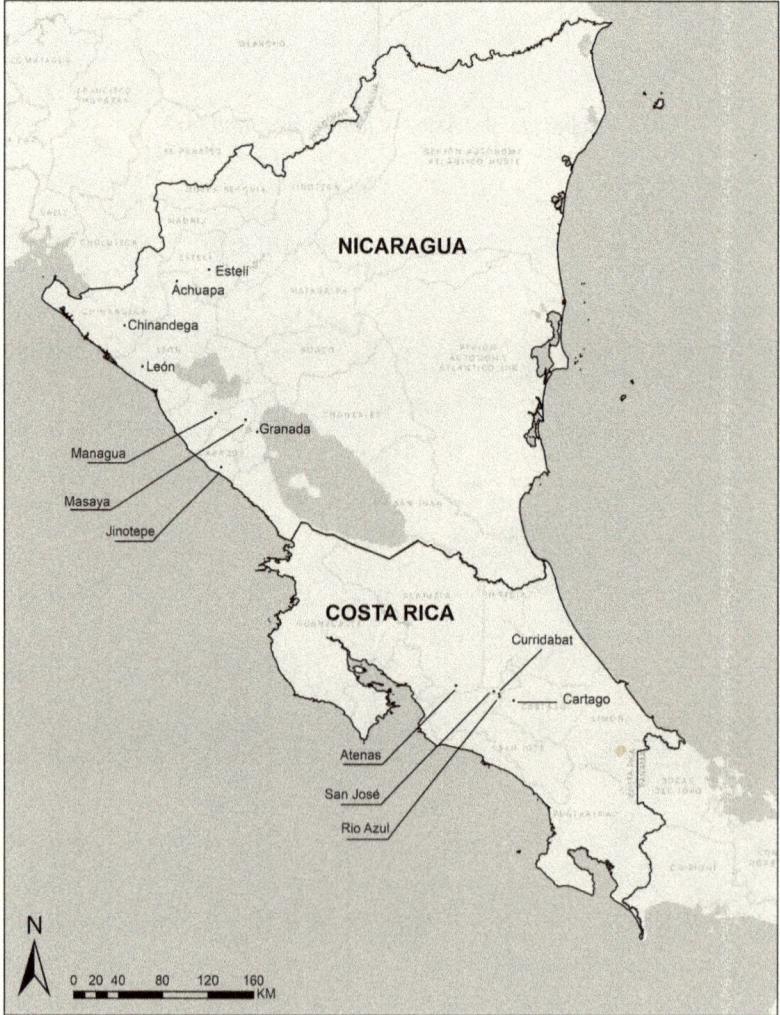

Map of Nicaragua and Costa Rica. Sites added. BaseMap Source Credits: Esri, HERE, Garmin, © OpenStreetMap contributors, and the GIS user community.

CONTENTS

ACKNOWLEDGMENTS

This book would not have been possible without the contributions of so many who cannot be named here for reasons of confidentiality, especially the families in both Costa Rica and Nicaragua who allowed us into their homes and shared meals, parenting advice, and more. To the women who continue to hold and support me in community both in Central America and in California through fieldwork, academic life, parenting, and the pandemic, I owe you immense gratitude.

The research for this book was generously supported by the Department of Anthropology and Center for Global Peace and Conflict Studies at University of California, Irvine, a Wenner-Gren fellowship, and an IIE Graduate Fellowship for International Study. Funding from California State University, Long Beach and a Wenner-Gren Engaged Research Grant allowed me to return to the field, follow up with the families with whom I worked, and share my research with them as well as with colleagues and students in Costa Rica. The open seminar Koen Voorend and I hosted at the University of Costa Rica in 2015 provided me with feedback and insight from a number of Costa Rican students, scholars, and community organizers who are cited or interviewed in this book.

My love for research and interest in migration in Costa Rica can be traced to a student Fulbright grant. For that, I owe the continuous support of Jane Morris and the Villanova University Honors Program and Center for Peace and Justice Education, especially Carol Anthony and Sue Toton. My understanding of the politics and pragmatics of the development and migration landscape in Costa Rica is largely thanks to my time working at the International Center for Development Studies and its predecessor,

El Centro Internacional del Desarrollo Humano, and the researchers and friends I met there, especially Mimi Prado, Marta Trejos, Jorge Nowalski, Bernardita Rodriguez, Laura Sariego, Aitor Llodio, and others. The project began to take shape while at Cambridge University with the support of the faculty, staff, and students of the Centre of Latin American Studies, especially Sian Lazar and David Lehmann.

I owe enormous debts to the mentors, friends, and colleagues who have helped me think through this project, from inception to writing. At UC Irvine, the mentorship and unconditional support of Leo Chavez and Susan Coutin in my professional and personal life allowed me to grow as a scholar and learn to balance family and academic work as well as any of us are able. Feedback from the Socio-Legal Studies Workshops at the UCI Center in Law, Society and Culture was crucial to my thinking about immigration policy and illegality. Mentorship and support from the Center for Global Peace and Conflict Studies was also critical in the early stages of research.

My writing has benefitted from participation in several writing communities. I appreciate those who have offered their insight especially Taylor Nelms, Eva Yonas, Lydia Dixon, Ather Zia, Janny Li, Stevie Rea, Sean Mallin, and other colleagues from UCI Anthropology. I am thankful for the generous scholarship and engagement of Leisy Abrego, Lynnette Arnold, Deanna Barenboim, Debbie Boehm, Carmen Caamaño, Katie Dingeman, Ruth Gomberg-Muñoz, Laura Paniagua, Megan Rivers-Moore, Jelena Radovic-Fanta, Leila Rodriguez, Carlos Sandoval, Koen Voorend, Joe Wiltberger, Nanneke Winters, and Kristin Yarris, among others. Tanya Golash-Boza's virtual writing retreat came at a crucial moment in the writing process. My colleagues at CSULB have provided invaluable writing support and encouragement, and I owe a special thanks to Yousef Baker, Laura Ceia, Norma Chinchilla, Christine El-Ouardani, Babs Grossman-Thompson, Lauren Heidbrink, Lily House-Peters, Jayne Howell, Richard Marcus, Jolene McCall, Karen Quintiliani, Deborah Thien, Kimberly Walters, and Kris Zentgraf. I also want to thank my editor, Zack Gresham, and the team at Vanderbilt University Press, who made the whole process much less intimidating. Zack's encouragement helped me push through the final writing and revising stages, despite the chaos of pandemic parenting.

My parents, Mary Eileen and Bob, have provided unconditional encouragement and support—from visiting us in Costa Rica and Nicaragua, to traveling to conferences to entertain my kids, to reading drafts of my manuscript. My siblings, Abbey and Andrew, and their partners, Jameson and Nicki, have only increased the levels of humor, sarcasm, and love in our family.

For more than fifteen years, my ex-husband Chris accompanied me as I pursued a PhD that moved us both far from our extended families and conducted research that had us packing suitcases frequently. My sister-in-law Melanny, nephew Alessandro, grandmother-in-law Tita Lali, and dozens of aunts, uncles, and cousins in Costa Rica and beyond embraced me and shared in the work of parenting. It has been a privilege to celebrate, grieve, and love with them. My mother-in-law Luz Marina and my brother-in-law Greivin both passed away far too soon, but what I learned from them about family, loyalty, bravery, and how to properly cook rice will stay with me forever.

This project was born alongside Magdalena, who appears quietly woven throughout these pages, though she was rarely quiet during fieldwork. Arlo arrived as I learned to balance research and writing with teaching and service. Their goofiness, unconditional love, and sense of adventure have accompanied me on many travels and through the COVID-19 pandemic.

"The Family Is a Little Society"

IN A SHADY COURTYARD inside a modest little hotel in Estelí, Nicaragua, my husband and I were enjoying a *cafecito* after a fruitless afternoon of calling migrants in Costa Rica. Families in several of the popular barrios we had been visiting in Estelí had offered us phone numbers for migrant relatives in Costa Rica, but most of those phone numbers were disconnected, or no one answered. Don Marco, a man in his sixties whose home and small artisanal workshop were next to the hotel, joined us to commiserate about the frustrations of working with migrants and their families. A former migrant himself, Marco often offered workshops for family members of migrants, hoping to provide them with skills to produce crafts for tourist markets so they would not have to rely on money sent from abroad. Too many, he said, had been abandoned or lost touch with loved ones in Costa Rica, Spain, or elsewhere. Migration, he felt, was the largest social problem facing Nicaragua. "The family is a little society," he said, "and migration can cause its disintegration at the level of family ties and emotional intimacy. What happens to the larger society," he went on to ask, "when all these little societies fall apart? On what does the larger society become based?"

Marco's provocative questions haunted me as I struggled to connect with, interview, and make sense of the transnational family lives of Nicaraguan migrants in Costa Rica. In Costa Rica and Nicaragua, migration is often blamed for family instability and breakdown as Nicaraguan migrant parents, especially mothers, leave families behind. When I first started out researching Nicaraguan migrants in Costa Rica and their families, one Costa Rican colleague, a sociologist and feminist scholar, told me that in her own research with Nicaraguan seasonal migrant workers, "the frequency of changing partners caught my attention. Nicaraguan women come one year with one partner, the next year with another." She cautioned me to focus my research on "relatively stable families," not those "where they're changing partners frequently." Both Marco and my colleague's statements link family, migration, and social breakdown. That is, to talk about the family and migration is also to talk about the larger society and the nation. Both statements also rely on an understanding of the family as the foundation of social life in addition to being stable and unchanging over time.

Yet "the little society," envisioned as a stable patriarchal, heteronormative nuclear family, has rarely reflected the ways Nicaraguans configure family life. Instead of this rigid, inflexible ideal, families employ a variety of flexible and changing configurations in the face of major economic and political challenges to their well-being. Indeed, half of all unions in Nicaragua take place outside of formal, official marriages, and almost a third of households are single-female headed (Castro Martín 2002; INIDE 2014). Rather than a set of brittle relations that snap or break in the face of economic and other pressures, Nicaraguan family relations bend, flex, fade, and reconnect in unexpected ways in response to the unpredictability of life. Even as public and political discourse revere the traditional nuclear family, Nicaraguans rely on a variety of family configurations and strategies for making do and getting by, including migration, in a context of extreme poverty, inequality, and ineffective public policies. How can we expect families or relationships to remain stable when jobs and access to food are not stable, when life is unpredictable even in its most simple, everyday aspects?

Migration is at once a response to and a result of these unpredictabilities. Indeed, what stuck with me after my conversations with Marco and my colleague was that migration, with its uprooting, leaving, adapting, and moving, was one of few constants in Nicaraguan family life. At its core, migration represents a gamble: migrants hope that by leaving they will be able to provide for their families, especially for children. But the emotional and other costs of their absence may outweigh the economic stability migration can bring. Indeed, the Nicaraguan migrants I worked with often expressed the seemingly contradictory position that migration leads to family breakdown but that people migrate for their families.

I have tried to make sense of how Nicaraguan transnational families build precarious and uncertain lives across borders. Transnational families, that is, families in which members live in two or more countries (Abrego 2009; Baldassar and Merla 2013; Zentgraf and Chinchilla 2012), are fraught with separation and challenge understandings of what—and who—constitutes a family. At the same time, members of transnational families engage in very mundane family-making activities: cooking and feeding, building houses, providing for children, and marriage. As Joanna Dreby (2010) has noted, transnational families are ordinary families in extraordinary situations.

Such families face not only the effects of chronic economic crisis and extreme poverty in Nicaragua but also intense xenophobia and increasingly repressive immigration laws in Costa Rica. Migration paradoxically both enables certain forms of care—by improving families' access to food security, education, and healthcare in Nicaragua—while it also generates new forms of instability and uncertainty through absence, separation, and the vulnerabilities Nicaraguans face as undocumented migrants in Costa Rica. Transnational families, then, provide insight into how people make and remake the meanings of family across borders.

However, a key premise of this book is that these transformations in family configurations and their meanings must be understood through the lens of the uncertainties and instabilities Nicaraguan families have long faced, even before migration. That is, the kinds of family reconfigurations migration entails or produces, including high levels of mobility, marriage instability, and grandmother caregivers, are part of a long history of flexible family configurations in Nicaragua that challenge both the normative nuclear family and assumptions about the importance of physical proximity for sustaining relationships. In particular, I examine two aspects of transnational family life often described as symptoms of family breakdown in public discourse: the decline of traditional, formal marriages and the predominance of cross-generational caregiving. They represent both the instabilities of family life more generally in Nicaragua and the strategies through which Nicaraguans attempt to provide stability and care for children.

Further, such family reconfigurations and relations emerge in relation to state interventions in the economy and the family. Through decisions about migration, families encounter the state on both sides of the border. Across the Costa Rica–Nicaragua border, regional and global trends in immigration law and policy intersect with Nicaragua's legacies of exclusionary politics and the Sandinista Revolution.

Migration within Central America

Although Nicaraguans migrate to various countries, including the United States, Panama, and Spain, over the past three decades, Costa Rica has emerged as the primary destination for Nicaraguan migrants. This book contributes to a growing body of scholarship on South-South (S-S) migration (Carte 2014; De Lombaerde, Guo, and Neto 2014; Fouratt 2014; Sadiq 2009). More than 3 percent of the world's population is on the move across international borders, most from developing countries. And about half of all migrants from developing countries migrate to other developing countries (Ratha and Shaw 2007; Sadiq 2009). Yet we know relatively little about migration within the Global South. Such so-called South-South migration includes not only movement between low-income developing countries but also migration to middle income countries, like Costa Rica, that serve as poles of attraction within developing regions (Khan and Hossain 2017; Kofman and Raghuram 2009).

Examining Nicaraguan migration offers insight into contested and relevant migration dynamics within the Central American region. While much scholarly, public, and political attention has been focused on migration from the northern countries of Central America, especially El Salvador, Guatemala, and Honduras, to the United States, this book looks south to migration dynamics between one of Latin America's most politically and economically stable democracies and one of the region's poorest post-conflict countries. Shared turbulent histories of political conflict and economic crisis have produced an intimate but unequal relationship among the countries of Central America and transformed Costa Rica into a major migrant destination within Latin America. While in sheer size Central American migration to the US dwarfs migration to Costa Rica, the country represents an important migrant destination within Latin America. Indeed, Costa Rica has the highest percent of foreign-born population of any Latin American country, followed by Argentina, which has functioned as another key center of attraction within regional migration systems (Cerrutti and Parrado 2015).

This case of South-South migration highlights the consequences of uneven processes of regional development. In Costa Rica's case, part of what makes it a migrant destination is its position vis-à-vis the US economy. Both the tourism and service sector more broadly have generated high demand for immigrant labor, filled primarily by Nicaraguans. In contrast, as I will discuss later, Nicaragua's experiences with global capitalism have resulted in deepening inequality and the absence of a social safety net. Much theory on migration assumes South-North (S-N) movements and the primary importance of wage differentials. However, S-S migration is also economically motivated, not always only by concern about wage differentials but also about access to services, escaping interpersonal and political violence, and more (Khan and Hossain 2017). Thus, Nicaraguan migration to Costa Rica provides a particularly fruitful site to examine the legacies of political and economic crisis in Central America through the juxtaposition of Nicaragua, a former socialist country plagued by political instability and extreme poverty, and Costa Rica, a poster child for liberal democracy, peace, and economic stability.

Key to migration dynamics within Central America is also the high rate of economic informality in the region's economies and among migrant workers. The informal economy includes all income-earning activities that are not regulated by the state but normally would be. It can include small businesses and informally contracted labor, as well as companies that avoid regulations, including taxes. While it has long been noted that immigrants are likely to work in the informal sector in destination countries like the United States, the larger size and scope of this sector in Latin America mean that migrants are highly likely to work within it both before and after they migrate. In Nicaragua, for example, 80 percent of workers are employed in the informal sector (Narvaez and Rivera 2016). In Costa Rica, 40 percent of jobs are in the informal economy, and they are concentrated in sectors in which Nicaraguan migrants are clustered: 80 percent of domestic worker jobs and 60 percent of construction jobs are informal (Delgado Jiménez 2013). Economic informality thus represents a factor both driving Nicaraguan emigration and attracting Nicaraguan migrants to Costa Rica. This high level of informality is important because jobs in this sector are less stable, have lower wages, and rarely provide access to health insurance or other benefits.

Other forms of informality also play a role in South-South migration dynamics. Informal settlements are often the first stop for many migrants in the global South (Alvarado 2020). These settlements, sometimes referred to as slums or squatter settlements, are not just zones of unregulated house construction but are also often at the margins of state services like water, electricity, and security even as they are heavily policed. In Costa Rica, all of the migrants I worked with lived in informal settlements at one point during their time in Costa Rica. Some made their homes there long-term; others used such communities as stopping points as they got settled, found work, and saved money to rent or buy homes in less marginalized and stigmatized areas.

In terms of transnational family life, migration within Central America entails different expectations for maintaining family relationships, sending remittances, and making return visits than migration to other, farther destinations. For example, during Easter and Christmas holidays, some seventy thousand Nicaraguan migrants in Costa Rica cross back to visit family (Solano 2013). Relatively short and inexpensive travel between the two countries also facilitates movement, and until recently, lax border enforcement made migration without documentation relatively low risk. At the same time, cultural similarities and a shared language make settlement relatively easy for Nicaraguans in Costa Rica. This has generated a situation in which there are high levels of both cross-border movement and settlement in Costa Rica, strengthening transnational dynamics.

Costa Rica has often been held up as a model of human rights because of its well-developed system of rights, hospitable orientation, and universal public welfare system. Yet over the past fifteen years, it has made accessing legal status and public services much more difficult for migrants. Although in the US we tend to hear a lot about undocumented migration, in reality, less than a quarter of all immigrants to the US are undocumented. In contrast, given the porousness of borders and weak border and immigration enforcement in developing countries, South-South migrations tend to be dominated by high levels of migrant irregularity or "illegality" (Khan and Hossain 2017). In Costa Rica, estimates of the undocumented population range up to 50 percent of the total foreign-born population (Acuña and Olivares 2000; Voorend 2016). Further, requirements to renew permanent residency every few years and other new laws have increased restrictions on regularizing status and accessing documents (Fouratt 2016; Sandoval García 2013). This contrast between the affordances offered migrants on paper versus the difficulties of accessing legal status, public services, and more offers insight into how even ostensibly welcoming host countries generate exclusion among migrant populations.

"A Multiply Wounded Country"

Costa Rica's national monument offers a striking image of the intimate and unequal relationship between Nicaragua and Costa Rica. The statue, located in the Parque Nacional in front of the National Library in downtown San José, portrays the Battle of Rivas (1856), a foundational event in Central American history that often features in regional origin stories. Five women, each representing a Central American republic (Costa Rica, Nicaragua, Guatemala, Honduras, and El Salvador), drive out the infamous William Walker, who led a group of American filibusters intent upon annexing Central America to the US as new slave-owning states (Gobat 2018; May 2002). At the Battle of Rivas, the young Central American republics united to push the US imperial forces out of Nicaragua. On the monument, Costa Rica occupies the central position in the tableau. Raising a flag in one arm, she leads the other republics to victory. With her other arm, strong and capable Costa Rica embraces a broken, nearly defeated Nicaragua who appears wounded and exhausted by the filibusters' invasion. This perception of Costa Rica as stronger and more capable than her neighbors persists today, supported by Costa Rica's relative economic, social, and political stability. And while it is easy to critique myths of Costa Rican exceptionalism, the country does enjoy a more robust economy, better social conditions, and a stronger democratic system than the rest of Central America (Rivers-Moore 2007; Sandoval García 2002). For all these reasons, it represents a primary destination for migrants within Latin America.

Nicaraguan migration to Costa Rica has deep historical roots in colonial and nineteenth-century regional economic developments, including the rise of Costa Rica's coffee industry, the construction of its railroad, and the establishment of the multinational banana industry. Contemporary migration, however, is linked specifically to political and economic instability in Nicaragua during the latter part of the twentieth century, including the Contra War in the 1980s, economic restructuring, and natural disasters. Four major stages of Nicaraguan migration since the 1970s highlight the litany of crises Nicaragua has faced in the last fifty years: 1) after the 1972 Managua earthquake; 2) during the conflict between Somoza government forces and Sandinista rebels until 1979; 3) during the Sandinista Revolution and Contra War of the 1980s; and 4) after the fall of the Sandinista Revolution in 1990. This last period, which continued until civil unrest and government repression generated refugee flows in 2018, has been characterized by mass economic migration. In the first three periods, fewer than one hundred thousand Nicaraguans migrated to Costa Rica, but by 2000, the Nicaraguan population in Costa Rica had quintupled its numbers from the 1980s (Castro Valverde 2007; Programa Estado de la Nación 2001).

This confluence of multiple intersecting political, economic, and social factors makes it impossible to disaggregate economic, political, and environmental reasons for migration in Central America, and Nicaragua specifically. For example, the devastation caused by the 1972 Managua earthquake was deepened by the mismanagement of international relief funds by the Somoza regime, prompting those who lost homes and businesses to migrate (Dosal 2009). The Nicaraguan economic crisis of the 1990s was intensified by years of political conflict during the Contra War of the 1980s. The most recent period (from the 1990s to 2018) has been marked not only by economic crisis in the wake of structural adjustment but also by natural disaster. In November 1998, the country's economic crisis was exacerbated when Hurricane Mitch swept through Central America, causing millions of dollars of damage to agricultural crops, telecommunications, and road infrastructure and leaving nearly eight hundred thousand people homeless in Nicaragua (Loebach and Korinek 2019). In a matter of days, what little economic stabilization the country had gained through economic reforms was reversed.

The layering of recurrent natural disaster on economic crisis on political instability makes it impossible to pinpoint a single event as *the* crisis in Nicaragua. Instead, the chronic state of crisis points to the ways multiple crises intersect to generate a pervasive sense of precariousness in people's everyday lives. Martha Cabrera (2002), a Nicaraguan psychologist who worked with victims of Hurricane Mitch, has called Nicaragua "a multiply wounded, multiply traumatized, multiply mourning country." When Cabrera found that Nicaraguans who had lost everything in Mitch could not process the emotional toll of the hurricane because they had never worked through previous trauma experienced under the dictatorship or during the Contra War, she and her team began to make an "inventory of wounds." Such wounds included not only the decades of dictatorship under the Somoza regime, followed by war, economic restructuring, and natural disasters that have left Nicaragua one of the poorest countries in the region, but also the personal sides of these collective tragedies, including skyrocketing levels of crime and violence as well as domestic and sexual abuse.

Perhaps the most important underlying wound has been poverty and inequality. In the 1980s and 90s, countries throughout Latin America implemented economic reforms often glossed over by the term "neoliberalism." While neoliberalism may be thought of as the state's withdrawal from the economic and social spheres, it is more complicated than that. The neoliberal state relies on the rule of law, free movement of capital, flexible labor, and individual freedom in the marketplace, guaranteed through privatization, deregulation, and individual responsibility for well-being (Harvey 2005). Social well-being is purchased through the market as the social safety net is dismantled. Failure to procure well-being is blamed on individuals rather than on the public spending cuts and economic adjustments that lead to the dismantling or to increasing unemployment. Although bound by common principles and promoted by multilateral organizations like the World Bank and International Monetary Fund (IMF), the implementation of neoliberal reforms and their consequences have differed dramatically in different places.

In Nicaragua, the Sandinistas began to implement economic stabilization policies in the 1980s but were hampered by the Contra War and the US embargo. When structural adjustment programs were implemented in full force in the 1990s, under Violeta Chamorro's National Opposition Union (UNO, for its initials in Spanish) government, the country was still trying to recover from decades of conflict. Continued free market policies, government corruption, public debt, and inadequate investment in the social safety net have deepened poverty and inequality. Today, Nicaragua's informal sector accounts for almost 80 percent of jobs (Narvaez and Rivera 2016).

Migration has been a response to this chronic state of crisis. Although there is evidence that Nicaraguan migration slowed between 2000 and 2018 (INEC 2011), about ten percent of Nicaragua's population continues to live outside its borders. During the period of my research, up to 40 percent of Nicaraguan households received remittances from relatives in the United States, Costa Rica, and Europe, and remittances represented the largest source of national income (Monge-González, Céspedes-Torres, and Vargas-Aguilar 2011). The majority of remittances contributed to basic household consumption—allowing families to cover their basic needs (Chaves et al. 2011).

While the implementation of neoliberal reforms in Nicaragua has driven emigration via high unemployment, shrinking public services, and low wages, in Costa Rica, similar reforms increased demand for migrant labor, encouraging Nicaraguan immigration. After the 1948 civil war, the Costa Rican government disbanded the army and invested heavily in education and healthcare. More than thirty years later, these investments in social welfare and Costa Rica's long history of state-led development provided a buffer against some of the negative effects of neoliberal economic reforms and the liberalization process (Burrell and Moodie 2013). In the 1990s, Costa Rica experienced the largest increase in exports in the Central American region, successfully incorporating the cultivation of nontraditional exports such as melons, pineapples, and ornamental flowers to its traditional exports, bananas and coffee (Nowalski 2002). In the second half of the decade, the Costa Rican labor force began transitioning into emerging jobs in services and technology, creating a scarcity of labor in the agricultural and industrial sectors (Morales and Castro 1999; Programa Estado de la Nación 2001). As a result, the San José metropolitan area became a major destination for both internal and international migration (Nowalski and Barahona 2003).

Ironically, it was not until the late 1990s, when Nicaraguan migration to Costa Rica also increased, that the effects of cuts to the Costa Rican public sector began to be evident. The high volume of Nicaraguan migration combined with the decline in public services in Costa Rica over the last thirty years has renewed anti-immigrant sentiment among many Costa Ricans who stigmatize migrants as criminals and abusers of their country's social services (Sandoval García 2002). Nicaraguan migrants are concentrated in low paying jobs, especially in the export and service sectors, where they earn lower wages, work longer hours, and experience higher levels of poverty than other immigrant groups. Nicaraguans represent a significant manual labor force, while migrants of other nationalities—including US and Canadian citizens—are primarily white-collar workers, investors, and retirees. Nicaraguan men are concentrated in agriculture, especially in banana, pineapple, and other nontraditional exports, and as seasonal workers on coffee plantations (DGME 2012). Nicaraguans have also developed labor niches in the construction sector and in private security for men, and in the service sector and as domestic workers for women (Programa Estado de la Nación 2001, 2016). As noted earlier, given the undocumented status of much of the immigrant population, many of those jobs are in the informal sector.

Over the last thirty years, this migration has also seen a shift from primarily the temporary movement of male agricultural laborers to increased migration of both men and women, long-term settlement, and the establishment of family ties, including having children in Costa Rica (Chen Mok et al. 2001; DGME 2012; González Briones 2013). However, from Nicaraguan migrants' perspective, they flee one form of insecurity in their homeland to face new kinds of insecurity—including xenophobia, labor instability, and repressive immigration policies—in Costa Rica. Many Nicaraguan migrants live in marginal urban neighborhoods in the San José metropolitan area, where violence and poverty are compounded by their precarious legal status. Though they may have children born in Costa Rica and attending Costa Rican schools, many migrants remain undocumented because of the high costs of applying for legal residency. Anti-immigrant sentiment, coupled with restrictive policies, have a direct impact on immigrants' social and economic integration as well as the welfare of transnational families. For example, Nicaraguans, whether documented or not, insured or uninsured, are less likely to seek medical care in Costa Rica because of such experiences of discrimination (Voorend and Venegas B. 2014).

Even as migrants work to maintain families in Costa Rica, they remain committed to households in Nicaragua, regularly sending a portion of their paychecks home to children and other relatives. Across the border in Nicaragua, children and adult caretakers, often elderly grandmothers, depend on these remittances to meet their most basic needs. They go months without seeing or even speaking to their loved ones abroad. I started the research for this book with a fundamental question: How do Nicaraguan migrants and their families maintain intimate connections in the face of these challenges?

Marco's comments about family, social instability, and migration would come full circle for me in April 2018, when I awoke to news of mass mobilizations and government repression in Nicaragua. The streets of Managua,

Masaya, and other Nicaraguan cities erupted in popular protests against President Daniel Ortega's plans to reform pensions. Protestors were met with riot police firing live ammunition. In the days that followed, students barricaded themselves in universities and churches. Paramilitary and police groups circulated through Managua, Masaya, León, and other cities—conducting extrajudicial detentions and beating protestors and their supporters. Over the course of the next few months, tensions intensified, violence increased, and state repression culminated in a law labeling protestors as terrorists. As of autumn 2021, the conflict continues, so far resulting in more than three hundred dead, thousands wounded, and an unknown number still missing or held as political prisoners.

While the events leading up to the protests and the ongoing conflict are beyond the scope of this book, my research serves to provide an understanding of the struggles of Nicaraguan working-class migrant families in the period just before these protests. Many of the families I worked with in the field participated in the protests in some way, most often as university students involved directly in the protests and blockades. Both young adults in Nicaragua and their relatives in Costa Rica texted and sent me videos of their children, nieces, nephews, and friends barricading themselves in universities or churches or running from state-sponsored paramilitary and police forces. Since 2018, more than one hundred thousand Nicaraguans have fled the country, with more than eighty thousand of those going to Costa Rica (Mantoo 2020).

The April 2018 protests gave voice to more than a decade of frustration with the Nicaraguan government, and with President Daniel Ortega's regime in particular. Although Ortega's motto, "Nicaragua: Socialist, Christian, and in Solidarity," echoes revolutionary values of the 1980s, the current Sandinista party looks very different from the party many people like Marco supported in the 1980s. This resurgence of revolutionary rhetoric has done little to improve everyday life for most Nicaraguans. As Karen Kampwirth (2008) has noted, the transformation may be best summarized by the transformed colors of the revolution—from the iconic black and red of the Sandinista Revolution, to the hot pink and neon colors of Ortega's administration. Since Ortega's return to power in 2007, he has consolidated authority—in his office and his person, strengthened clientelist relationships at all levels, and ridiculed dissent and protest. As Julienne Weegels (2018) has noted, "Ortega governs from a position beyond the law." Mass migration, then, signals Nicaraguans' frustrations with life in Nicaragua and the breakdown not of the "little society," but of the nation-state, as Nicaraguans scramble to provide for their loved ones and enact solidarity at the micro-scale.

Migrant Ethnography

Following David Fitzgerald's (2006) call to conduct multi-sited ethnographies of migration that integrate sending and receiving sites and to historicize case studies, I conducted interviews and participant observation with migrants and their families in Costa Rica as well as their families back in Nicaragua. In practice, this meant "following the people" (Marcus 1995). As Ulla Berg (2017) notes, this kind of "ambulant ethnography" is less an a priori dedication to multi-sited ethnography than an attention to the multiple spatial and temporal realities of migrants' lives. Between 2009 and 2012, I conducted almost twenty-four months of ethnographic fieldwork in Costa Rica and Nicaragua (two and a half months in 2009, two months in 2010, and eighteen months of continuous fieldwork from August 2011 to December 2012). In June 2015, with the support of a Wenner-Gren Engaged Anthropology Grant, I returned to both Costa Rica and Nicaragua for a total of two and a half months to present findings to the organizations and families I had worked with previously. This served both to provide feedback from research participants about the conclusions I was drawing and to follow up on changes in immigration status and family configurations. In the summers of 2016, 2017, and 2018, I returned to Costa Rica. I still maintain regular contact with many of the families interviewed for this project.

Most of my fieldwork was spent moving between various sites in Costa Rica and Nicaragua, tracing the movements of migrants and their links to nonmigrant family members in Nicaragua. As such, I was privileged to live and work in a number of locations in both countries. In each site, I combined participant observation and formal and informal interviews to understand both the particular family dynamics at play and wider community dynamics and histories of migration, kinship, and gender. Thus, instead of spending a year or more in one location with a particular group of people, I spent time traveling, adjusting, readjusting, and adapting to life in two different countries, among different people, within the same family networks.

In addition to "following the people," I followed policy changes. In 2012, I attended a workshop for relatives of migrants in Managua where I learned about a temporary legalization program in Costa Rica. I returned to Costa Rica to continue participant observation and interviews to understand how these particular measures were being implemented, how migrants were navigating the complicated bureaucratic process, and generally how migrants and family members confronted legal structures and state institutions. During this period, I also continued archival research on the new temporary measures, immigration reform since 2005, and current immigration law. Since then, I have continued to trace the impacts and implementation of these reforms.

In following these transnational families, I conducted interviews with multiple members of the same families in both Costa Rica and Nicaragua. I began with Nicaraguan migrants living in the San José metropolitan area, where I divided most of my time between Rio Azul, a poor, urban neighborhood outside of San José, and La Asociación de Trabajadoras Domésticas (ASTRADOMES, the Domestic Workers Association). I first encountered ASTRADOMES in 2004 as a Fulbright scholar studying issues of xenophobia. ASTRADOMES provides advocacy, employment orientation, a job bank, and literacy and other classes for domestic workers.

The majority of domestic workers in Costa Rica are Nicaraguan migrant women, and so their work is always intimately tied to migration policies. Indeed, the organization is a member of Costa Rica's Civil Society Network for Migrations and the Permanent Forum on Migration and has played a critical role in improving legislation protecting domestic workers and advocating for migrants. While I was in the field, I had the privilege of witnessing the Costa Rican National Assembly pass a law providing minimum wages and benefits to domestic workers and, in 2011, adopt the International Labor Organization Resolution 189 on the rights of domestic workers. These achievements are a direct result of decades of work by the group and its founder and leader, Rosita Acosta.

Participant observation at ASTRADOMES allowed me to examine how migrants and their families navigate the legal and institutional landscape of transnational migration. Their small office in Curridabat, a suburb on the east side of the San José province, functions as a meeting space, classroom, and refuge for domestic workers. I have spent countless afternoons in the office, sharing coffee and stories, offering help with English and computer class homework, and attending workshops on labor rights, migration, and gender. Across town, in Sabanilla, the Red de Mujeres Migrantes (Network of Migrant Women), hosted by Centro de Derechos Sociales de la Persona Migrante (CENDEROS, Center for Migrant Social Rights), another organization working for migrants' rights, offered similar refuge and support for migrant women, most of them also domestic workers. Observations and interviews with ASTRADOMES and the Network of Migrant Women helped me to understand better how new immigration policies were being implemented, how migrants were navigating the complicated bureaucratic procedures of adjusting status, how migrant women developed social networks and friendships, and generally how migrants and family members encountered state institutions.

I also spent time in Rio Azul, an urban settlement outside San José, where most families live in crowded, self-built houses pieced together from aluminum scraps. In 2006, the Costa Rican Ministry of Health closed the community's largest landmark—a landfill—in an effort to secure neighboring communities from runoff and landslides from the dump's unstable topography. In his novel *Única mirando al mar* (1993), the Costa Rican novelist Fernando Contreras Castro immortalized Rio Azul as a place where objects go at the end of their usefulness and find new life, whether they be edible, recyclable, or human. The community continues to be a marginalized place where discarded sectors of Costa Rican society—the poor, the unemployed, and migrants—build makeshift homes on hillsides. I spent most of my time at a local community center that serves hot meals to more than three hundred children daily. At least half of them are children of Nicaraguan immigrants. I spent time talking to staff, volunteers, children, and parents at the community center, and I also visited families' homes, learning about living conditions, rents, access to public services, and violence in the community. In-depth interviews with migrants and observations of their daily lives and living conditions in Rio Azul allowed me to examine family relationships and the social conditions in which migrants live in Costa Rica as well as to observe practices of long-distance caring such as phone calls, sending and receiving remittances, and internet communication with families back in Nicaragua.

Nicaraguan migrants may be concentrated in the San José metropolitan area, but they come from sending communities throughout Nicaragua, so fieldwork in Nicaragua required travel to various localities. Indeed, given the small size of Costa Rica and the extensive migrant networks developed over the past thirty years, Nicaraguan migrants are unlikely to settle in specific towns or neighborhoods in Costa Rica based on their Nicaraguan hometowns or even kin networks. In Rio Azul alone, I met families from every *departamento* of Nicaragua. I asked interviewees to identify family members I could contact in Nicaragua.

Tracing these family networks, I ended up spending time ranging from several weeks to months in rural and urban communities in the Nicaraguan departments of Carazo, Chinandega, Estelí, Granada, Jinotega, León, Managua, and Masaya. We lived for several months in both Granada and Managua, using both cities as home bases for meeting with families in nearby towns as well as in those cities themselves. These cities were also hubs for ASTRADOMES and the Network of Women Relatives of Migrants, a group founded by daughters and mothers of the Network of Migrant Women in Costa Rica. I attended two workshops with the Network in Managua in 2012 and interviewed various network members. In the end, families in Nicaragua were chosen both because of their willingness to engage with the project and speak to us about migrant relatives and because of the ease of transportation and accommodations for my own family.

As in Costa Rica, I combined informal and formal interviews with participant observation in families' homes and neighborhoods, where we spent afternoons sipping Coca-Cola or instant coffee, introducing my daughter to other families, and talking about babies, the price of food, and the costs of migration. Here, I focused on the Nicaraguan side of transnational families, looking at everyday life in the absence of loved ones and the economic, social, and emotional repercussions of migration for those who stay behind, especially children and caretakers.

Over the course of fieldwork, I worked closely with ten families that included fifty-two of my 150 interviewees (thirty women, seventeen men, and five children under eighteen). In these families, I interviewed multiple family members, at least one on each side of the border. They do not necessarily represent typical transnational family formations, but rather offer insight into the range of migration experiences and family configurations. My years of experience living and working in Costa Rica, studying Nicaraguan migration, and my ongoing conversations with Costa Rican and Nicaraguan academics and activists lead me to believe that these families' stories highlight important elements of Nicaraguan transnational family life. In the chapters that follow, I draw heavily on the experiences of these ten families, as well as on interviews and conversations with family members, other migrants, and members of transnational organizations, NGO staff, and local officials in both receiving and sending communities. Here, I highlight some of the key family dynamics that cut across these diverse families, introducing key themes I will tackle in subsequent chapters and introducing some of the families with whom I worked.*

Family and Gender in the Field

It is no accident that all the field sites I chose in Costa Rica were populated primarily by women and that women's concerns as mothers, grandmothers, sisters, daughters, and wives are a central concern of this book. Although I

---

* All names used in the book are pseudonyms, even in the case of interviewees who asked me to use their real names. I have used pseudonyms throughout because, given the conflictive situation in Nicaragua, I do not want anyone to be identifiable. I am deeply aware that comments that seemed innocuous in 2009 might be enough to label someone an opposition member today.

have conducted fieldwork in migrant organizations with a lot of men's participation, like the male-dominated Confederación de Solidaridad in Costa Rica, it was almost always more difficult for me to interview men. Men happily answered questions about employment and work, xenophobia, and discrimination, but they rarely were open to discussing their families, marital histories, or views on gender. I identified and met migrant men either through their partners, sisters, and mothers, or through local community networks. I also encouraged my husband Chris to approach and develop rapport with migrant men before asking if I could interview them. In the case of several men, Chris conducted preliminary interviews himself. The transcripts of those interviews gave me insight not only into migrant men's thinking on fatherhood and marriage, but also on my own husband's views in light of both our research and our changing family life. Thus, although one of the intentions of the project was to examine men's as well as women's experiences with migration and family, cultural gender norms and practical fieldwork considerations shaped my access to migrant men. These challenges themselves represent data about men's participation in families and households and how they view their roles within families.

Further, like many scholars of transnational migration, at various moments throughout my fieldwork, I found myself tracing and retracing the paths and experiences migrants themselves traveled. When I first began the preliminary research for this project, I was newly married without children. I enjoyed a certain cultural capital as the wife of a Costa Rican, and certain privileges as a US citizen. Over the next ten years, I would embark on a bureaucratic odyssey to gain residency in Costa Rica—one interrupted by graduate school, employment, children, and cross-border movements. When I speak of the bureaucratic labyrinths of Costa Rican immigration law, I know them firsthand—not just from observations and policy research, but from my own waiting in lines and missteps in government offices. It was not until 2020 that I received my Costa Rican *cédula* or ID card.

When I moved to Costa Rica in 2011 as a pregnant woman, relationships with my interlocutors shifted as they began to see me as another mother. After her birth in November 2011, my daughter, Magdalena, and my husband, Chris, became my constant fieldwork companions. Certainly, these experiences as a mother became integral not only to building rapport with my Nicaraguan interlocutors, but also to my expectations of how I would undertake fieldwork and my understandings of kinship and family. Like migration, fieldwork entailed myriad decisions over who should stay or go where and when.

The most important decision we took regarding fieldwork was to bring our daughter with us wherever we went. Migrants who had done the same both argued that no one could care for a child like her mother and commiserated about the difficulties of travel and work with small children in tow. Vaccinations, nutrition, and breastfeeding, heat exhaustion in infants, and who to trust to care for your child all became topics other mothers and grandmothers brought up with me. However, the majority of migrants, who had left children back in Nicaragua, questioned whether we were really giving her the best care by dragging her along on our travels. I was often asked, "Don't you have a mother or mother-in-law to leave her with?" People especially wondered why I had brought her to Central America at all instead of leaving her in the US with my own mother. Our conversations about why I could not or would not leave Magdalena behind became part of the way I came to understand not only Nicaraguan conceptions of gender, kin expectations, and intergenerational care, but also the work of maintaining family ties. Debates over creating economic and emotional stability and the structural issues that made childcare difficult to find or access informed our decision-making and our conversations with each other.

Magda's presence in interviews, during travel, and while observing families and communities not only helped Nicaraguans open up to me but also made me open up, and made me vulnerable in ways I never expected. This experience of mothering and fieldworking has made me think a lot about the labor involved not only in migration but in doing family and doing fieldwork. In September 2012, during our fieldwork in Nicaragua, my mother-in-law in Costa Rica suffered a stroke. Overnight, we packed our bags, closed up our apartment in Managua, and made the eight-hour bus ride back to Costa Rica. While I would eventually finish my planned fieldwork in Nicaragua, my husband became my mother-in-law's primary caregiver in those first months after her stroke. Such shifting of care responsibilities and expectations upended what we thought we knew about parenting, fieldwork, and migration. In the years since, we have faced more challenges of transnational family life. In 2015, just weeks after our second child was born in California, my mother-in-law passed away in Costa Rica. In 2018, my husband's brother would pass away from cancer. In 2021, as I completed this manuscript, Chris and I divorced, and he moved back to Costa Rica. Thus the emotional labor of transnational family life, negotiations about marriage, parenting, and caring for relatives, tensions over sending money, and our own cross-border movements have become part of my understanding of what it takes to create, maintain, and nurture a sense of family across distances and national borders, through tragedy, grief, and joy as well as across cultures, class, and languages.

I do not mean to suggest that my experiences as a transnational researcher or even as a member of a transnational family with privileges of dual citizenship, education, and relative financial stability map neatly onto the experiences of the Nicaraguan transnational families I examine here. However, these ethnographic encounters have highlighted the partial connections we share—encouraging us to understand the "other" in her connection to us and understanding our own otherness in connection with those who jostle us, extend our capacities, and refuse to be subsumed in our experiences (Haraway 1988; Strathern 2005b).

Flexible Families: Key Transnational Family Dynamics

What constitutes a family has been a fundamental area of inquiry for anthropology since its inception as a discipline. Feminist scholars have de-centered Western ideals of the patriarchal nuclear family and biological relations, breaking down traditional notions of gender and kinship and broadening our understanding of what it means to be related in new cultural, legal, and political contexts. According to David Schneider (1984) a distinction between relations of substance—biogenetic or blood relations—and relations of code—relations of law or conduct—underlie Western (for Schneider, specifically US) kinship systems. In Schneider's distinction, relationships of substance are immutable, unchangeable because they are based in "nature," that is, human reproduction, like parent-child relationships. Relations of code, like marriage can be ended because they reflect choice.

However, by examining surrogacy and in vitro fertilization (IVF) clinics, LGBTQ+ kinship, international adoption, and other contexts, feminist scholars have denaturalized these ideas about the immutability of biological substance and relatedness. Taking a cue from science-studies-informed approaches to new reproductive technologies (NRT), this literature has emphasized *how* kinship is produced through active and dynamic processes by focusing on people's experiences and understandings of family, rather than on formal kinship systems (Franklin and McKinnon 200; Yanagisako and Collier 1987). For example, among IVF patients and families using surrogates in an infertility clinic, arguments about biological and genetic relatedness are deployed in different and sometimes conflicting ways to assert who counts as legitimate parents (Thompson 2002). These conflicting arguments, however, highlight the role of intention, economics and financial transactions, and genetics in aligning biological facts and socially meaningful categories of kinship. Key insights from this feminist scholarship have been the intersection of affect and economics, the denaturalization of "pure" relationships based only on love and centered in the domestic or private spheres, and the values of women's nonwage labor in sustaining kinship.

A particularly fruitful point is how relatedness is produced through the sharing of substances such as food and everyday domestic practices of caring (Carsten 2000). Of course, ideas about gender inform such practices of caring. Women and feminine spaces of the home are central to domestic processes of creating relatedness within households and the political process of integrating newcomers. Everyday, seemingly trivial acts like cooking, sharing a meal, and clothing children are integral aspects of creating relatedness (Carsten 2004). This focus on everyday processes of creating relatedness within the home contrasts the assumed naturalness of mother-child bonds with these dynamic processes of relating and the ways mother-child bonds are mediated not just by reproductive technologies and choice, but by globalization, poverty, and access to resources. Thus, we need to pay attention to how kinship is mediated, assisted, and configured not only in light of new technologies, but in everyday life, as people attempt to solidify and fix enduring kin ties.

Such a focus entails attention to the emotional, creative, and dynamic potentials of kinship as well as to the ways people themselves draw boundaries around different forms of relatedness. In other words, families are not a static and unchanging foundation of society, but are rather always contested and in process. What kinds of activities create and maintain relatedness becomes a question to be explored in particular families, communities, and nations. By examining the work that goes in to forging and sustaining transnational kinship, I am interested in the meanings of social relations as people practice them over time, as well as how the patriarchal nuclear family has been codified and normalized through law and deployed by those in power.

Indeed, how ideas and language about kinship are deployed is highly political. The language of family is used to blame the poor for their irresponsibility and lack of respectability, and it informs the discourse on the redistribution of responsibilities between the private and public sectors in neoliberal reforms. For example, the defunding of public early childhood education may be justified through appeals to traditional family values that envision mothers as primary caregivers in the home. This language naturalizes particular conceptions of gender as well as the nuclear family. Other kinship patterns, particularly those that depend on women's networks and "fictive" kinship, including single mothers or households that depend on multigenerational care networks, are devalued (Rapp 1987). This link between women, kinship networks, and domestic, intimate acts of care and survival serves not only to devalue women's work but also to make such labor appear unconnected to the economy, politics, or the larger world.

Transnational families are particularly fruitful sites for examining both the practice and politics of relatedness because they challenge the nuclear family norm and provide insight into how families are linked to larger economic, social, and political processes (Boehm 2012; Caamaño Morúa 2011; Haenn 2019; Heidbrink 2020; Vogt 2018).

Transnational families challenge deeply held assumptions about the importance of physical proximity for emotional intimacy and "normal" or "healthy" family life (Baldassar and Merla 2013, 38). Indeed, academic, political, and public critiques of transnational families often assume that long-distance forms of care are incomparable to face-to-face care. Underlying this are taken-for-granted assumptions about the Western patriarchal nuclear family as the norm and the importance of intensive physical and emotional contact that underlies the naturalization of mother-child bonds. However, transnational families challenge us to see how the kinds of separations, distances, and absences typical of transnational family life are part of wider features of family life today as choices about kin and care are constrained and shaped by global and regional economic, social, and political forces (Baldassar and Merla 2013). Scholars of transnational migration have noted that family survival, threatened by cycles of debt, poverty, and violence, motivates individuals' migration (Abrego 2014; Boehm 2012; Haenn 2019; Heidbrink 2020; Parreñas 2005). In contexts of economic precarity, migration represents a form of care—a way to contribute to the ultimate well-being of one's family. In this sense, transnational families highlight not just issues of care within families but also a crisis within the larger "community of care," the nation (Moodie 2011). They point to family relationships as key "tense and tender" ties through which we can understand both people's experiences as migrants and citizens and state attempts to govern people's intimate lives (Renda 2001; Stoler 2001; Wilson 2015).

Transnational families, then, show the dynamic and flexible nature of kinship in Nicaragua. They are one of many ways Nicaraguan families organize themselves, along with single mothers, multi-generational extended families, and more. However, these configurations that deviate from the dominant patriarchal nuclear family ideal are devalued and marginalized. Shifting the focus from transnational family breakdown to the making and remaking of families opens up possibilities for thinking not only about intimate dynamics of parenting, marriage, and domestic tasks of caring, but also about political, social, and economic transformations. Indeed, like other marginalized communities within Latin America and beyond, Nicaraguan working-class families have developed strong, flexible kinship systems to survive (Olwig 1985, 2013; Stack 1974; Weismantel 1995).

This is not to say that family members always value such flexible kin relations or that people do not suffer from feelings of disappointment and disconnection in transnational families. Indeed, scholars have described such families as "fragmented" and focused on the emotional and physical impact of separation and absence, particularly for families left behind (Boehm 2019; Parreñas 2005; Yarris 2017). A focus on *how* people reconfigure both their ideas and their practices around family in the transnational context highlights these moments of tension, where connection and disconnection are at stake. Further, a transnational perspective widens the frame to include those that migrate as well as those that stay behind, positioning the care that members of transnational families enact on both sides of the border as part of "a contested emotional field," as members interpret migration, separation, and long-distance care differently (Mckay 2007, 190; McKenzie and Menjívar 2011). Such interpretations of the meanings of migration and transnational family life rely on already existing concepts of gender, family, and care. Assumptions about gender underlie our ideas about the "facts" of sexual reproduction that form the basis of notions of kinship—the centrality of mother-child bonds and universality of the family, for example. In other words, gender and kinships are mutually constitutive and must be critically examined together.

CARE AND THE WORK OF RELATEDNESS

In August 2012, I attended a workshop with the Network of Women Relatives of Migrants in Managua on care as a human right. As the participants discussed their own experiences caring for husbands, children, grandchildren, their elderly parents, and others, a picture emerged of the immense care responsibilities these women—some as young as fifteen, some as old as seventy—took on in the name of family. As we discussed the low wages earned by those who worked in the care sector outside the home—as domestic workers and nannies—the facilitator complained about such work being called "unskilled." "It's specialized work; we've learned it from the time we were young girls," she argued, and went on to specify "who's more qualified than us, *las chiquillas*, who've been taught to carry our baby dolls since we were small?" Within Nicaraguan families, the lion's share of care responsibilities fall to women. In the context of economic crisis and neoliberal reforms, it is often women who take on new additional care responsibilities, through engaging in paid work to increase household income or developing strategies for coping with scarce resources, including sharing care responsibilities within extended families and kinship networks (Chant 2003; González de la Rocha 1994).

Transnational migration intensifies this situation for both those who migrate and those who stay behind. Women migrants and female caregivers back home become nodes in what scholars have described as "global care chains," in which migrant women provide paid care as nannies and domestic workers for women in the host country, while other relatives, often their own mothers, provide paid or unpaid care labor by raising their children back home (Hochschild 2000; Kofman and Raghuram 2009; Yarris 2017; Yeates 2009). Marina, for instance, was raising her migrant daughter Dulce's two children. In Costa Rica, Dulce worked first as a daycare assistant, then a nanny, and most recently a housekeeper—three jobs typical of migrant women employed in the service sector and closely related to gendered ideas around care work.

Back in Managua, her three other adult daughters, two of their partners, and their children lived with Marina, making for a large, extended-family household. Marina managed household budgets, remittances, and scarce resources to ensure that everyone had enough. She often sacrificed her own meals so that her working daughters or her grandchildren would have enough to eat. Such care work is both physical—the feeding and clothing of children—and emotional—comforting lonely grandchildren and constantly worrying about how to make ends meet. In the workshop, Marina described care work as "Work that keeps us busy almost 100 percent of the time—in both actions and thoughts." Care and kin work is more than social reproduction, it is emotional labor and emotionally taxing.

In the transnational context, the already heavy burden of grandmothers' care work is deepened by the work of mediating migrants' physical absence and maintaining long-distance family ties using phone calls, text messages, and remittances to generate forms of imagined co-presence (Baldassar 2008). As another participant at the workshop put it, "when migrant women leave, other women take on forced maternities," that is, doing both "the work of those who are here" and the care work once performed by "those who have left," not to mention care and worry for migrant loved ones abroad. Such arrangements reinforce traditional gender norms that emphasize women's continued sacrifice for children across space and generations (Parreñas 2005). In this context, ideas and ideals about the family and women's roles take on new significance. In Latin America, in particular, discourses around sacrifice, suffering, and women's capacity to care, modeled on the figure of the Virgin Mary, inform both migrant and nonmigrant women's care work and society's critiques of their family configurations. This care work within transnational families contributes not just to care in the meantime, but through practices that include sharing substance, whether food, remittances, or love, also serves to transform people's sense of relatedness and the meanings of family.

RELATIONSHIP INSTABILITY

It is only recently that migration studies have turned to exploring men's experiences with migration, masculinity, and fatherhood (Gallo, Gallo, and Scrinzi 2016; Kilkey 2010). As Jason Pribilsky (2007) and others (see for example Hirsch 2003) have argued, some Latin American men see the key cultural markers of masculine identity—for example, land and house ownership, marriage, and the ability to support a family—as often only accessible through the economic opportunities provided by migration. Given this cultural understanding, in which international migration is seen as a rite of passage, a key form of economic provision, and a hallmark of responsible fatherhood, Nicaraguan men are often physically absent from Nicaraguan households. Further, cultural ideas about men's sexuality also inform a social tolerance for infidelity and men's leaving households and marriages. This is heightened in the context of migration. Many people in both countries repeated to me the idea that migrant "women come to support their children, men come to find new partners." Even when men are physically present, there are relatively few expectations for them to participate in the emotional and care work within families, in contrast to women's heavy care burdens.

Of course, men's absences appear visible only against the dominant image of a patriarchal nuclear family. Yet, while the patriarchal nuclear family may represent an ideal in public and political discourse, Nicaraguan family configurations are much more complex, including high rates of extended households, cohabiting couples, and single mothers (Castro Martín 2002; Rubenstein 1983). Although family configurations prior to migration contribute to decisions to migrate and the reconfigurations of kinship as a result, scholarship on transnational families has rarely taken into account practices of caregiving and family configuration in communities prior to migration. For example, when studies take father-away and mother-away families as comparable, they obscure the fact that mother-away families are often headed by single mothers before migration, leaving no other parent at home when mothers migrate (Abrego 2009). In contrast, father-away families usually include a mother who stays with children. Ignoring the differences in these dynamics risks reinforcing assumptions of a stable patriarchal nuclear family as the norm in sending communities and stigmatizing migrant mothers. In Nicaragua, where there are high levels of divorce and relationship instability, men often leave marriages and families long before migration. Relationships in Nicaragua are characterized by their informality and instability, themes I address in Chapters 3 and 4.

Many of the women migrants I interviewed had first migrated in the wake of financial abandonment by a spouse or partner. Take Marina's migrant daughter, Dulce, for instance. Dulce first left Managua when her daughter, Lisseth, was two years old. Lisseth's father had never been in the picture and so, as Dulce put it, "For my daughter, I've always been mother and father." Like Dulce, the Nicaraguan women I met included migrant labor and political and community work under the umbrella of "mothering," as a form of care for loved ones, especially children. Such mothering was usually another kind of forced maternity in the absence of a partner's financial support. Despite this, mothers were still more vulnerable to criticisms of abandonment or lack of care because of their physical absence from children left in Nicaragua (Abrego 2009, 2014; Parreñas 2005).

On the other hand, focusing only on fatherly absences obscures the active engagement of Nicaraguan men within families in the context of marriage informality. While some men were absent presences in homes because of their drinking, violence against their partners or children, or unemployment, most struggled to craft meaningful relationships with partners, children, and their own parents. Further, the men I interviewed expressed a wide range of understandings of marriage, fathering, and family that largely did not conform to stereotypical notions of masculinity or machismo. And, perhaps most importantly, in the context of marriage informality, men are not only fathers, but participate actively within Nicaraguan families as brothers, sons, uncles, and grandfathers.

EXTENDED FAMILIES

As may be surmised by my observations about women's roles in transnational households and marriage instability, few families in the neighborhoods where I worked in both Costa Rica and Nicaragua conformed to traditional nuclear family households. Most were some form of blended families, with children from previous relationships either joining parents in Costa Rica, or remaining with other relatives in Nicaragua. As I will discuss further in Chapter 5, Nicaragua has a very high rate of extended family households. Such households allow families to weather economic hardship by pooling resources to ensure the well-being of children. Thus, in Nicaragua, as in many Latin American and Caribbean countries, forms of social parenting and child fostering—raising children outside their natal households and among several (female) caregivers—are common. This is particularly true among the working class and poor, where flexible and strong kin networks have long represented both a response to and consequence of high levels of mobility and migration (Cardoso 1984; Olwig 2013; Rubenstein 1983; Soto 1987). Indeed, in the context of relationship instability and the paucity of paternal financial support, Nicaraguan single mothers often live with their own mothers, who take on active roles in raising grandchildren. For example, Marina was not only raising Dulce's two children, but also provided the day-to-day care for other grandchildren in the household while their mothers worked locally.

Extended families and family networks are also key in lowering the risks of migration for family members on both sides of the border. For instance, Digmar, a security guard in our neighborhood outside San José, had four other siblings who were abroad, some in Costa Rica, some in Spain. While Digmar's only son was born and lived in Costa Rica, his other siblings had left their children on the family farm outside Chinandega. Digmar's mother, doña Teresa, was in her seventies and, with the help of other adult children who had not migrated, was raising three granddaughters. The extended family lived together on a modest farm, each adult child with their own little house, while Teresa's house remained the center of family life, with teenage grandchildren and her adult children and their partners coming and going, helping with farm chores. While some of these family configurations are the result of migration, the family has lived on the farm for generations, using the family compound to pool resources, ensure sufficient labor to farm, and provide a safe environment for the children—both those whose parents lived on the property and those whose parents were abroad.

SHIFTING TRANSNATIONAL CONFIGURATIONS

The one constant among all the families we worked with was that they were constantly changing. Both children and adults moved back and forth between Costa Rica and Nicaragua or between cities and towns within the countries. These were not necessarily short return visits, but rather longer attempts to build lives on both sides of the border. People formed new relationships and household configurations. For women caught between care and family responsibilities in both countries, spending a few years in one country then the other over the course of more than a decade may allow them to be present for various family members at critical times—for example, when children hit their teenage years or when elderly relatives require more care. In 2011, I found I had to begin interviews with a new group of families in Rio Azul because nearly all those I interviewed in 2010 had moved—either elsewhere in Costa Rica or back to Nicaragua. Indeed over the course of fieldwork, three migrant women in the core group of ten families moved back to Nicaragua after our initial contact in Costa Rica. The two countries' proximity, ease of transportation, and the relative laxity of border controls and immigration enforcement, as well as the economic demands for migrant labor in Costa Rica, have encouraged high levels of migration, settlement, return, and remigration. While the transnational lens makes visible the lives of those "left behind," it is important to remember that neither staying nor migrating is a singular act along a linear trajectory, but rather part of "an ongoing, multidirectional process" of mobility and immobility among transnational families, particularly within this South-South migration system (Heidbrink 2020, 18).

Gabrielle Oliveira (2018, 2019) describes transnational configurations like Marina's or Teresa's as "transnational care constellations," set patterns of transnational families characterized by decision-making, communication, daily interaction or care activities that cross borders. However, unlike celestial constellations separated by immense distances and fixed in their positions in the sky, Nicaraguan transnational families are characterized by constant and high levels of movement and changes in family configurations. While transnational care constellations focus on the role of a migrant mother in the center, with all the related care relationships and activities in which she participates, focusing more on circulation and flexibility helps us to see the dynamic nature of Nicaraguan transnational families and the changing kin relations and roles individuals play within them. Indeed, the circulation of care framework developed by Baldassar and Merla (2013) recognizes not only the movement of care responsibilities and activities across borders but also the physical mobility and movement of those who participate in such circulation of care.

The changes to the Urbina family, whom I first met in 2009, reflect the temporariness of any family configuration over time as children grow up, move out, and start families of their own. These multiple movements show why it is so hard to understand Nicaraguan migration to Costa Rica through the binary of temporary or permanent. But they also reflect how decisions about migration are inextricably linked to "doing" family. In 2009 we met Agnes at her grandmother doña Esmeralda's house in Estelí. Agnes, her mother, and two sisters were visiting Nicaragua but had been living in Costa Rica for years. When we visited them a month later at home in Costa Rica, where they lived just outside Rio Azul, we learned that Agnes had stayed behind in Estelí with doña Esmeralda and her younger cousins. Esmeralda was having health issues and it had become increasingly difficult for her to raise her youngest four grandchildren, whose parents were all working in Spain.

In Costa Rica, Agnes's parents, Martín and Claudia, had a small sewing workshop in their house, where they filled contract orders for children's clothing. Valeria, Claudia's eighteen-year-old daughter from a previous relationship, worked with them, while their youngest, Yessica, attended school. A year later, in 2010, Agnes had returned to Costa Rica to continue studying and working, leaving another cousin, Luisa, to care for their grandmother. Valeria had moved in with her Costa Rican partner and in-laws in a house across the street and was eight months pregnant.

In 2011, no one answered when I tried to call Claudia and Martín. One day, Chris and I stopped by unannounced and found their house empty. From across the street, Valeria called to us from her second floor balcony. She and Yessica were having coffee; Agnes was at work. We met Valeria's one-year-old daughter and learned that Agnes was *ajuntada*, that is, informally married, with an infant of her own. Over coffee, Valeria explained that her mother had left for Spain a few months before because the sewing business was not going well. Martín was thinking of leaving too. Six months later, when Agnes, Valeria, and I met for empanadas with our three babies, I learned that Martín had attempted to join Claudia in Spain, but had been refused entry, returned to Costa Rica and was looking for work. All three sisters were working and studying in Costa Rica, with Valeria supervising Yessica, who continued to live across the street with Martín. Back in Nicaragua, one of doña Esmeralda's other daughters had returned from Spain to help care for her.

In several other cases, women migrants returned to Nicaragua during the course of my fieldwork. For example, Juana, a domestic worker in her forties who had lived in Costa Rica since 2005, returned to Jinotepe in 2012 because her eighteen-year-old son suffered an aneurism. While he was recovering from surgery, her father passed away unexpectedly. What she thought would be a short visit home soon extended to several months. Although she was working part time as a secretary for a doctor in Jinotepe, she felt she needed to return to Costa Rica to repay debt incurred by her son's medical bills, as well as to pay for her house and help support her now widowed mother. Similarly, Elena, a domestic worker in her late forties, returned to Nicaragua in 2012 because her ex-husband was trying to gain the title to her house. When her twenty-three-year-old daughter separated from her husband and moved back in along with her two children, Elena decided to stay in Granada to help her daughter get back on her feet.

Again, the importance of gendered care and kinship responsibilities are fundamental in determining women's constrained choices around family and migration. None of the migrant men I interviewed returned to Nicaragua because of family obligations.

CHANGING PERSPECTIVES ON TRANSNATIONAL FAMILY-LIFE

Recent scholarship on transnational migration has challenged earlier depictions of children as passive recipients of transnational care or victims of abandonment. Instead, such work has shown how children and youth are integral to families and care provision and actively participate in migration processes and decisions (Heidbrink 2014, 2020; Menjívar 2002; Poeze and Mazzucato 2013; Punch 2012). They have looked at how young people make sense of their own transnational responsibilities as well as resentment and appreciation around family separation (Coe et al. 2011; Hidalgo Xirinachs 2016; Oliveira 2018). As active participants in transnational families, children's views on migration and family separation change over time along with shifting transnational configurations.

Elena's family provides important insight into how children's perspectives on parent migration shift over time. She first left her three children after their father left the family, when they were very young. Early on, Kobe, Scarleth, and Jefferson felt resentment toward Elena. When she first returned to visit a year later, four-year-old Jefferson refused to speak to her until she bribed him with candy. However, over time, they came to understand her migration as a form of motherly sacrifice for their well-being. By the time I met them in 2012, they expressed articulate and critical understandings of why their mother had migrated and how her return to Granada had changed their family dynamics yet again. All three lived in the home that Elena had built through remittances. Scarleth, in particular, noted that when she had her own children, she came to understand better why her mother had left her behind to provide for them.

Similarly, Rosa had left her two young daughters in Managua with her mother in the mid-1990s in order to work in Costa Rica. Rosa would go on to become active in organizations promoting migrant rights and form part of the Network of Migrant Women. She and her daughter Tania participated in a workshop with relatives of migrants, where Tania learned about her mother's struggles to send remittances and her battle with depression and loneliness. Tania would go on to participate in the Network of Women

Relatives of Migrants, to raise awareness about the hardships migrants faced, promote understanding within transnational families, and to advocate for migrants with the Nicaraguan government.

While I also interviewed families with younger children, speaking to families like Elena's and Rosa's with adult children in Nicaragua allowed me to ask about how their perceptions of parents' absences and migration had shifted over time. Indeed, in these interviews, many adult children discussed how their understanding of their parents' migration had changed when they themselves became parents for the first time.

CAUGHT IN A LEGAL LIMBO

I first met Gloria, a thirty-five-year-old Nicaraguan woman, in 2011 at the Rio Azul community center as she nursed her newborn daughter on the shady patio. I was eight months pregnant at the time, and we talked about newborns, nursing, and Gloria's family in both countries. Gloria was married to a Nicaraguan man from her hometown. He worked in construction, and she sold tortillas from their house. They had four Costa Rican–born children under ten, including the oldest, Isaac, who later would often meet me at the bus stop and carry Magda up the steep hills to their house.

Gloria, like many parents at the community center, was undocumented, even though her Costa Rican–born children made her eligible for legal residency. Gloria saw little hope for affording residency, though she also saw herself as permanently established in Costa Rica, with no plans to return to Nicaragua. Nicaraguan migrants like Gloria leave for Costa Rica looking for a way to care for their loved ones. However, they flee one form of insecurity in Nicaragua to face new kinds of insecurity—including xenophobia and labor instability—in Costa Rica. For many, their vulnerability is exacerbated by irregular immigration status.

Most of the families I worked with were "mixed-status"; that is, they had some members who were permanent residents or Costa Rican citizens and others in a range of temporary, irregular, or "undocumented" statuses. On paper, Costa Rican immigration law provides extensive provisions for family reunification; in practice, legal status is hard to attain. For parents in this situation, their precarious economic situations made it difficult to afford the costs of the residency process. Further, the complicated bureaucratic procedures residency required were confusing.

In the past, immigration status may not have been such a pressing issue for Nicaraguan transnational families, as the border was fairly porous and there were a number of ways around restrictions on healthcare access and other services. However, since 2005 Costa Rica has passed two new immigration laws (Ley No. 8487, Nov. 22, 2005, Ley de Migración y Extranjería, SINALEVI; Ley No. 8764, Aug. 19, 2009, Ley General de Migración y Extranjería, SINALEVI), both aimed at restricting legal immigration and eliminating "illegal" immigration (Fouratt 2014; Voorend 2014). These two laws are only the latest in a series of immigration measures over the last thirty years that have vacillated between an overall tendency toward increasing immigration restrictions and moments of exception or loosening of restrictions; both have primarily targeted and benefitted Nicaraguan migrants. The regularization process has become more difficult and expensive, and deportations have increased, making illegal status more dangerous. The tightening of immigration laws is part of a wider "securitization" of migration—the conflation of migration policy with national security concerns (Menjívar 2014; Menjívar and Kanstroom 2013). Within Central America, such securitization is tied to regional discourses of organized crime, transnational gangs, and the war on drugs that position migrants as "preemptive suspects" who are inherently dangerous (Stephen 2018; Zilberg 2011, 2018).

For migrants in Costa Rica, these restrictions, coupled with new immigration requirements across a range of public institutions and rising xenophobia, have contributed to a deepening sense of "illegality." Such illegality manifests in both a sense of "deportability" and feelings of unworthiness (De Genova 2002; De Genova and Peutz 2010). However, actual levels of deportation in Costa Rica are relatively low, and most migrants experience illegality and deportability not as imminent threats, but as a sense of "stuckedness" or a form of waiting (Hage 2009; Jacobsen, Karlsen, and Khosravi 2020).

Further, the recent incorporation of immigration status requirements as prerequisites for access to state services and institutions means that without residency, migrants like Gloria have trouble accessing the universal healthcare system, even for their Costa Rican–citizen children. They cannot access credit and are ineligible for grants to improve their makeshift housing; they are less likely to report labor abuse and more likely to earn less than minimum wage. Further, these restrictions follow increasing xenophobia and negative public sentiment toward Nicaraguans in Costa Rica. Yet, Nicaraguan migrant families find creative, quasi-legal ways to enact their own "temporary measures" to access services, find a sense of security, and avoid deportation. These alternative strategies are only partially effective, trapping Nicaraguan migrant families in transitory states somewhere between legality and illegality.

DISCONNECTION

While many families find ways to mitigate the difficulties of absence and separation, others do not. For instance, Diana, a mother in her forties from Granada, left behind her mother, stepfather, and two teenage sons when she moved to Costa Rica with her new partner. She rarely spoke with her parents and older children. Yet when we asked to contact her family in Nicaragua, she readily put us in touch with them. It became clear that, in part, she had moved to Costa Rica to escape her previous relationship and the father of her two sons, who had repeatedly assaulted her, even throwing boiling water in her face once. To cut off ties with him, she also had to cut ties with her sons. She also chose not to communicate with her mother because of a strained relationship with her stepfather, who was highly critical and held deeply conservative views. Unfortunately, such disconnection also fed into the control her current abusive partner held over her, cutting her off from potential support networks in Nicaragua.

Likewise, Hazel, another Nicaraguan woman in her forties, had lost touch with her two adult daughters back in Masaya, Nicaragua. When I first met her, she had not spoken to either one in several years. When she gave me their last known address and the numbers of neighbors who could help us contact them, I thought we would never find them. We did, though, living on a farm the two sisters had purchased together with their husbands, about a twenty-minute walk from the house their mother owned just outside Masaya. Her adult daughters were bitter about their mother's lack of communication and blamed the disconnection on her caring more about her ten-year-old Costa Rican–born daughter. In contrast, they had nothing but good things to say about their father, Hazel's ex-husband, who was in the US. I soon learned the difference was that the women knew their father had sent them remittances to pay for university, while they felt that Hazel had abandoned them physically, financially, and emotionally. Hazel, in turn, felt they were ungrateful because they never recognized the efforts she had made when they were younger to send remittances that paid for their housing, food, and primary and secondary schooling. It would not be until 2015, when Hazel moved back to Masaya with her youngest daughter, that the three women would reconcile and begin to rebuild their relationship.

Much of the literature on transnational migration has focused on the fragmentation, separation, and absences of transnational family life and their negative consequences. Often connection, return, and reunion are framed as the ultimate goal or objective of transnational families. However, it is important to recognize that disconnection and cutting ties are both analytically important and often personally desirable for members of transnational families. As Marilyn Strathern (2005a) argues, moments of disconnection make connections visible and show how cutting off ties leads to making others. This brings into relief what relations are valued and devalued. Indeed, in the transnational context, migration can represent an exit strategy for some (Drotbohm 2009). Of course, given gendered expectations of childcare and family roles, such "voluntary dissociation" may be easier for men than for women. Indeed, many of the women I met in Costa Rica had migrated precisely because their ex-husbands had already migrated, leaving them without economic support. On the other hand, disconnection can also be an unintended consequence of the unpredictability of transnational life, including new financial needs back home or new relationships in the host country. However, connections are cut not just across transnational households or along kin networks, but in encounters with state agencies and offices in both sending and receiving countries—in a lack of access to exit permits for children, precarious legal status, and unfulfilled child support orders.

Organization of the Book

In what follows, I examine the intersections of family remaking, state policies, and migration. The next chapter, "State, Family, and Solidarity in the Nicaraguan Nation," looks at the transformations of state and economy that have pushed Nicaraguans to migrate, as well as parallel shifts in the meanings of the family. During the series of political and economic crises since the 1970s, Nicaraguans have depended on family and the unpaid labor of women as mothers and wives in the face a "sink or swim" neoliberal world (R. Montoya 2013, 46). The Sandinistas' return to power in 2007 has generated a resurgence of revolutionary discourses of solidarity. Yet my working-class interviewees critiqued such discourses as political posturing by self-interested politicians, arguing that the renewed Sandinista party has done little to improve conditions for most families. Instead, families enact private, intimate forms of solidarity along kin networks to ensure family survival.

In the following chapter, "Locked up and Waiting," I examine how migrant "illegality" is produced by the Costa Rican state and experienced by Nicaraguan migrants. Without real access to legal status, Nicaraguan migrant families find creative, quasi-legal ways to enact their own "temporary measures" to ensure their security. Like survival strategies in Nicaragua, these measures rely on family relations and are informed by perceptions of gendered risk—men often feel more vulnerable to immigration authorities, while women feel safer as mothers. However, these alternative strategies are only partially effective, trapping Nicaraguan migrant families in a legal limbo—neither legal permanent residents nor completely undocumented and deportable.

I then shift to looking at family configurations, both in the context of migration and in Nicaragua more broadly. Chapter 3, "Single Mothers and Absent Fathers," examines how family configurations often attributed to migration, particularly single mothers and absent fathers, are tied to flexible kinship practices in Nicaragua. Contrasting the reality of Nicaraguan family life with ideals of the traditional nuclear family, I examine how Nicaraguan men and women understand the gendered roles of parenting and marriage relationships. These understandings emerge in the context of different state attempts to transform family relationships through policy from enrolling families in revolutionary projects in the 1980s to shoring up traditional family values since the 1990s. Chapter 4, "Reconfiguring Relationships across Borders," builds on the analysis of informal marriage to examine migrants' experiences of transnational parenting. While my interlocutors often noted the absence of fathers in transnational families, my observations and interviews with multiple family members highlighted that fathers might be absent, but men were not. Nicaraguan men play dynamic roles in transnational families as sons, uncles, grandfathers, and stepfathers. I also address children's shifting understandings of parents' migrations, and the ways transnational family life shapes how young adults envision their own family-making. I pay particular attention to moments of tension and conflict and new cultural models of family and parenting migrants encounter in Costa Rica.

Chapter 5, "Mamitas: Grandmothering in Transnational Families," looks at the importance of grandmothers in transnational families. Practices of child fostering and rearing by grandmothers represent not simply a response to migration, but part of a larger repertoire of arrangements developed by Nicaraguan families in the face of decades of social, economic, and political instability. This chapter provides insight into the particular challenges grandmother caregivers face in the context of migration. Through an attention to the work it takes to create a sense of family, I argue that relationships, practices, and understandings of family are themselves constantly shifting and should be understood as always tenuous and changing.

Chapter 6, "'I eat all my money here': Remittances in Transnational Family Life," addresses the tensions involved in the work of maintaining transnational family relationships through remittance sending and other forms of transnational connection. I argue that remittances, the money migrants send home, have high costs both for undocumented Nicaraguans in Costa Rica and families back in Nicaragua, but they are also the substance through which a sense of transnational relatedness is maintained. Balancing family expectations and managing remittances create tensions for transnational family members. However, remittances provide a way for migrants to invest in families' futures and sidestep the state to purchase services for education and healthcare in the private sector.

Finally, Chapter 7, "Returns and Reunions," looks at the tensions in family plans for reunification and migrants' returns. Reunification is uncertain as migrant illegality and poverty in Costa Rica may prevent parents from bringing their children abroad. When reunification is achieved, it creates new tensions. For example, reunification for parents and children represents another separation and sacrifice for grandmothers. However, given the diversity of Nicaraguans' destinations, reunification abroad is not always the goal. Many hope to reunite in Nicaragua, but these dreams are delayed by conditions in Costa Rica and continuing financial needs back home. For others, returning to Nicaragua continues the cycle of intergenerational caregiving, as migrant women return to become grandmother caregivers so their own children can work or migrate. Ending by touching on the political protests and state repression in 2018, this final chapter asks what kind of intimate and political futures Nicaraguan families hope to build through migration and transnational family life.

Conclusion

As the families in this book make clear, labor migration and families are mutually constitutive. Family relations and household configurations are characterized by the mobility of some members—generally those with work prospects abroad—and the immobility of others—particularly older women with heavy care responsibilities for children and families in Nicaragua. Such mobility is not only generational but also gendered; men were the most mobile, moving countries and switching households much more easily than women. Children were also mobile and had a say in their own movements as they got older, though they too were beholden to cultural gender norms. Agnes, for example, wanted to stay in Estelí in 2009 to be close to her friends, and her parents supported this decision because it allowed her to provide care for her ailing grandmother and younger cousins. The next year, they were adamant she return to Costa Rica because, as Martín noted, she was entering a "difficult age" and they wanted to be able to keep a closer eye on her.

The reconfigurations of family this work entails are often temporary, their outcomes uncertain. Making sense, then, of the creative ways people make do in situations of absence and separation requires recognizing the limits of family. In tracing family ties between places like Rio Azul and the barrios of Managua, I have tried to remain open to the uncertainties and temporariness of such reconfigurations, movements, and the work of caring for loved ones. Moments of both connection and disconnection in transnational families point to how it is largely in and through families that people respond to the demands of the global economy, navigate the contradictions of legal status across physical and political borders, plug the gaps in provisioning of livelihoods, and attempt to shape futures for themselves.

CHAPTER 1

State, Family, and Solidarity in the Nicaraguan Nation

ALONG THE PAN-AMERICAN HIGHWAY heading north from the Costa Rica-Nicaragua border toward Managua, as in many other prominent places around the city and the whole country, there are bright pink billboards with larger-than-life photos of a smiling Daniel Ortega, the former Sandinista *comandante* and current president. The billboards read, *Nicaragua: Cristiana, Socialista, Solidaria!* (Nicaragua: Christian, Socialist, and in Solidarity). In Managua at night, bright streetlights illuminate the billboards and strings of Christmas lights crisscross the urban highways and roundabouts. The year-round lights, hot-pink billboards, and flashy presence of Ortega highlight the contradictory politics of life in Nicaragua, where the Sandinistas returned to power in 2007 after a decade of economic restructuring under a series of liberal democratic administrations. Since then, revolutionary discourse centered on solidarity and focused on the persona of president and Sandinista leader Daniel Ortega has made a resurgence. At the same time, working-class Nicaraguans have faced increasing difficulties in making ends meet. These difficulties have been reinforced by the Ortega administration's promotion of big business and foreign investment and continued neoliberal economic reforms.

Throughout my research, Nicaraguans of all political persuasions expressed profound frustration with life and politics in Nicaragua. Like other Central American societies after the civil wars of the 1980s, Nicaraguans have faced an extended moment of disillusionment, built on several decades of post-war disappointments (Silber 2004, 2011). There are multiple frustrations linked to various political attempts to steer Nicaragua forward, from the failure of promises of equality under the Sandinista Revolution, to the *"sálvese quien pueda"* (roughly, sink or swim) neoliberalism of the 1990s (R. Montoya 2013, 46), to current failures of solidarity under the neo-Sandinista party.

This chapter examines the intersections of state constructions of family life and Nicaraguans' relationship to the state to understand transformations in state-family relations over the past four decades. I trace the history of political and economic transformations, focusing on their interventions and impacts on families and the gender norms that underlie them. The entanglements of national crises and family emergencies, of failed state policies and flexible practices of care and kin in Nicaragua occur in the face of what James Quesada (2009) has called the "vicissitudes of violence" of the past four decades.

Nicaragua underwent two major political and economic transformations in a relatively short time—first from a market economy and authoritarian dictatorship under the Somoza regime (1936–1979) to a state-regulated economy and revolutionary government under the Sandinistas (1979–1990), then to a liberal democracy and neoliberal market economy after the 1990 elections (Babb 1998). Subsequent administrations included major transformations not only of policies, but of the logic and function of the state (Close 2016). These transformations took place in the context of deeply entrenched inequality that was a legacy of both the Somoza regime and a decade of warfare between the Sandinistas and Contra forces. Many scholars have discussed these histories of transformation and exclusion (Babb 1996; Close and i Puig 2011; Lancaster 1992; Montoya 2013; Randall 1994). Here, I focus on state interventions in the family during and after the Sandinista Revolution of the 1980s, situating structural adjustment, poverty, and the privatization of social services within Nicaragua's particular history of exclusionary social regimes.

Such shifts in state-family relations have not only generated conditions that pushed thousands of Nicaraguans to migrate but have also had profound impacts on kin and care arrangements within the country and transnationally. Indeed, despite their stark differences, the Sandinistas, the neoliberal regimes of the 1990s, and the current Sandinista administration under Daniel Ortega have all relied on family flexibility and the unpaid work of women to make up for the poor provision of care through public services (Martínez Franzoni and Voorend 2011). Today, Nicaragua's social service system remains poorly funded and uncoordinated, resulting in poor coverage and quality of care of the most basic services.

Even as the current government calls on Nicaraguans to participate in building a solidary, post-revolutionary society, working class families find it almost impossible to participate in this national project of development given high levels of poverty and unemployment. While wealthy Managuans flit across the city in cars, sip coffee at cafes, and shop at international malls, others look for new ways to get by, including through migration. By 2009, the families I worked with had little use for revolutionary discourses as they struggled to put food on the table, afford ever-increasing rent and utilities, and find work. To explain the frustrations Nicaraguans felt at this situation, I draw on Ellen Moodie's (2011, 2013) concept of a "community of care," which implies desires for belonging and equality. While Moodie and others have used the term to describe desires for democracy in post-war Central America, I am extending it to understand desires for solidarity, a key Sandinista and Nicaraguan national value.

From Dictatorship to Revolution: The New Man and New Woman

By 1979, the Somoza family dynasty had ruled Nicaragua for forty-four years. Don Eloy, my seventy-five-year-old neighbor in Granada who proudly identified as a *Somocista*, argued that under the Somoza regime, "there was an abundance of everything." Nicaragua, he claimed, was known as the breadbasket of Central America and achieved economic growth thanks to development projects financed from abroad. Indeed, between 1950 and 1977, annual per capita income doubled to US$3,349 (World Bank 2017). However, this wealth was concentrated in the hands of a few, particularly among the Somoza family and their associates. In the first half of the twentieth century, much of Latin America underwent policy transformations that expanded state interventions in social welfare and the economy. However, in Nicaragua the Somozas, with US support, crushed peasant demands for land and rights (Collier and Collier 2002). From at least the 1930s through 1979, when the Sandinistas overthrew the Somoza dynasty, Nicaragua was characterized by state-enforced exclusion and inequality. For example, after the 1972 Managua earthquake devastated the capital city, millions of dollars in international aid went directly to the pockets of the Somozas and their allies while Nicaraguans struggled to rebuild.

The Somozas grew wealthy while the majority of the population lacked access to land, education, healthcare, and other services. At the end of the 1970s, half the Nicaraguan population was illiterate; only one-third of the urban population and only 5 percent of the rural population had access to potable water, and even fewer to sanitation (Martínez Franzoni 2008, 191). In this context, poor Nicaraguans, who were the majority of the population, depended on family networks for care provision, and women contributed heavily both to these informal care networks and to income-generating activities. Thousands of Nicaraguans participated in seasonal migration within the country and to Costa Rica for cotton and coffee harvests. Indeed, don Eloy's own parents had migrated seasonally to Costa Rica and Panama to make ends meet. Discontent with the Somoza regime grew among many sectors, including the business community, leftist activists, students, and the Catholic Church.

The Frente Sandinista de Liberación (FSLN, Sandinista National Liberation Front) came to power in 1979 as part of a broad coalition to overthrow the Somoza regime. They would commence a decade-long experiment in social and economic reform that included attempts to transform family configurations and gender relations and to promote a vision of a society and nation built on solidarity. These ideas were rooted in new ideals of gender roles—the "new man" and "new woman"—and in a vision of solidary family and social relationships.

Sandinista visions of the "new man" and "new woman" sought to transform these relations and promote both men's and women's integration into the economy, military service, and volunteer work, while generating particular affects around such revolutionary ideas. As the former Sandinista leader and poet Gioconda Belli (1982, 19) wrote, "solidarity is the tenderness of the people."* In that same poem, Belli evokes the sense of sacrifice and hope at the beginning of the Sandinista Revolution, along with the continued work to make that dream of Revolution a reality. In transforming gender roles, the Sandinistas sought to enlist both the private and public spheres to create a solidary society that strived for social transformation, through both hope and sacrifice aimed at care for fellow Nicaraguans. Thus, Sandinista notions of solidarity included ideals of mutual sharing, responsibility toward fellow citizens, and active participation in revolutionary efforts and ethos.

Sandinista revolutionary projects of the 1980s sought to create a unified nation in part through gender equality and family stability. Such state intervention to transform the patriarchal family has been a common reform in socialist states as new governments seek to dismantle social relations of the "old" society (Molyneux 1985a). As Ann Laura Stoler (2001, 831) has argued, the "tense and tender ties" of families, households, and intimate relationships are important "microsites of governance." It is, after all, within the family that citizens first learn about rights and duties, labor, and power relations. Interventions into the family represent highly gendered inter-

---

* All translations from Spanish are my own.

ventions into the basic social fabric. In Nicaragua, the traditional patriarchal family represented the society of the past, particularly its deep gender inequality and rigid hierarchy.

The Sandinistas attempted to redefine relations between the sexes and create legislation to protect women's rights at home and in the workplace. They tried to legislate equitable relations within the home by requiring men to participate in household work. Underlying the solidary family was a vision of the "new man" who was both a social revolutionary and a benevolent patriarch. This "new man" would be a model of solidarity publicly and privately—both building a revolutionary society in the streets and nurturing solidary relationships within the home. This "new man" was embodied by three revolutionary figures: Che, Christ, and Sandino—the Nicaraguan peasant who first stood up to the Somoza dictatorship (R. Montoya 2003).

The image of the "new woman" naturalized women's role as nurturers and caregivers to enroll mothers in the service of the revolution and the nation. During the Revolution, women participated in armed conflict, income-generating activities, and government literacy and vaccination campaigns. The iconic photo *Miliciana de Waswalito* (1984) by Orlando Valenzuela highlights the idea that to mother the nation was to fight for its liberation. In the image, a young woman with a rifle slung across her back nurses a baby in her arms. Her radiant smile projects optimism and hope for the Revolution. The image circulated internationally as a symbol of the revolution and appeared on murals, posters, and other materials sponsored by the FSLN and the Asociación de Mujeres Nicaragüenses Luisa Amanda Espinoza (AMNLAE, the Sandinista women's organization). Certainly, the image evokes Belli's "tenderness of the people." At the same time, the young woman's full arms point to how such "tenderness" within both families and the larger nation was undergirded by the labor of women.

The Sandinistas emphasized economic and social development as national projects requiring the participation and contribution of all citizens. While much of Latin America experienced a retrenchment of social services under structural adjustment during this period, Nicaragua underwent an expansion of programs and services under the Sandinistas. For the first time, large numbers of Nicaraguans saw increasing access to public services as education and healthcare became key goals of the Revolution. This expansion of services largely depended on the unpaid and voluntary work of citizens. For example, Dennis Rodgers (2007) describes how in the early 1980s, residents of a Managua *barrio* that had once been a notorious urban slum participated in urban redevelopment projects by collectively building local infrastructure including houses, roads, drainage, and public spaces. Further, women represented the primary volunteers in literacy and vaccination campaigns as well as nutrition and medical brigades (Chinchilla 1990). As the Contra War intensified in the latter half of the 1980s, many of these same women joined the popular militias.

For the Sandinistas, voluntary work represented revolutionary principles of the people's participation and ownership of the Revolution. It was also the only way for an overstretched, under-resourced government to provide such services to the population. The Sandinistas, often seen as socialists, attempted to create a mixed economy in which a strong and expanded state sector existed alongside a private sector. At first, as they sought to dismantle the agro-export economy, the Sandinistas implemented broad agrarian reform and nationalized key sectors of the economy. However, as the decade wore on, Sandinista efforts at social and economic transformation stalled, in part because of the US trade embargo and the ongoing Contra War. Defense spending increased and the government's capacity to fund social welfare decreased. By the mid-1980s, Sandinista economic policy shifted from revolutionary social transformation to economic stabilization (Babb 1998; Metoyer 2000). They cut state spending and public sector jobs in an effort to combat hyperinflation and slowing economic growth. The end of consumer subsidies especially impacted women and children (Lancaster 1992). Wage increases and other actions meant to protect poor Nicaraguans from these adjustment measures were unable to cushion the blow. US support for the Contras and influence in international lending agencies also meant no new international loans for Nicaragua. As in previous periods, women's unpaid domestic labor compensated for economic impacts, consequences of war, and community needs. Indeed, collective and cooperative survival strategies relied heavily on kin-based networks, including remittances from relatives abroad (Higgins and Coen 1992; Pérez-Alemán 1992).

As families struggled under the weight of economic reforms, war, and more, Sandinista visions of solidarity began to fracture. Women, and by extension the families they cared for, suffered under cuts to the public sector toward the end of the decade. Families faced separation, polarization, and death because of the divisiveness of the war and compulsory military service. Daniel, a Nicaraguan migrant in his thirties who lived in Río Azul, had moved to Costa Rica with his mother as a young boy in the 1980s. "I came because there, the war and that Sandinista regime stuff started— either you were with the *Somocistas* or you were with the Sandinistas. So my *mamá* said, 'Here they're going to militarize everything and I don't want my children going off to war and being killed.'" Like many other families, Daniel's mother sold her farm and took her children out of the country.

For many, ending the Revolution seemed like the only hope for ending the war, since the US continued to support the Contras. A number of scholars have attributed the Sandinista's 1990 electoral defeat, at least in part, to their failure to address family issues and women's concerns because of their focus on the war (Babb 2001; Molyneux 1985b; Randall 1994). Violeta de Chamorro, who won the 1990 election ending the Revolution, cultivated an image of an apolitical mother and widow, appealing to Nicaraguan mothers' frustrations with war and loss (Kampwirth 1996; Metoyer 2000). For example, in Managua doña Ester talked about the heartbreak of having her then fifteen-year-old son sent off to the mountains to train as part of his military service. She said she felt "great relief" when the Sandinistas lost the 1990 election, not because she did not believe in the Revolution, but because she was scared of losing her son. The Sandinistas left behind a mixed record: the institutionalization of democracy, a culture of citizen participation, and important social reforms, as well as a highly polarized society and an economy in shambles (Close and i Puig 2011). Although no longer in power, the party, and particularly party leader Daniel Ortega, vowed to continue to fight from below, promising the party's continued push for solidarity and social reform.

1990–2006: Free Market Democracy, Economic Crisis, and Traditional Family Values

The promises of peace and economic well-being on which Violeta Chamorro campaigned never came to fruition for many Nicaraguan families. When the Sandinistas peacefully handed over power to Chamorro's UNO party, they became only the second party to relinquish power peacefully in the country's history. Similar political shifts were occurring throughout the region, with promises of democracy that would provide a path toward peace and collective well-being (Coronil 2011). However, as Jennifer Burrell and Ellen Moodie (2013, 24) point out, many Central Americans found they could not access "the community of care," the peace and security many associated with the transition to democracy. Nicaraguans struggled to rebuild physical infrastructure, political institutions, and the economy as well as families fractured by war. In the 1990s, the Chamorro regime accelerated the implementation of neoliberal structural adjustment begun under the Sandinistas, and the impacts were intensified.

Further, the end of the Sandinista Revolution saw a shift in political discourse from the language of revolution to the language of reconciliation and democracy (R. Montoya 2013). The language of democracy as tied to obligation, concern for the well-being of others, equality, and justice was challenged by neoliberal interpretations of democracy. The first, which Moodie

(2013) refers to as a desire for "a community of care," contrasts directly with the second, which includes neoliberal rationalities of individual responsibility and self-care. In Nicaragua, notions of democracy as participation in the free market confronted ideas about social justice and solidarity, leading to the erosion of revolutionary ideals in the public sphere. Neoliberal reforms that included the privatization of much of the public sector, cuts in social services, and the removal of protective tariffs on imports were implemented very quickly, leaving already struggling small producers and business owners unprepared for the transition. Unemployment and under-employment rose to almost 60 percent (Babb 1998). As the economic crisis deepened, Nicaraguans continued to rely on families and particularly the unpaid work of women to ameliorate the devastating consequences.

As in other Latin American countries, women suffered disproportionately under structural adjustment as policies shifted responsibility for survival from the state to individuals and families (González de la Rocha 1994; Safa 1995). First, women were not only among those who took advantage of Sandinista programs promoting small producers and cooperatives that were cut in the 1990s, but they also represented large numbers of workers in sectors hard hit by an influx of cheap imported goods in the 1990s (Babb 1998). Women faced heavier burdens at home during economic restructuring because of cuts to childcare, health care, and education. Throughout Latin America, this "feminization of survival" extended beyond households to place the burden for the welfare of communities and nations on women as growing unemployment, declining government revenues, and rising national debts made alternative means of making a living, earning income, and raising government revenue necessary (Sassen 2000).

In Nicaragua, these reforms were accompanied by a state-led push to return to traditional gender roles and uphold the nuclear family. Chamorro had won the election by not only positioning herself as an apolitical mother figure but also by emphasizing the importance of the traditional family. The Chamorro campaign was silent on issues of gender equality, and Chamorro herself identified not as a feminist, but as a traditional woman concerned with family and home (Kampwirth 1996). Chamorro's promotion of "traditional" family values encouraged women to exit the labor force, leaving them to bear the brunt of responsibility for dealing with the economic crises of the 1990s from the less visible position of the house. The emphasis on peace and reconciliation within both the nation and the family helped to delegitimize opposition to an economic order that generated further suffering.

The 1990s also saw continued reliance on voluntary or community work in the provision of social services and programs, as cuts to state spending made the provision of care more difficult. In childcare and educational institutions in particular, families became responsible for remodeling buildings, digging latrines, and fundraising to cover operating costs and teacher wages (Martínez Franzoni 2008). Voluntary work was transformed from a revolutionary ideal into a cost-saving measure. As revolutionary rhetoric was eroded in the public sphere, neoliberal values and discourses of individual responsibility dominated.

The Alemán (1997–2002) and Bolaños (2002–2007) administrations continued neoliberal policies of privatization, encouraging foreign investment, and economic liberalization. Their administrations saw the establishment of free trade zones and tax breaks for real estate developers and were rife with corruption (Rodgers 2008). At the heart of this system was a pact struck between President Arnoldo Alemán, a liberal, and Daniel Ortega. The pact led to constitutional amendments that heightened presidential powers and made the chief executive less accountable. The FSLN, under Ortega, continued to push to return to political power, even as there was dissent within that culminated in the fracturing of the party when the Movimiento de Renovación Sandinista broke away.

Political corruption, high levels of unemployment, and the lack of a cohesive and hopeful vision for the country disillusioned many Nicaraguans. The promises of democracy—a sense of order and justice, a perception of belonging, and possibilities for future economic well-being in the form of development—seemed beyond reach for working-class families struggling to make ends meet. It was during this period that Nicaraguan migration to Costa Rica intensified. Migration became a labor market "adjustment mechanism," as 71 percent of the economically active population worked in the informal sector by 2000 (Agurto and Guido 2001). While just over 1 percent of the population lived outside the country in 1970, by 2000, almost 20 percent lived abroad (Idiáquez 2001, 102), the largest proportion of the population to live outside its country of origin in the Central American region. Nicaraguans left looking for work and to ensure household financial stability, particularly for their children. The tenderness of the people or of the state toward the people had given way to a sink-or-swim society in which individuals and families had to look out for themselves.

Nicaragua: Christian, Socialist, and in Solidarity

In 2007, almost thirty years after the beginning of the Sandinista Revolution and the toppling of the Somoza dictatorship, the Sandinistas regained power in Nicaragua through the election of former Revolutionary leader Daniel Ortega to the presidency. But far from representing a radical challenge to the neoliberal administrations of the 1990s and early 2000s, the Sandinistas of today reflect a contradictory and conflicting incorporation of revolutionary discourses of solidarity and justice with neoliberal discourses of responsibility and free market values, a kind of Sandinista 2.0 or neo-Sandinista politics (Collombon and Rodgers 2018).

Ortega's return to power was not just the result of people's disenchantment with neoliberal regimes. Rather, it was the result of carefully orchestrated agreements between Ortega and the Sandinista party and the Alemán and Bolaños administrations. Between 1990 and 2006, Ortega remained a key political player, asserting major influence over political and legal changes that expanded executive power and restricted oversight of the president (Close 2016). For example, Ortega made a deal with Alemán to reduce the percentage of votes needed for a president to be elected in exchange for promising to commute Aleman's sentence for embezzlement to house arrest (Kampwirth 2008). Eventually, Ortega's quest to regain the presidency would lead to political alliances with the Right.

These transformations in the meanings of revolution and Sandinista discourses of solidarity are represented clearly in the shift from the traditional red and black of the Sandinista party to the Ortega administration's vibrant hot pink (Kampwirth 2008). Like the colors, under the current Sandinista administration, the meanings of the legacy of the Revolution have shifted—particularly from liberal liberation theology Catholicism to conservative Catholicism, from feminist to antifeminist, from anti-imperial, class-conscious revolution to a rhetoric of peace and reconciliation (Kampwirth 2008). Since 2007, this transformed, post-Revolutionary Sandinista party has maintained power at both the national level and in municipalities across Nicaragua. In 2009, Ortega successfully had the Supreme Court of Nicaragua declare articles barring re-election unconstitutional, paving the way for his 2011 and 2016 re-elections and consolidation of power within his family. In 2021, Ortega was re-elected again after jailing his political rivals and repressing all opposition.

Ortega's presidency relies heavily on revolutionary discourses and images of solidarity, popular participation, and equality. Slogans of *el pueblo presidente* (the people are president) and *poder ciudadano* (citizen power) echo Sandinista yearnings for a people's revolution and situate solidarity as foundational to what it means to be Nicaraguan. Yet, Ortega has assiduously courted big business, continued supporting the neoliberal market economy, and sought to increase foreign investment in Nicaragua, which has come to participate in the global economic system primarily through weakening protections for its labor force at home and exporting more and more workers abroad (Quesada 2009).

In the public celebration of the anniversary of the Revolution on July 19, 2009, I listened as the iconic revolutionary music of the Mejia Godoy brothers played over loudspeakers and Ortega spoke of solidarity, the achievements of the Revolution, and the need to defend Central America from imperialism. He spoke at length about the then recent coup in Honduras and Nicaragua's willingness to fight for its legacy of revolution and social progress. However, he also praised a number of big-business men and called for a referendum to amend the Constitution and allow (his) presidential re-election, an amendment that eventually passed.

Revolutionary rhetoric has been diluted by vertical, authoritarian power structures within the FSLN and the administration and widespread corruption. For example, Citizen Power Councils (CPCs, Consejos de Poder Ciudadano in Spanish) have been local tools of direct democracy in Nicaraguan communities. However, the FSLN has used the CPCs to build clientelist relations by putting them in charge of allocating goods provided by the state, from latrines to zinc roofing (Montoya 2013). The FSLN has also refused to engage with existing departmental, municipal, and other organizations not affiliated with the party (Prado 2007). In Estelí, families in popular barrios complained that if one was not on the "right side" of the current administration, it was impossible to obtain grants or free zinc to repair your roof. In Achuapa, a rural town in León, if you did not publicly support the FSLN, it was nearly impossible to obtain credit from the local cooperative, whose leaders were all Sandinista Party members.

Further, even as it upholds solidarity as fundamental to the nation, the Ortega government has undermined both social equality and family stability. While Ortega's administration has worked to improve health and education coverage, public services are still "not for everyday life," as my friend Andrea put it. Nicaraguan social spending in absolute terms is the lowest in Central America and focuses only on education and health, with housing receiving much less priority in funding (Martínez Franzoni and Voorend 2011). Shortly after regaining power in 2007, the FSLN under Ortega pushed through a ban on therapeutic abortion, essentially jeopardizing the health of hundreds of pregnant women annually.*

Voluntary contributions—either of labor or money—are often requisites for accessing services in Nicaragua. For example, families in Nicaragua talked about having to take their own sheets and purchase syringes and

---

* See Kampwirth (2008) on this issue, and on the importance of therapeutic abortion rights in the context of the Global South and healthcare systems like in Nicaragua.

other medical supplies for hospitalized relatives. Others opted to seek services in the private sector, paying for services or relying on clinics staffed by international organizations and volunteers. Andrea noted that such clinics, often financed through international agreements with Venezuela or Cuba, were "only temporary." Indeed, while the Ortega government has expanded healthcare and education, the impact on most of the population has been relatively limited (Montoya 2013).

For working-class families, who have long relied on family strategies including migration for survival, the resurgence of discourses of solidarity did little to change their day-to-day lives. Nicaragua remained the second poorest country in the Western Hemisphere, behind Haiti (World Bank 2021). In 2010, almost 60 percent of the population lived below the poverty line (ECLAC 2013). During the first decade of the twenty-first century, Nicaragua's social spending was the lowest of all Central American countries in absolute terms, and as a percentage of GDP, the country's entire investment in social spending was comparable to what Costa Rica spent on education alone (Martínez Franzoni and Voorend 2011). Further, in 2008 and 2011, sharp increases in basic commodity prices intensified the crisis for many Nicaraguans (R. Montoya 2013).

At the same time, the Ortega government has emphasized the importance of family to national projects of unity. In 2014, the CPCs would largely be replaced by new Cabinets of the Family, Community, and Life in the new Family Code, centering families as a locus of government control (Miranda Aburto 2013; Jiménez 2015). Although these Cabinets were implemented just after I finished the majority of my fieldwork, the discourses around the family they institutionalized were circulating widely in the communities where I worked. The new Family Code, for example, establishes the family as the "fundamental nucleus of society" and promotes "unity, harmony, love" and "family values" (Ley No. 870, Código de Familia, Art. 36, October 8, 2014, *La Gaceta, Diario Oficial* No. 190 [Nicar.]).

This is a very different framework than revolutionary visions of the family as the foundation of radical equality and solidarity. Here, family life ought not challenge social hierarchies, but rather in the name of harmony and unity contribute to notions of *Vivir bien, vivir bonito, vivir sano.* Roughly translated as "Live well, live beautiful, live healthy," the Ortega government's new tagline connotes not only physical health and economic well-being, but moral wholesomeness rooted in traditional family values. That is, no longer is the family a cauldron of revolutionary ideas, but rather a bastion of unity and "rescued," that is, traditional, values. Rather than work toward the transformation of society from its foundation in family life and gender relations, family members should prioritize harmonious coexistence in public and private life.

Twinkling Lights and Electric Bills

Such contradictions between neoliberal discourses of individual responsibility and revolutionary discourses of solidarity and justice manifest in the ways people express a deep sense of disillusionment about the possibilities of life in Nicaragua. A woman I met in a doctor's office waiting room in Granada in 2012 described the state of the country as a "wonderland." She used the term not to refer to an enchanted place, but rather to reality turned on its head, one whose logic seemed undecipherable even to those who resided there. "This is a wonderland," she said, "where values are lost, public officials prostitute themselves, and foreigners buy up everything historic or beautiful." She complained about local officials who turned a blind eye to foreigners who broke rules regarding downtown development and supported projects that would get them reelected or that provided contracts for friends' or relatives' businesses. Her very presence in the waiting room at a private clinic implied dissatisfaction with the public healthcare system. People in every city and town I visited in Nicaragua repeated this sense of disillusionment with national and local governments and state institutions. Indeed, others often used the word *irrealidad*, unreality, to describe this sense of disillusionment and betrayal.

This unreality is visible in the juxtaposition of international malls like Metrocentro in Managua and modern well-lit highways next to poor urban barrios, for whose residents such infrastructure is clearly not intended (Rodgers 2008, 2012). Investments in private security and the improvement of roads and construction of roundabouts to connect areas of the city frequented by urban elites have undergirded both the development of such commercial centers and the neglect of areas of the city where the poor live and work. When we lived near Metrocentro, my husband often noted how walking just a few blocks further into residential areas, or taking a bus or taxi just down the road, brought us face to face with ruins left from the Contra War or even the 1972 earthquake. As we moved further off the highways and roundabouts, pavement became more riddled with potholes and electricity became more unreliable. Meanwhile, in the mall itself, wealthy Nicaraguans shopped for imported homegoods and electronics.

On the heels of decades of political and economic instability, the current contradictions of Nicaragua have generated global desires for development and consumption without providing the means for most Nicaraguans to achieve them. If, as Florence Babb (2001, 56) has noted, the changing face of Managua and the growing number of shopping centers like Metrocentro represent both neoliberal desire for foreign investment and "middle-class longings," such desires are unattainable for most of the families we met. Indeed, in many ways this urban development has created a disembedded and fortified network for urban elites (Rodgers 2004). These shifts in urban development, in which large sectors of society are left behind or displaced by new highways, roundabouts, gated communities, and commercial centers, index the disconnection working-class Nicaraguans feel around the country. In this context, discourses of solidarity serve as a nostalgic brand or screen for individualistic and neoliberalized reforms.

In her working-class barrio just a mile from the Metrocentro mall, Marina argued that the misplaced priorities of politicians showed how little they cared about the Nicaraguan people:

> Here in this country, I have to be honest, that like, this president, like no, he only thinks about running around building houses for the people, with little parks, but we don't live off of that. Imagine how expensive electricity is! Why? Because all over Managua they're putting in streetlights. Lights in the street. And who's going to pay for that? Low income people.

Although publicly Ortega has promoted campaigns to build houses in slums and revamped programs for zinc roofing in poor communities, Marina criticized him for spending his time dedicating parks instead of making policies that would contribute to real improvement in the lives of working-class Nicaraguans. For her, voting for the Sandinistas had created little real change in the lives of poor Nicaraguans and poor Managuans, in particular:

> *Ahorita* [in a little bit] we'll have the elections for, I believe it's for mayor. And who's running for the position? Another Sandinista, *Dios mío*! Lord help the voters, open their eyes. Because change, we can't expect it. We don't expect it. The majority, 100 percent of the people already know that another Sandinista is on the way. And change for *el pueblo* [the people]? Because what good is another roundabout to me, if it's just more taxes? More bills: water bills, light bills. What good is more lighting to me? What good is lighting when I'm walking in the barrio? I don't live in the street. There should be light where I'm sitting at home. And that streetlight is going to show up on my bill!

Marina critiqued Sandinista discourses of solidarity with *el pueblo*, the people. She viewed streetlights and roundabouts as projects for those who traverse the city in cars, who are out driving at night, something she found pointless, because what she needed were lower electricity bills to keep the lights on at home. Instead, investments during the Alemán (1997–2001) and Bolaños (2002–2006) administrations focused on rebuilding government offices and encouraging foreign investment, through tax breaks for foreign developers for large international malls for example. These kinds of developments continue today under Ortega.

Elena's son, Kobe, who had interned in the office of the first lady, criticized Ortega's "beautification" campaigns in Managua, especially what he felt was "wasted money" spent on Christmas lights. In 2011 and 2012, the Ortega administration invested heavily in the "beautification" of Managua, decorating and landscaping roundabouts and lighting highways. In Managua, the Christmas lights along the roads remained in place all year. Heading south out of the roundabout, toward the highway to Masaya, the highway was illuminated by more lights, both strings of festive twinkling lights and evenly spaced street lamps. "I think they spend more money on lights than on healthcare," he told me in an email. As a journalism major, he wanted to investigate but was afraid he would lose his prestigious internship in the Ministry of Culture, headed up by first lady and at the time minister of education, culture, and sports and government spokesperson, Rosario Murillo.

Just a year later, giant illuminated metal tree sculptures would begin to appear along the highways. The trees, called *Arboles de la vida*, Trees of Life, were sponsored by Rosario Murillo to commemorate the thirty-fourth anniversary of the Sandinista Revolution. Each tree, critics have claimed, cost US$25,000 to install (Pastor Gómez 2018), and up to US$1 million in electricity/year to operate. In 2013, Kobe wrote to me, angry about the trees and Christmas lights:

> I mean, we're talking about more of those trees full of lights. It's not glitter or anything, they're electric lights! And then they put up Christmas lights starting November fifteen, like [Rosario Murillo] announced months ago. And she demanded that their mayors do the same in the main parks of every town in every department around the country. I know so much about it because I'm working for them, but, well, I can't say anything because of my job.

Like Kobe, others levelled their complaints and critiques in living rooms and on front porches, in hushed tones. They also often looked around to make sure no one else could hear them or reminded me to use their pseudonyms when recounting these stories. Fear of the material consequences if CPC leaders or other Sandinista supporters heard their criticisms kept many from doing more than making vague complaints about "how things are."

Despite the rhetoric of solidarity, Nicaraguans like Marina and Kobe noted an absence of a sense of obligation, compassion, or concern for the well-being of families on the part of the government. The CPCs, the Sandinista party, and Ortega and Murillo demand loyalty, not solidarity. The country is suspended in what Nicaraguan author William Grigsby Vergara (2014) has called a "forced fantasy," and a "constant Christmas Eve." Trees of Life line highways and light up roundabouts that link gated neighborhoods and exclusive communities to malls like Galerias de Santo Domingo and Metrocentro. There, wealthy Nicaraguans browse electronics, appliances, and brand-name clothing at department stores. They can eat at McDonalds, Burger King, or Quiznos. International business executives stay next door in the luxurious Intercontinental Hotel, where rooms start at US$129 a night. Meanwhile, a few blocks away, Marina and her family struggle to feed themselves and keep the lights on at home.

"Entre Todos": Forging Communities of Care

Families like Marina's find themselves caught—able to neither procure the material goods that would signal their participation in global desires for consumption nor provide the kind of solidary social support that underlies the renewal of revolutionary longings. Marina, Kobe, and others employ a revolutionary vocabulary of people, nation, and solidarity to critique the state. If people articulate their relationship to the state through their disillusionment with infrastructure projects and absent or failing social services, they articulate desires for a community of care through more private and intimate forms of solidarity. As Ann Laura Stoler (2001, 831) has pointed to with respect to race and empire, the intimate domains of kin and care "confound or confirm" relationships between people and the state. Faced with the betrayal of revolutionary ideals and broken promises of democracy, equality, and prosperity, Nicaraguan families find ways to enact solidarity—these revolutionary ideals of sharing and compassion—within the private sphere. They also run up against obstacles to that solidarity and care.

The families I interviewed in Nicaragua contrasted the individualistic and selfish priorities of politicians and the government with what they themselves did within their families. When I asked Marina how her family got by, she said simply, "entre todos" (between us all). Marina and her husband, for instance, lived with three of their daughters, two of whom were married, and their daughters' children, as well as the two grandchildren they were raising while their mother worked in Costa Rica. In total, the household included seven adults and more than ten children. She noted that sometimes her oldest daughter would complain that she did not feel like cooking for her little family, "Then, I say to myself, it's not the cooking, it's that she doesn't have anything to cook." And Marina would make rice and eggs for all the grandchildren in the large extended household.

In contrast to public discourses of solidarity in which *el pueblo* and the state work together to realize the revolutionary society and nation, families enact practices of making do and getting by to secure the needs of their most vulnerable members in the face of the state's neglect. Such kin and care work serves to highlight which relations are valued and which are devalued, both by the state and within families. João Biehl (2005) and Clara Han (2012), for example, point to the ways state attempts to create economic stabilization and growth in Latin America—often linked to the privatization of public forms of care like health, education, and social security—generate forms of insecurity that are born primarily by families. As noted earlier, for Nicaraguans this privatization is exacerbated by the "dissolution of revolutionary ethos" in the public sphere and the conflation of democracy with neoliberalism (R. Montoya 2013, 46).

Such fragile arrangements to care for one another are organized within households and along kinship networks. Extended households represent important strategies for pooling income, resources, and care labor. In Nicaragua, as in other places around the world, the expansion of households tends to follow economic downturns, while the contraction of households occurs during economic upswings (Agurto and Guido 2001; Martínez Franzoni 2008). However, the past three decades have seen few upswings, and so families—configured in extended households—have remained the primary way through which Nicaraguans have guaranteed some level of security for themselves and loved ones.

However, just because households are organized along family ties and various extended family groups live together, it does not mean that they always work cooperatively to meet each other's needs. There are many lines of division and conflict within kinship networks and households. Feminist scholars have long argued that households are not unitary entities, and the naturalization of women's roles as caregivers disguises hierarchies of power and resources within homes, often along gender and generational lines. Dennis Rodgers (2007), for example, details the non-cooperative relationships within poor households in Managua in the 1990s. For Rodgers, such non-cooperation is indicative of how families and households are not "natural" units of cooperation and solidarity. It also highlights the difficulties of engendering a solidary community or "community of care" even at the micro-level.

Indeed, within households, the sharing of burdens and survival strategies is highly gendered. Marina never let her husband, who worked as a long-distance truck driver and came home only every few weeks, know just how difficult things were at home:

> Yes, because if I tell my husband, "oh there's this and that," I mean, he's coming from work. He leaves, and he's here three or four days with me. The poor guy comes home. And supposedly, he says, "Ah, I'm going home to rest." And I start with, "Ay, this gutter is broken, it needs to be fixed now." Poor guy, to fix it. "Ay, look at this chair, it broke and now you've got to nail it back together." And then, I mean, if I put the weight of the house on him and I put all my burdens on him by saying, "Ay, I feel terrible, ay no. I feel like I can't go on. I feel like I can't do it." What's he going to say, back there [at work]? "Neither the house nor she are any good to me. I should just leave."

Indeed, both Nicaraguan gender dynamics and economic instability affect possibilities for longterm relationships or marriage, as I explore in Chapter 3. Social institutions, agencies, and dynamics contribute to relationship instability by naturalizing women's domestic and care work and men's economic provision. Men often take temporary and low-paying jobs in the informal sector, making their contributions to households erratic and uncertain.

It is within this context that migration emerges as a welfare strategy within Nicaraguan families. Migration represents a strange combination of neoliberal individualism and intimate solidarities: migrants leave to pursue their own welfare, but they do so through the support of family networks and in order to support those families back home. These decisions to migrate are often negotiated between couples and within extended families including among adult siblings. For example, Rosa first came to Costa Rica twenty years ago because her partner encouraged her, saying that it was easier for women to find work in Costa Rica than men. In Estelí, part of the reason Claudia's sister returned from Spain was so that someone would be close by to help their aging mother, Esmeralda, while her other sisters were abroad.

Conclusion

Practices of Nicaraguan family-making must be understood within changing ideas about family and gender that emerged during economic crisis and political upheaval and that have been promoted by the state over the past three decades. In particular, revolutionary ideas around gender and men's and women's roles within the nation and the family have shaped Nicaraguans' understandings of the "community of care." So too has disillusionment with the promises of democracy and revolution. In 2010, journalists from Nicaragua's *Magazine* by *La Prensa*, a leading daily newspaper, sought out the famous *Miliciana de Waswalito* from Valenzuela's 1984 photo. They found doña Blanca "without a gun and without a home," but with fifteen children to feed (Garth and Gertsch R. 2010; Navarete 2011). The child she nursed in the photo was now a university educated twenty-seven-year-old young man, unemployed and struggling in poverty.

In the face of a government more concerned with the spectacle of revolutionary symbols than with the actual "tenderness of the people," with loyalty rather than solidarity, Nicaraguans have drawn on intimate solidarities to ensure the welfare of their loved ones. These forms of intimate solidarities build on and are bound to kinship networks, but are not limited to such networks. Solidarity represents one of the enduring legacies of the Sandinista Revolution as well as the language that binds family and society into a unified nation.

However, the kinds of practices through which solidarity is enacted within transnational families destabilize official visions of the solidary society. Indeed, in migrating to send money home, in taking on the costs of care—health, education, and more—Nicaraguans are enacting neoliberal ideals of self-sufficiency. Yet given the long history of exclusionary regimes in Nicaragua, many families had already long shouldered immense burdens in terms of care provision. Both during the Sandinista Revolution and during the 1990s, women's unpaid labor was central to social provisioning. In the 1980s, Nicaraguan women participated in nation-building and development as soldiers, workers, and social brigade volunteers. Since the neoliberal regimes of the 1990s, their contributions have been framed as those of apolitical agents of reconciliation and domestic support in the face of economic crisis.

As migrants in Costa Rica they encounter new possibilities for creating communities of care and enacting solidarity, especially within organizations like ASTRADOMES. Both migrants and their relatives in Nicaragua explicitly contrasted the lack of social services, programs, and opportunities in Nicaragua with the kinds of assistance and support available in Costa Rica in the form of healthcare for children and programs and organizations like community centers and daycares. For many, migration not only provides the funds needed to access services from which they might be excluded in Nicaragua, but also access to such services and possibilities for the future in Costa Rica. In Costa Rica, many also found solidarity, friendship, and support through ASTRADOMES and other groups organized around labor rights, mutual aid, and justice work.

At the intersection of desires for solidarity and disillusionment with national development projects, migration becomes a new way for poor Nicaraguans to enact a community of care even as it threatens their place in the solidary society and nation. Blaming individual migrants for family breakdown obscures these dynamics of neoliberal individual pursuit of well-being in the context of the retrenchment of the state from social provisioning, despite recycled rhetoric of solidarity. Families' participation in nation-building takes place through both "voluntary" contributions and informal mechanisms for making do and getting by that rely on kinship and particularly on women's roles as mothers and wives. In this sense, reliance on extended family—and particularly women's care work—has underwritten and made possible the transformation of state and economic policies in Nicaragua, buffering the devastating consequences of government policies and absent social services.

CHAPTER 2

Locked Up and Waiting

AMONG THE MORE THAN three hundred children, ages two to fourteen, who fill the benches in the Rio Azul community center, almost half are the children of Nicaraguan immigrants, most of them undocumented. One afternoon in late 2011, I sat and talked with Gloria, as she nursed her six-day-old daughter on the community center's patio. Although the center ostensibly only served children, they had a standing policy to serve lunch to pregnant and nursing mothers too. The center hummed with the chaos and ebullience of the children, some returning from classes, others on their way to school, girls smoothing their braids and ponytails, boys slouching and teasing one another about favorite soccer teams. As the kids laughed and chatted, Gloria explained about her lack of legal status: "I have the right, but I haven't been able to because of a lack of economic resources." Like many of the children at the center, Gloria's four children were all born in Costa Rica.

Because Costa Rica allows foreigners to claim residency based on a first-degree family relation, migrant parents can apply for residency as soon as they have the child's birth certificate. However, given Gloria's economic insecurity and lack of familiarity with Costa Rican immigration procedures, she never applied even though she was eligible. Gloria described the confusing process of applying for residency, the incredible cost to gather the documents needed, and the financial strains on her growing family. She first entered Costa Rica in 2000 on a passport and tourist visa. Like many Nicaraguans, she overstayed her visa and began working as a *doméstica*, a domestic worker. She met her husband and became pregnant with their first child, Isaac.

This chapter looks at the experiences of family members living in Costa Rica, where Nicaraguans face stigma, xenophobia, limited economic opportunities, and complicated immigration laws that limit their integration. As I argued in the last chapter, when Nicaraguans leave for Costa Rica, they are both responding to economic insecurity as responsible neoliberal subjects by securing their own livelihoods *and* enacting intimate, domestic solidarities that challenge state discourses of individual responsibility. When they reach Costa Rica, migrants encounter the consequences of neoliberal reforms in Costa Rica. There, economic restructuring has generated demand for migrant labor in the service, construction, and agricultural sectors that have grown thanks to foreign investment. The different implementations of neoliberal reforms heightened uneven processes of development within Central America, where Costa Rica's stronger traditions of the social welfare state buffered many of the worst social impacts of public-spending cuts and economic restructuring. At the same time, these logics of flexible labor and free market have oriented Costa Rican immigration policies away from values of human rights and hospitality.

Instead, immigration reform has ensured migrants are largely unable to obtain permanent status. Increasingly restrictive immigration laws coupled with an ever more expensive process of legalization help to maintain a large proportion of the Nicaraguan population in Costa Rica undocumented. Although most Nicaraguans enter the country legally on a ninety-day tourist visa, they easily slip into irregular statuses by working without a permit or overstaying their visas. Few accurate estimates exist, but scholars, activists, and others often emphasized that up to 40 or 50 percent of the Nicaraguan population was undocumented.

Intense xenophobia and discrimination compound the challenges of undocumented status. Even when Nicaraguans have residency or legal status, they often encounter discrimination on the street, on buses, and in clinics and schools, making it more difficult for them to access public services to which they have a right and to participate fully in Costa Rican society. In Costa Rica, this anti-immigrant sentiment is visible in everyday insults and attitudes, graffiti lining highway overpasses calling for "Nicas out" (*Nicas fuera*) or "No more lowlife Nicas" (*No más nicas muertos de hambre*), jokes making fun of Nicaraguans, and the insults school children hurl, accusing classmates of being stupid, dirty, or uncivilized like "Nicas."

Restrictive immigration policies and border controls work in tandem with xenophobia to ensure not the exclusion of migrants, but rather the differentiation of migrants' access to employment, housing, education, and healthcare as well as permanent legal status and belonging. Migrants are integrated in Costa Rican public institutions through forms of "bureaucratic inscription" that make them visible to the state without conferring the same rights or benefits granted to citizens (Horton 2020). In this way, the Costa Rican immigration system participates in a system of "global apartheid" based on legal distinctions that serve to create a vulnerable, flexible, and expendable workforce (Sharma 2006; see also Heyman 2012; Horton 2020; Spener 2011).

I begin by recounting a very public episode of xenophobia that occurred in 2005. This episode and the media coverage surrounding it remain a touchstone for how Nicaraguans perceive and experience xenophobia in Costa Rica even more than a decade later. Next, the chapter turns to new immigration policies that have enshrined this xenophobia in law, making it harder for Nicaraguans to gain permanent legal status. The final two sections turn to how Nicaraguans experience this confluence of xenophobia and legal restrictions. While many feel locked up and paralyzed, migrants also actively navigate this complex landscape of repressive laws, confusing legalization processes, and discrimination through informal measures. Such measures create a provisional sense of security for their families. In many cases, this temporary sense of security requires circumventing state institutions—by avoiding official channels of legalization or accessing services in the private sector.

The Death of Natividad Canda

In the early hours of November 10, 2005, Natividad Canda, a twenty-three-year-old Nicaraguan man, entered a car repair shop near Cartago, a city in Costa Rica's Central Valley, and was attacked by two Rottweiler guard dogs. Police officers, firefighters, neighbors, the shop owner, and a guard watched. At least one spectator filmed the event. By morning, Canda had died of his injuries, and the attack, unusual in its violence, was major national news complete with replayed footage of the attack. Costa Rican public discourse and media coverage, instead of being outraged at the violence or horrified at the death of the young man, overwhelmingly supported the dogs and condemned the victim, an alleged criminal and "illegal" immigrant. Violent text messages glorifying the dogs, vilifying Nicaraguans in general, and advocating further violence against immigrants circulated by cell phone and internet for weeks.

I arrived in Costa Rica to visit friends and family just weeks after Canda's death and watched the video footage with horror. I listened with disgust to taxi drivers, acquaintances, and people on the street retelling grotesque jokes about killing Nicaraguans. A taxi driver who was surprised that I did not know any "Nica jokes," shared the following poem:

> From heaven fell a Rottweiler
> and ate a Nica,
> how lovely it would be if 600,000 fell
> to clean up Costa Rica.

Flyers on the internet showed Rottweilers running for president (Mendoza 2005). The dogs became new national heroes; one meme circulating joked that the statue of Costa Rican national hero Juan Santamaría would be exchanged for one of Hunter, one of the dogs that attacked Canda. Rottweilers featured in xenophobic versions of the National Anthem:

> Noble dog, your race is Rottweiler,
> Expression of caring you give.
> As long as you have a Nica in your sights,
> Our hero you will be.

These jokes, which circulated by word of mouth, text message, and email, sanctioned the violence against Canda by turning the dogs into heroes. These citizen-protectors were figured as cleansing the nation of "impurities" and asserting citizens' rights over and against the presence of unwanted, threatening noncitizens. The jokes were denounced by government officials but continued to circulate for weeks. When Canda's mother arrived in Costa Rica to seek answers, the media and public ridiculed her while government officials all but ignored her pleas for justice.

Although this event took place more than a decade ago, Nicaraguans in Costa Rica still frequently reference Canda's death and the public reaction around it when discussing how they feel in Costa Rica. Even nonmigrant family members in Nicaragua brought up Canda's death in talking about life in Costa Rica. They pointed to both Canda's death and the cruel treatment of his mother as examples of the kinds of sacrifices migration entailed for families and the ways migrant families were ignored, or worse, by host countries.

The vehemence and violence of Costa Rican reactions to Canda's death were made possible by a distinct form of Costa Rican nationalism based on racialized discourses of inferiority and the undesirability of foreign others who do not belong (Hage 2012). This xenophobia is rooted in foundational myths of Costa Rican national identity as well as the result of specific historical political, social, and economic relations between the two countries. Indeed, the National Monument in San José recalls the implicit hierarchy embedded in this conception of national identity; in an isthmus of violence, dictatorship, and underdevelopment, Costa Rica has risen above its Central American neighbors.* The image of Costa Rica as the "Switzerland of the Americas" conjures an image of the country with cultural, racial, and political similarities to Europe, in contrast to the rest of Central America. Today, Costa Rican tourism marketing emphasizes the country's exceptionality in the region: a peaceful, democratic country renowned for its natural beauty.

This exceptionalism has long been constructed in contrast to Nicaraguan others. Negative perceptions of Nicaraguans serve to highlight positive aspects of Costa Rican identity. Where Nicaraguans are seen as "inherently violent," Costa Ricans are peace loving; where Nicaraguans are poor, illiterate, and uncultured, Costa Ricans are middle class and educated; where Nicaraguans are *mestizo* and dark skinned, Costa Ricans are "white" (Sandoval García 2002, 2004). While Costa Ricans hardly ever use the term *mestizo* to describe themselves, race is a silent but powerful element of discourses of national identity, marking difference and claims to the nation from within (Bustos Mora 2000; Rivers-Moore 2007; Sharman 2001). For example, Limón, the coastal region with a large Afro-Caribbean population, is still equated with "danger and pollution," which are codes for blackness (Sharman 2001, 47).

Given these contrasts, Nicaraguan migration is represented as a demographic, cultural, and racial threat to Costa Rican national identity and its exceptionality in the region. These "threats," reproduced and disseminated through television and print media, contribute to a general disrespect for Nicaraguans in Costa Rican society. In many ways, these stereotypes of Nicaraguan migrants resonate with perceptions of Latino migrants in the US, like the "Latino Threat Narrative" outlined and debunked by Leo Chavez (2008). Ironically, Costa Ricans sympathize with Mexican migrants in the US, even as Nicaraguan migrants in their own country face similar obstacles of poverty, exploitation, and racism (Alvarenga 2004).

This anti-immigrant sentiment has grown since the 1990s, when Nicaraguan immigration increased and Costa Rica faced the consequences of neoliberal structural adjustment. Neoliberal reforms in Costa Rica encouraged Nicaraguan migration by expanding and promoting an export sector that demanded large-scale manual labor. Immigrant labor was particularly important for coffee, banana, ornamental flowers, and other agricultural exports. However, these same adjustment policies also reduced the Costa

---

* While there are certainly a proliferation of counter-hegemonic readings for these dominant narratives and counter-identities that problematize these notions of "whiteness" and exceptionality, I focus here on the prevailing notions of Costa Rican identity as they are projected in the Central Valley, where San José is located.

Rican state's capacity to ensure the welfare of its population. Costa Rica already had higher levels of social spending than other Latin American countries, which helped buffer the negative social impacts of adjustment. However, by the mid-1990s, just as Nicaraguan immigration increased, the impacts of declining public investment began to emerge (IDESPO, UNFPA, and Foro Permanente sobre Población Migrante 2000).

In part, the vehemence of this xenophobic discourse is linked to a perceived crisis of citizenship as economic, social, and political changes transform the meaning of formal membership and access to what were once substantive elements of national belonging (Calavita 2005). Anti-immigrant sentiment represents a response to the ways Costa Ricans have begun to feel that the instabilities and inequalities that have haunted the rest of the region are beginning to take shape in their country. Rising crime and declining quality of life as a result of reduced public investment threaten Costa Rica's self-perception as exceptional. Crowded classrooms, understaffed public schools, and an overworked and underfunded health system became symbols of a welfare state in crisis. Anti-immigrant sentiment, then, represents a way for Costa Ricans to assert their own fuller belonging in a context where political and economic realities threaten Costa Rican notions of inclusion.

Finally, renewed conflict over the San Juan River, which forms the border between the two countries, represents another source of growing tensions since the early 2000s. The conflict flared up again in 2010, leading to a renewed wave of nationalist discourse (Sandoval García 2013). However, rather than focus resentment on Ortega's administration in Managua, Costa Rican public opinion has targeted Nicaraguan migrants living in Costa Rica, insisting that the Nicaraguan government's attitude represents ingratitude for Costa Rican "hospitality" toward immigrants. Alma, an immigrant rights' advocate, pointed to the dispute as a major catalyst in intensifying hostility toward Nicaraguans: "Costa Ricans started to say 'ungrateful,' 'jerks' [desgraciados]. They're blaming not the Nicaraguan government, but the people [pueblo] who are in Costa Rica." Rosa, an immigrant activist concurred, "Always, when the governments argue, we're the ones who suffer."

Producing Illegality

These tensions have found expression in increasingly restrictive immigration policies that target Nicaraguans in Costa Rica. Between 2005 and 2010, Costa Rica passed two new comprehensive immigration laws. Both increased restrictions on immigrants, making applying for residency more complicated and expensive. Further, these new laws focus on restricting legal migration and policing undocumented migration within a framework of national security (Fouratt 2014). This repressive tone, with its emphasis on national security and immigration control, represented a notable shift in policy for Costa Rica, where a tradition of hospitality and refuge for displaced populations from Latin America had dominated political rhetoric (Hayden 2003). Further, because the law incorporated immigration requirements as prerequisites for accessing services in various public institutions, effectively breaking down "bureaucratic firewalls," it made legal status more important for migrant families (Horton 2020, 2).

On paper, permanent residency is relatively easy to gain in Costa Rica, which recognizes birthright citizenship, granting Costa Rican nationality to anyone born in its territory. Under this system, known as *jus soli*, from the day a child is born in Costa Rica, his or her parents may claim residency through that Costa Rican citizen-child. This contrasts with the US, where undocumented parents must wait until the child turns twenty-one and petitions for them. Other countries, like Ireland, have eliminated birth right citizenship because of controversies over fears of immigrant fertility (Luibheid 2013).

However, higher costs and complicated procedures under the new law make it difficult for low-income migrants to complete the residency process. The law institutes high application fees and a US$100 per month fine for each month a migrant has been in the country in "irregular" status. But the average Nicaraguan migrant only earns somewhere between US$160 as a domestic worker to US$390 in certain construction jobs (Leon Segura 2012). For example, Gloria estimated that by the time she could pull together her documents and pay the fees, she would accrue more than US$2,000 in fines under the new law, an amount impossible to pay on her husband's US$300-per-month salary. Although the implementation of the fine was postponed several times while I was doing fieldwork and was postponed again in 2020 with the COVID-19 pandemic, the very specter of the fine, coupled with misinformation within migrant communities, made many like Gloria feel paralyzed about initiating the legalization process.

Further, applicants must present a number of documents that can add up to between US$300 and US$800 (Goldade 2011; IIS et al. 2012). Until 2014, these documents had to be emitted and authenticated in Nicaragua, requiring applicants to return and face the costs of the trip for each family member needing documents, as well as lost wages and often jobs because of these absences. These incredible costs relative to income, coupled with the expensive and complicated process of obtaining documents and applying for residency made the law a bureaucratic labyrinth that was difficult for low-income Nicaraguan migrants to navigate. In the many offices, lines, and bewildering requirements to acquire documents one already has a right to, Nicaraguan migrants encounter the Costa Rican state not as a "distant and faceless" entity, but as concrete and embodied by unsympathetic clerks who serve as barriers to accessing rights and services (Horton 2020, 4).

Of course, the costs of residency are due not only to Costa Rican law but also to the bureaucratic procedures of the Nicaraguan state, which sets the costs for obtaining documents in Nicaragua. Digmar detailed out the costs of getting the necessary documents for him and his wife:

> We would spend around two thousand dollars in papers and travel there to Nicaragua, because there every document they charge you forty or fifty dollars. The procedure for the visa to re-enter Costa Rica, for permits, transportation, and all that, you spend a lot. And beyond that, you can't go to your family in Nicaragua to get the documents and come back. It's not like that. Your family always expects the best of you. You have to save up so that when you go, you can take them something too.

Digmar used the word *vuelta* to describe the various office visits needed. The term, used to refer to errands, literally means *laps* or *returns* and evokes the multiple comings and goings that such bureaucratic procedures imply in Central America, as Nicaraguans visit and revisit offices in both countries with new paperwork to fulfill requirements. Further, as Digmar notes, there are not only the legal or institutional costs of documents and processing, but family costs—migrants must return with gifts and money for family members back in Nicaragua.

The process is further complicated by the larger inefficiencies of the Nicaraguan registry system. The European Union's Electoral Observation Mission (2010), for example, observed that in order to obtain a national ID card, Nicaraguans had to complete a fifty-two-step process. In parts of Nicaragua, up to 50 percent of births go unregistered (Duryea, Olgiati, and Stone 2006), and many Nicaraguans lost their birth and marriage certificates when civil registry offices and archives were destroyed in the war or natural disasters over the past forty years.

Even after 2014, when Costa Rica began to accept documents emitted by the Nicaraguan consulate in Costa Rica, many migrants felt the Nicaraguan government was still throwing obstacles in their way. In 2020, Rosa, who often helped other migrant women through the documentation process, explained:

What are the actions our government has taken for those of us who are outside Nicaragua? The actions they have taken are that, in the Nicaraguan embassy, we have to pay in dollars, and we don't earn in dollars. Instead of facilitating life for us with the work permit process, where Costa Rica asks for the police record, birth certificate, everything is dollarized. But also, to get your police record from Nicaragua, they ask you for a ton of things, and if you don't have a Nicaraguan national ID, they can't give it to you. So, when I've had contact with the embassy, I said, why do you make things so difficult for us? Because there were children who came here very young. They didn't know Nicaragua; they already had family here. How were they going to get all that documentation?

From the high costs of obtaining personal documents to inflexibility of procedures in cases where Nicaraguan citizens cannot meet requirements, Nicaraguan immigrants' legal problems are as much a consequence of the Nicaraguan state's incapacity and perceived unwillingness to facilitate papers to its population as of the Costa Rican state's bureaucratization of the legalization process.

Even as it makes legal status more expensive and thus difficult for Nicaraguans to achieve, the Costa Rican law is oriented toward integration. This simultaneous and contradictory incorporation of integration with repressive and exclusionary measures is part of a global system of immigration control aimed at the temporary admission of migrants. As Pilar, a Costa Rican immigration lawyer who worked for a national NGO, argued to me, "what the law is doing is maintaining the population undocumented." Expired entry permits and residency cards coupled with the expansion of immigration data collection across public institutions subject migrants to more intensive state surveillance through frequent renewals and immigration requirements for accessing even basic services. Integration programs and policies serve to inscribe migrants within bureaucratic systems that make migrants legible to the state without offering permanent legal status, durable rights, or long-term security (Horton 2020).

Such surveillance is implemented and enforced not just at immigration offices, but across public institutions. To access most public services, migrants must first complete all the *vueltas* to "fix" their status. For example, an academic and activist colleague of mine in Costa Rica inquired with the Instituto Nacional de Aprendizaje (INA), a public institution that offers vocational training, about admissions to vocational courses for undocumented minors. The INA insisted that such immigrants would first need to "regularize" their status before applying. No matter how my colleague approached the issue, INA officials were unable to respond outside the legal/illegal framework that made migrants themselves responsible for their status, and thus, integration. By making legalization a prerequisite for any meaningful economic or social integration, the law incorporates integration and security within a neoliberal framework of personal responsibility. In this context, migrants must act as responsible and ethical subjects in order to gain recognition and legal status from the state.

This is part of a transformation of government in Costa Rica, characterized by the dismantling of the social welfare state, introduction of market rationalities, and increased policing and militarization. The emergence of what Jonathan Inda (2006, 12) calls the "post-social state" has displaced the responsibility for dealing with the need for security, health, and welfare onto individuals. For example, the current law requires migrants to pay into the social security system but does not impose new requirements or enforcement measures to ensure that employers fulfill their obligations to contribute to the system. Indeed, in 2013, the Costa Rican congress announced further reform that would reduce the fines faced by employers who hired undocumented immigrants (Ruiz Guevara 2013). The law puts the onus of compliance on migrants rather than on those who hire them.

By linking integration to legalization and making migrants responsible for complex, institutional processes of documentation and residency, the integration framing legitimizes a law that, in effect, makes both legalization and integration more difficult for low-income Nicaraguan migrants. As each step in the process requires migrants to have fulfilled other requirements, a lack of coordination among banks, the social security institute, and immigration offices (the Dirección General de Migración y Extranjería, or DGME) has created nearly unresolvable conflicts in the process of obtaining residency. This confusion between immigration offices, banks, and other government agencies shows how the new law serves not to weaken state control on migration but to disperse the production of knowledge and governance of migration across a range of governmental and nongovernmental institutions and actors and to generate more uncertainty for migrants themselves.

Life without Legal Status

These liminal statuses often leave Nicaraguans feeling *encerrados* or "locked up," paralyzed by their legal situation. This sense of being locked up delays their planning for the future and blocks economic and social mobility for family members in both countries. It may also generate anxiety as spaces like public streets and transportation, markets, and places of employment feel unsafe for migrants under laws focused on detention and deportation. Like in other migrant-receiving contexts around the world, undocumented Nicaraguans live "in the shadows" (Chavez 1992) or "en route" (Coutin 2005) but never fully incorporated into Costa Rican society, where their illegal status creates a sense of abjectivity (Gonzales and Chavez 2012; Willen 2007). However, in Costa Rica, the pattern of constantly changing legal context has generated a sense that the current law is always only temporary, replaceable by another set of policies. Together, these conditions contribute both to uncertainty and hope for the future among undocumented Nicaraguans.

Many undocumented residents of Rio Azul restrict their lives to the confines of the informal hillside settlement. In 2010, when Chris and I served as chaperones for a community center field trip to a local recreation center in the nearby mountains, nearly half of the one hundred or so children had never visited the area, whose peaks were visible from their homes and only a short twenty-minute bus ride away. The Urbina family from Estelí, for example, described their life in Rio Azul as feeling "locked up." When I first visited their home in 2009, Claudia pointed out the high metal wall that enclosed their house and a large yard that doubled as parking. "This is my world. Sometimes I spend weeks enclosed by this gate," she explained. For Claudia, being locked up restricted her but also offered refuge and protection. When she first arrived in Costa Rica, she slept outside on park benches, feeling exposed and vulnerable to the rain as well as to passers-by and Costa Rican authorities. Now, the walls of the house both enclosed her and protected her from the world beyond. Indeed, the family set up a sewing workshop in the house and took on jobs, manufacturing children's clothing for local contractors with three sewing machines in their living room.

For Claudia's three Nicaraguan-born daughters, being locked up was also a temporal condition. They described their enclosure in the family compound in direct contrast to their lives in Nicaragua, where they felt they had a freedom of movement. A few years after our first meeting, Claudia's youngest daughter, Yessica, then fourteen, reminisced about arriving in Costa Rica, "It was a totally drastic change. Because there [in Nicaragua] we could go out and all with our friends, with our cousins, with everyone. And here [in Costa Rica], no. Here is like being locked up. It's a jail." For a time, Yessica had even returned to Estelí to live with her grandmother, but eventually chose being with her parents over the freedom implied in living in Nicaragua. Indeed, a number of young people remarked on this difference between Costa Rica and Nicaragua, which is the result not only of feelings of vulnerability among the undocumented, but also perceptions of urban crime and violence in the low-income Costa Rican neighborhoods in which they lived.

Poverty is an integral part of feeling locked up because migrants with undocumented status or no work permit are paid less and work in less stable jobs. This job instability contributes to a sense of economic paralysis and exploitation. For example, Nestor, a forty-year-old Nicaraguan immigrant, and his Costa Rican wife, Melissa, struggled to make ends meet and feed their two young sons. Melissa lamented that her husband's undocumented status made him subject to exploitation at his work as a security guard:

> There's nothing to do, because there where he works, they exploit him a lot. More and more because right now he doesn't have the *cédula* [national id card]. He just has a passport. And they exploit him a lot. They pay him like [US]$500. They don't pay him his days off; they don't pay him holidays; they don't pay him his *aguinaldo*.* And that is what we're living on. But God has given us a hand. Because sometimes we barely scrape by.

At his wife's urging, Nestor had even submitted a formal complaint to the Labor Ministry. Even though the Ministry had found in Nestor's favor, his employer continued to refuse to pay the full *aguinaldo*. As Melissa noted, "I think that these people, because they see him without papers or only with a passport, they think that they don't have to treat him well."

Nestor's lack of legal status reinforced his job insecurity, which in turn made it more difficult to afford residency. He felt he was in a catch-22. Before having kids, he could have afforded residency, but because he and Melissa were not legally married, he had not been eligible. Now he was eligible for legal status through his children, but could not afford it because of the cost. Nestor described his stress as an inability to "take the weight off," as both physically and emotionally draining, which prevented him from planning for the future. Illegality and poverty mutually reinforce Nicaraguans' vulnerability and raise the stakes of uncertainty in their lives.

This waiting oriented migrants toward the future even as they could not resolve their problems in the present. Claudia's husband, for example continued to hope that they would be able to "someday get out of where

---

* The *aguinaldo* is a thirteenth monthly salary paid in December and required by Costa Rican labor law. Although sometimes translated as a bonus, it is not "extra," but rather a calculated part of salaries. Poor and working-class migrants often depend on *aguinaldos* to pay debts or make major purchases or home repairs, send remittances to Nicaragua, and pay for Christmas festivities in both countries.

we are, this big hole we're locked up in." If laws can change, and one's relationship to the law can change—through, for example, the birth of a child in Costa Rica—then one's sense of illegality is only ever temporary. In this sense, migrants develop different creative ways to navigate Costa Rican immigration law and minimize the impacts of illegality on their lives, generating a space and time for waiting, even if their waiting was restricted to the narrow confines of their houses and neighborhoods. That is, waiting may be a result of uncertainty, but it also generates a time and space for future possibilities.

For Nicaraguans in Costa Rica, waiting entails enacting defensive, present-oriented tactics that play off the uncertain boundaries between legality and illegality and generate temporary senses of security for migrant families. These informal, temporary measures generate new, if makeshift, understandings of the law and of state power that are intimately tied to transnational family life. First, families prioritize and invest in residency for certain members over time. Gloria's husband, for example, is a resident. As a construction worker, a sector known for low wages and poor job security, Gloria's husband could earn more as a resident. Women like Gloria are often the last to attain residency. As Yolanda, an undocumented mother of four, explained, her husband had residency, her seventeen-year-old Nicaraguan-born daughter had residency, and her two Costa Rican–born children had citizenship, but she remained undocumented: "He got his residence permit almost three years ago, because, you know, he was working. We did it on purpose, so that he would earn better. He works in construction. In domestic work, one does not earn that well, and they don't demand [the residence permit]. In construction they do." Thus, families invest in residency little by little, with women usually the last to gain legal status. In 2012, Digmar was slowly pulling together the documents to apply for residency for his wife and himself, taking advantage of a temporary program to facilitate legalization: "We are taking advantage [of the program]. For us it is more difficult and it costs us more because we don't earn the quantities needed for these *vueltas*. We have to do them gradually." Even with the reduced costs of a temporary government legalization program, Digmar calculated they could only complete his paperwork that year, leaving his wife still undocumented.

In the calculations of residency, Nicaraguans balance the cost of applying for women against the earnings potential of men. Women who work primarily in the service sector as domestic workers in private homes may be less vulnerable to deportation in the first place, compared to men who work primarily in public places like construction sites and fruit plantations. Further, because women's migration is still a relatively new phenomenon;

sometimes men, who may have migrated years before their partners, have already achieved residency through employment or in the 1999 amnesty. That is, they were able to legalize their status before the latest restrictions and requirements were imposed. Investing in residency for men both mitigates the relative danger and vulnerability men experience on the street and provides access to higher wages and better working conditions.

Many women felt that as long as they carried their newborns or small babies, they would be safe because "who's going to detain me with a baby?" As newborn Costa Ricans, infants index their mothers' right to residency and in so doing they secure their mothers' de facto right to residency. Indeed, Judith, who had lived in Costa Rica since 2010, explained that she had never had a problem with migration police or officials because, "I say that when you're really delinquent [*vago*] you have problems with migration. I'm a moral woman [*mujer sana*]. When I go out, it's to take the kids somewhere or with my husband." For Judith, going out with her children or accompanied by her husband marked her as a mother and wife instead of a delinquent, thus protecting her from policing measures, which she believed pertained to "criminal" migrants, for whom she used masculine terms (*vago*, not *vaga*). Such forms of self-profiling, like restrictions of movement more generally, mean that migrants attempt to embody forms of legality and avoid both legally and morally suspect movements.

Juana, a domestic worker whose son and daughter-in-law also lived in Costa Rica, had discussed with her daughter-in-law how to use Costa Rica's more robust paternity laws to protect her family:

> My daughter-in-law, what has she said about this immigration problem? Well, "If they catch him," she says, "immediately what I have to do to keep him is go put a, like a child support, so that they won't let him cross the border." It's a wedge, to avoid the father's deportation and so the children won't be left alone. It's the only option they have.

Drawing on Costa Rican legal provisions for responsible paternity, Juana planned to parlay one form of legality (paternity laws) into a legal immigration status. According to her, the child-support order would supersede the deportation order, creating a kind of wedge that blocked the border from closing, forcing the authorities to allow her son to stay. Here, Juana drew on her understanding of Costa Rican family law—which gives children the right to their fathers and gives fathers the responsibility to financially support their children—to counter illegality generated under immigration law. However, the Costa Rican Supreme Court has ruled a number of times that alimony or child-support claims should not delay or nullify a deportation (see for example Sala Constitucional, Resolución No. 14618 – 2020; Resolución No. 00161 – 2006; Resolución No. 03132 - 1999). Thus, these strategies are only temporary and ultimately do not resolve migrant illegality.

Accessing Care

These restrictions, bureaucratic hurdles, and xenophobia intersect in migrants' attempts to access public services such as healthcare and education in Costa Rica. Nicaraguans identified both as important and problematic sites of incorporation in Costa Rica, particularly for families. Such tensions are particularly important for Costa Rica, where both the universal healthcare and education systems have been foundational to national identity and discourses of Costa Rican exceptionalism. Access, or lack thereof, can be read as indicative of wider tensions about immigrant incorporation and belonging. Examining access to these two services is particularly important because they represent sites in which day-to-day interactions with state agents occur—moments at which the Costa Rican state ceases to be a faceless encounter with lines and paperwork and instead concretizes in interactions with clerks, school administrators, and doctors.

Before 2010, migrants were able to obtain health insurance and access the national healthcare system relatively easily, either through employers (for documented migrants) or by paying a voluntary insurance fee (for undocumented immigrants). The primary barrier to access was the cost of insurance. However, under current law immigrants without legal status cannot register with the Caja Costarricense de Seguro Social (CCSS, or la Caja for short) and, through this, access healthcare services. Healthcare for children, as well as prenatal and emergency care are exempted from this insurance requirement. However, even access to prenatal care has become a matter of debate. In 2013, not long after I left Costa Rica, the CCSS drafted a resolution to restrict the access of pregnant women in irregular status to emergency care only (Sandoval García 2015). Disagreement within the CCSS and advocacy by academic, NGO, and civil society networks pushed the CCSS for clarification and eventually reaffirmed women's right to prenatal care no matter their legal status. However, once women give birth, they are no longer eligible for care within the public system (Sandoval García 2015). This conflict over access to care for pregnant women highlights the importance of legal status for access to services and rights for migrants in Costa Rica. The conflict over access for pregnant women also demonstrates that, as with immigration law, implementation of restrictions has been plagued by lack of clarity within and across state institutions, which has translated into more degrees of freedom for counter clerks and other public sector employees working at the operational level to determine their own criteria for providing access to care.

That said, migrant parents emphasized that they were usually able to access services for their children, and that the quality of care was much higher than in Nicaragua. Services for children are relatively easy to access for a number of reasons. First, Costa Rican law guarantees children's access to healthcare and education regardless of immigration status. Second, many Nicaraguan migrants have Costa Rican–born children, who are citizens, which gives them a leg up in accessing services.

However, even in accessing services for children, migrants faced barriers. For example, children were sometimes turned away from clinics and hospitals because of their undocumented status (Fouratt and Voorend 2018). A number of times, I listened as the community center social worker called to remind clinics of migrants' legal eligibility for prenatal or pediatric care and watched as she helped migrant mothers make sense of extra steps and requirements they were being asked to fulfill. Similar issues emerged in accessing education. The social worker noted that she frequently intervened in cases where local school officials requested extra documents to enroll Nicaraguan children. This points to the ways tying integration to legalization and giving power to counter-level public officials produces new distinctions between deserving and undeserving that determine migrants' access to services.

When denied access to public services, immigrants sought alternatives in the private sector, particularly for health services like doctors' appointments and medication. Some had medicines sent from Nicaragua, where they can be purchased more cheaply. Many went to the *pulperria*, or corner store, for basic medicines. Others went to pharmacies and consulted with a pharmacist before purchasing medications. This is a common strategy, even among Costa Ricans, given the long wait times for appointments in public clinics. Migrants also relied on the private sector for specialists and diagnostic exams, reserving the public system for unavoidable emergencies.

However, even for those with access to healthcare and other services, xenophobia represented a major barrier to quality care. As Mariela, a legal resident, noted, "With papers it is a bit better, but I feel that there is still that discrimination. Maybe not for not having papers, because even with papers there still is [discrimination], just because of our country [of origin]. I have my papers in order, but I have had problems." Similarly, Ruth, who had a Costa Rican–born daughter and was insured by the CCSS, described the attention she received during her pregnancy in 2010: "I feel that there's also a terrible medical attention for immigrants. Yes, when I was pregnant . . . I got pregnant soon after arriving [in Costa Rica], and the doctor spoke to me like I was stupid. They think that because you're Nicaraguan you're illiterate, ignorant, stupid, and it's not true."

Mistreatment within the healthcare system is not only degrading, frustrating, and humiliating for Nicaraguans, but in some cases has long-term health and legal consequences. For example, Darling, who had first entered Costa Rica with her partner, Abel, in 1998, had moved back and forth between the two countries a number of times. But things became more complicated when their son was born in 2005. When Darling gave birth in the San Juan de Dios hospital in San José, she was forced to give birth without her husband with her; she was treated brusquely and unkindly by hospital staff and medical professionals. Such mistreatment is common in public hospitals, where advocates have long protested obstetric violence and poor treatment of pregnant and laboring women (Levine 2015; for more on obstetric violence in Latin America more broadly, see Castro and Savage 2019; Dixon 2020; Pérez D'Gregorio 2010; Sadler et al. 2016; Williams et al. 2018).

Costa Rican public hospitals do not routinely offer pain management like epidurals or medication for women in labor. However, neglect of patients, disregard for their pain, and humiliation are particularly severe for immigrant women (Goldade 2009; Spesny Dos Santos 2015). After Darling gave birth, the lack of compassion continued:

> When he was born, Abel, my husband said that if it was a girl, to give her the name Nercy. And if it was a boy, Omar. And since I was still with contractions, because I was still having contractions after he was born, I was in agony, and the woman came and said, "What are you going to name him?" And I couldn't even remember because of that pain, and so I told her, "I don't know." And she looked at me, and said, "What do you mean you don't know?" And so I said, "Nercy." And he still appears on his papers with that name. And the boy has suffered because he doesn't want that name.

At the time, Darling had not yet even held her baby boy. The insistence of an impatient nurse has followed the child ever since. Although Darling was able to get his birth recorded in Nicaragua with the name Omar, his Costa Rican birth certificate still bears the name Nercy. Darling returned to Nicaragua with the baby until 2011, when they moved back to Costa Rica to enroll him in school. Thanks to his Nicaraguan documents, teachers acquiesced to calling him Omar, though he is officially registered in school and at the local health clinic as Nercy. The process to complete the name change in Costa Rica was confusing and difficult, and Darling and

Abel had been unable to complete it because they could not afford a lawyer. Abel explained:

> We have to get an authenticated copy of our IDs, mine and hers, copy of our passports with a valid Costa Rican visa, a copy of his ID card and birth certificate here, go to the bank to pay, you know, like you would an ID card, more or less. I don't know how much it is. Then to the registry, to start all the paperwork. There in the registry, you have to pay some official stamps so they get his papers out of the archive and start the registry process all over again, as if he was just born again. So that he can legally have the name Omar. It takes about five months, they told me. But you have to pay.

Besides the costs involved in the process, the requirements to present the parents' passports with a valid Costa Rican visa or residency made the process almost impossible for Darling and Abel to complete.

Further, the children of Nicaraguan migrants, whether they were born in Nicaragua or Costa Rica, face severe discrimination from the wider society, particularly from peers and teachers within schools. Although Costa Rican-born children are citizens under the *jus soli* principle, these children are largely not considered "true Costa Ricans" and are caught in a "symbolic ambiguity [. . .] and will most likely always be perceived as first generation migrants" (Spesny Dos Santos 2015, 5). As Claudia noted, "what happens is here they discriminate a lot" and her daughters, "hide because they feel discriminated against." All three of Claudia's Nicaraguan-born daughters had faced discrimination. Her middle daughter feared admitting she was Nicaraguan to her boyfriend, "If I say I'm Nica, I feel like I'll lose him." Her oldest, Valeria, faced nasty comments from her mother-in-law when she first moved in with her partner. Her mother-in-law suggested that Valeria was going to cheat on him, implying that Nicaraguan women are promiscuous.

Rather than face such comments, Claudia's fourteen-year-old daughter Yessica regularly told people she was Panamanian. "She resists saying she's Nica. She hides her ID card," her mother complained. Yessica explained, "Because of everything that's on the news." One time, "a classmate said, 'My cell phone was stolen and it was a Nica.' So see? That's why." To avoid insults and discrimination in the streets and schools, many, like Yessica, tried to pass as a nationality other than Nicaraguan. While Yessica passed as Panamanian because of her dark skin, many Nicaraguans try to pass as from Guanacaste, the northwest region of Costa Rica that was annexed from Nicaragua in the late nineteenth century (Alvarenga 2004). Indeed, residents of this region sometimes are known pejoratively as "borrowed Nicaraguans." Migrants and their children, whether Nicaraguan or Costa

Rican born, felt that they could not leave behind their Nicaraguan-ness, no matter how long they had lived in Costa Rica.

Conclusion

Nicaraguan immigrants are caught in a legal limbo as they may have rights to residency but find it difficult to put together the elements necessary to achieve that status. It is in this sense that Costa Rican immigration law manages to both promote integration and maintain Nicaraguans' otherness, so that they may be physically present but legally outsiders (Calavita 2005). Undocumented immigrants are trapped not just by frequent legal changes or increasing restrictions, but by complicated bureaucratic procedures that prevent them from resolving their legal dilemmas. Although Costa Rican law produces illegality, the many changes in the law also mean that Nicaraguans rarely perceive their unauthorized status as permanent. Future changes in the law may provide avenues for legalization. One's family or job circumstances may change, making it easier to comply with existing requirements. Further, through their own creative measures, Nicaraguan migrants not only find quasi-legal ways to navigate immigration law but enact new forms of legality that challenge state-enacted legal measures. Rather than clearly resolve immigrant illegality, these temporary measures create conditions that allow migrants to wait and to defer the ultimate determination of their legal status.

In addition to their legal precariousness, Nicaraguan migrants face intense discrimination and xenophobia. While xenophobia may be rooted in historical notions of Costa Rican national identity, the increasing intensity of such discourses is the result of social, economic, and political tensions between the two countries, and social and economic changes in Costa Rica. Migrants often reported to me feeling unsafe or uncomfortable on public transportation, walking through the city, and in interactions with education and health professionals in the public sector. As discourses about immigrants as a burden to the nation-state increase in intensity, access to health and education services represent important sites of conflict and tension over inclusion and exclusion. Indeed, because the governance of migration has been dispersed among social service providers and public institutions, access to services has as much to do with who is sitting at the counter as it does with legal status.

The ad-hoc implementation and the bureaucratic procedures entailed in applying for residency and accessing services demonstrate how immigration laws aimed at resolving problems of illegality may actually reinforce migrants' vulnerability by generating new forms of marginalization. In this case, legality is determined not at one particular moment in an encounter with the immigration system but at several points along the process. Determinations of legality are part of the bureaucratic inscriptions that make migrants visible to state institutions and agents. The result is that while integration efforts and government officials assume that legality is an all-or-nothing, black-or-white issue, in practice most undocumented immigrants occupy varying gradations of liminal statuses that contribute to their social and economic exclusion. The higher fees and fines as well as the public perception that Nicaraguans are undeserving and do not belong, trap Nicaraguan families between their legal rights and their illegal status. In other words, because migrants like Gloria are legally entitled to residency but find it practically impossible to complete the process, the new law has produced liminal statuses that are neither completely legal nor illegal (Kubal 2013). Such exclusion impacts not just individual migrants or their children and partners in Costa Rica, but their children and extended families back in Nicaragua as well.

CHAPTER 3

Single Mothers and Absent Fathers

IN 2009, ELENA AND I sat drinking coffee and chatting in the front room of the ASTRADOMES office. At the time, I was asking her some preliminary questions about her migration story. Elena interrupted me, "You have to understand my life before I left to understand my life here in Costa Rica." As I would learn over the next three years of close contact with Elena, her life before she left and as a migrant was marked by a complicated relationship with her husband, his infidelity, and her drive to make life better for her children.

Elena had talked extensively about her three adult children back in Nicaragua. Her two sons were studying at university. In 2011, during another *cafecito* at ASTRADOMES, she told me about how her oldest son, Kobe, had struggled with drug addiction and dropped out of university, but had turned himself around and was studying again. Her daughter had moved back home with her two children after separating from her partner. As she looked pointedly at my pregnant belly, she asked me how many children I wanted to have, but did not wait for my reply. "I only ever wanted two children," she declared. I was taken aback for a moment, because in the two years I had known her, I had learned that Jefferson, her third and youngest child, was her pride and joy. She went on to explain, "I had been separated from my husband for five years, and I started to work. And in this job, I had to drop my kids off at a daycare, and my ex-husband worked nearby. And he started to tell me stories, and I, the idiot, because there is no other word for it, no better word, stupid, I listened to him." Elena's husband was jealous that she had an admirer at her job, and so began to woo her all over again.

Years earlier, he had left her for another woman when she was four months pregnant with her daughter, Scarleth, just before the end of the Sandinista Revolution. At the time, Elena was a primary school teacher. Once her husband left, she managed to care for her young son and her newborn daughter with the help of her family and with the friendship of a German teacher, who had come to visit Nicaragua through the Ministry of Education and lived with her for a few months. For five years, Elena and her husband were separated, and then in 1990, as her husband flirted and tried to reconcile with her, history repeated itself; she became pregnant with her youngest child, and her husband left her again. A few years later, when Jefferson was three, Elena would migrate to Costa Rica for the first time, to provide for her children.

Infidelity would mark her early experiences there, too. She stayed with her brother and his wife, but her brother was also seeing another woman. Three days after arriving in Costa Rica, her brother's wife "threw me and some of my clothes out on the street. She kept the clothes she liked." Elena was lucky in that her brother's new girlfriend allowed them both to move in with her. She was a domestic worker and taught Elena how to use all the "equipment" necessary for the job in middle-class Costa Rican households—the vacuum, blender, and washing machine.

Elena and her husband would reconcile a second time in 2004, when the children were teenagers, but that reconciliation would not last either. Economic need made her return to work in Costa Rica. In 2009, she went back to Granada and "found everything a mess. He had a new woman. He didn't have her in my house, but he wanted to move her in [while I was in Costa Rica]." There was also an issue with the house title, which he had managed to put in his name at some point. They separated again, but when she returned to Costa Rica, he continued living in the house she was building with her remittances. In 2012, he was still living in the house part-time and trying to claim the property title, despite maintaining his other partner in a house in town. Despite his frequent betrayals, Elena was willing to take her husband back because of the power of legal and religious marriage and national discourses of family unity that have further entrenched concepts of the traditional patriarchal nuclear family.

As I argued in Chapter 1, families have been a key resource for navigating the uncertainties of life in Nicaragua. It is important, then, to understand both how migration and separation shape or interact with existing family dynamics—including understandings, expectations, and practices of mothering, fathering, and marriage— and how these relationships have influenced Nicaraguans' decisions around migration. Thus, rather than examine transnational kinship as a deviation from "normal" family life, this chapter examines how one key feature of Nicaraguan family life—marriage informality and instability—shapes transnational families. In Chapter 1, I examined state attempts to mold the family according to state visions of solidarity and sacrifice; here, I turn to people's own negotiations of their roles within the dominant framework of the nuclear family.

The reification of the nuclear family as the fundamental social unit of the Nicaraguan nation has contributed to a discourse of "crisis" in the family. That is, if the basis of the family is marriage, then divorce and separation constitute the root of family, and thus social, breakdown. Such family instability is seen as both the cause of social problems and declining moral values and a consequence of migration (Chant 2002). However, distinctions between stable and unstable families reify the two-parent patriarchal nuclear family as the fundamental social unit, dissociating families from the precarious economic, social, and political context in which they live. Contrasting the reality of Nicaraguan family life with ideals of the traditional nuclear family, this chapter examines how Nicaraguan men and women understand the gendered expectations of marriage and parenting. I turn to two related "problems"—single mothers and absent fathers—to show how Nicaraguan men and women understand what it means to be a husband/father and wife/mother given not only cultural gender norms but also current economic and social realities in the country.

A key feature of family life in Nicaragua is marriage informality—that is, *uniones libres* or de facto marriages. I focus particularly on these unions because the vast majority of Nicaraguans I have interviewed in both Nicaragua and Costa Rica were in or had been in *uniones libres* rather than formal marriages. Elena, who referred to her husband as her ex-husband, though they were not formally divorced, was my only interviewee who had *only* been in a legal marriage. Most others had been in multiple informal relationships. That men and women described both de facto and civil or religious commitments as "marriage" underscores the ways religious, legal, and political frameworks condition how people understand the meaning of family and enact family relationships. Although family configurations often exist outside formal legal frameworks and structures, family continues to represent a fundamental institution in people's lives and in the larger society.

Marriage Informality in Nicaragua

Half of all unions in Nicaragua take place outside the legal and religious frameworks of formal marriage (Castro Martín 2002; Laplante et al. 2015).

They are alternately called consensual unions or de facto marriages—
uniones de hecho or *uniones libres* in Spanish. State officials and religious
leaders often view these relationships as less stable than legal or religious
marriages and more prone to breakdown. Although perceived as problematic, they are also widespread and socially accepted in both Nicaragua and
Costa Rica, especially among the working class and poor, who may find
the financial costs of formal marriage prohibitive. Among almost all of the
families I interviewed, those who described themselves as "married" were,
in fact, in de facto unions. And such couples used the terms *casados*, that
is married, or *juntados*, literally paired or joined, interchangeably. They
also interchangeably described their partners as *parejas* (couple or partner) *marido* (husband), *esposo/a* (husband/wife/spouse), or *compañero/a*
(literally, companion, but also significant other). Most of the Nicaraguan
men and women I have interviewed over the years have been *juntados* several times in their lives and have children from different unions but have
never been formally or legally married. For example, Jasmina, one of our
neighbors in Granada, had three children by her *ex-esposo* and three children with her current partner. In both cases, the unions had been informal and not legal marriages.

Though such unions often are seen as a new social problem, historically,
they have been prevalent in Nicaragua and much of Latin America. Since
the colonial period, formal marriage and the patriarchal nuclear family generated through it existed alongside widespread practices of extramarital
unions. For example, Raymond Smith (1984, 1987) has described the existence of a "dual-marriage system" in Latin America and the Caribbean
in which "nonlegal unions" were integral to kinship and family. Formal
marriage and the nuclear family were particularly important for elites and
emerging middle classes for ensuring property transmission; only children born within legally recognized marriages could inherit (Castro Martín 2002; Olwig 2013). At the same time, scholars estimate that throughout Latin America more than 30 percent of births in the colonial period
occurred outside of wedlock (Kuznesof and Oppenheimer 1985). Men commonly maintained various households—often a legally legitimate family
and another informal union, with children in both cases. Among the working and lower classes, flexible and extensive kin networks were the norm
(Olwig 2013, 134).

Through the nineteenth century, though the patriarchal family was institutionalized as an ideal through religious and political discourse, rates of
official marriage and households' resemblance to the patriarchal nuclear
family varied greatly with region, class, and ethnicity (Dore 1997). Other
family patterns—unmarried cohabitating couples, single-female headed

households, illegitimate children, and child abandonment—were seen as aberrations, abnormalities or pathologies that threatened social stability, but they were also common. This pattern has held into the twentieth and twenty-first centuries. In the 1990s, consensual unions represented 55.9 percent of all unions in Nicaragua; this pattern is repeated throughout Central America (Castro Martín 2002; Laplante et al. 2015). Further, in Latin America, informal unions have not represented a transitional or trial period before marriage (as we have seen in the US and Western Europe with cohabitating couples), rather many unions never formalize, implying that a significant number of families are built outside the traditional framework of marriage (Castro Martín 2002, 35).

Although such informal unions have been widespread and recognized, they have not enjoyed the same level of prestige as formal marriage. Until 1979, Nicaraguan family law defined formal marriage as the only legitimate basis for the creation of family relationships. Beth Stephens (1988, 142) notes that the Nicaraguan civil code defined marriage as a "lifetime contract" in which the family was a means for producing indisputable and legitimate heirs. The law made no provision for children born out of wedlock, unless the father specifically chose to recognize them. Recognition did not erase such children's status as illegitimate but brought them under their father's authority. This dual system contributed to a social structure in which consensual unions were widespread but represented serious disadvantages, especially for women and children.

The social and economic costs of illegitimacy were high for mothers and children. Unrecognized children born out of wedlock were not entitled to their fathers' financial support, much less inheritance. They could not claim social security through the father, and there were major difficulties if a parent or other adult tried to travel out of the county with unrecognized children. The adult would have to file a notarized document declaring the child fatherless because they could not produce paternal permission in order to obtain passports or exit permits. Further, children born out of wedlock were not entitled to their father's last name—permanently and publicly marking them as illegitimate. This legal code also perpetuated the dual marriage system because it lowered the incentives for responsible fatherhood. As Stephens (1988) points out, if a man wanted to maintain both a "legitimate," legal family and one or more additional unions to which he contributed nothing, this legal system not only made it possible, but protected his right to do so.

However, recognition could also be dangerous for women and children. In Nicaragua, like elsewhere in Latin America, the law granted men *patria potestad*, or absolute authority over minor children born into legal marriage, as well as over illegitimate children they chose to recognize. Women exercised legal authority over children only in the absence of a legally recognized father. Because of this, Nicaraguan women often feared that a child recognized by his or her father might be taken away and given to another paternal female relative to raise (Stephens 1988).

During the 1980s, the Sandinista reforms focused on gender equality mentioned in Chapter 1 altered the legal status of *uniones de hecho* by eliminating the category of "illegitimate," recognizing de facto unions, and holding absent fathers accountable for child support. The 1987 Constitution elevated de facto unions "to the same constitutionally protected status as legal marriage" and made them eligible for the same social benefits (Kampwirth 1998, 57). Under the new constitution, children were entitled to two surnames and to their father's recognition and financial support.

Such reforms were difficult to enforce, though, and their impacts were often contradictory for families. For example, Diana, a Nicaraguan woman in her forties originally from Granada, had her first child, Kenneth, and separated from the child's father not long after the reforms were put in place. In 1989, when Kenneth was born, his father refused to give him his surname, implying that Diana had been unfaithful to him, and marking Kenneth as illegitimate, despite the new law. Kenneth explained, "As a small child, my papa hadn't established me with his surname. My mom went that day and registered me with her last name." But several years later, Diana left Kenneth with her mother and migrated to Costa Rica. Conflicts between Diana's family and her ex's over custody of Kenneth escalated. Her ex-husband hired a lawyer and legally recognized the boy. He then was able to remove the boy from his maternal grandmother's care. His maternal grandmother would not regain physical custody until many years later. As Kenneth's case shows, legal recognition of children by their fathers can have negative consequences in the context of marriage informality and relationship instability. Other women, like Elena, complained that even though from the 1980s onward legally fathers had to provide child support, compelling men to do so was far from easy because many worked in the informal sector, where it was impossible to dock wages or otherwise compel payments.

As the Contra War intensified, families faced more pressures to provide for themselves through flexible care arrangements and strategies. Separations occasioned by military service compounded other forms of paternal absence and irresponsibility, while Sandinista social programs both offered new forms of support to single mothers and depended upon women's unpaid work as volunteers. Legal marriage, in this context, provided few advantages over informal marriage or *uniones de hecho*. With the end of the Contra War, families faced a new set of challenges as the new administration aggressively promoted traditional family values, while cutting social support to the most vulnerable households. Further, high unemployment, heightened by the demobilization of thousands of soldiers on both sides of the conflict, generated a situation in which this traditional family model, while publicly exalted and politically reinforced, was almost untenable for the majority of families.

Discourses of reconciliation at the national level, both from Violeta de Chamorro's administration and today under Ortega's, have translated into an emphasis on "family unity." This push to "strengthen" the family resulted in a new Family Code in 2014, one dedicated to the unity of the traditional family (Jiménez 2015). The new code also formalized what counts as a de facto union and, in so doing, lowered their status. Before 2014, what constituted a stable de facto union was not clearly defined, providing a lot of flexibility in terms of claiming constitutional rights guaranteed under the 1980s reforms. However, the new code established that de facto unions would not count until they had been established for at least two years and formalized by a judge or notary. This formalization of informal marriages left the partners "in a legal limbo and without recognized rights" (Jiménez 2015).

At the same time, informality continues to offer flexibility. Women in formal marriages have little power over their spouse's infidelity and may find it harder to escape violent relationships (Lancaster 1992). In contrast, *uniones de hecho* are easy to dissolve. Elena, for instance, was still legally married to her ex-husband simply because it was too costly and complicated to divorce. In Granada, he was a stubborn presence, refusing to move out of the house she had built with her remittances, even though relations between their children and him were strained. Formal marriage made removing him from the house more difficult, despite the fact that he had another partner whom he maintained in another house in town. Indeed, in 2012, Elena was trying to find legal solutions to her husband's continued insistence that the house belonged to him.

Further, Nicaraguans express growing desires for companionate marriage based in affection and mutual understanding and fostered by global media, migration, and shifting gender ideals (Hirsch 2007; Padilla et al. 2007), as well as national discourses of solidarity, empowerment, and equality promoted during the Sandinista Revolution (Babb 2001; Quesada 1998). Given both global discourses about love, care, and family and national rhetoric of revolution, marriage is increasingly seen by Nicaraguan women, and men, as a partnership of equality, mutuality, and sharing—a substantive, solidary relationship between equals. In this context, consensual unions reflect choice and substance over regulations and traditional family norms. Still, while the patriarchal nuclear family may not reflect the diversity of Nicaraguan families today, it remains the primary model in terms of which people define their participation in family life and their dissatisfaction with it.

Absent Fathers

In the context of marriage informality, stereotypes and stories of absent fathers circulate widely. Some attribute marriage instability to *machista* concepts of masculinity. Other public discourses connect men's absences from family life in Nicaragua to migration. While each of these may contain a grain of truth, they blame individual men for being bad husbands and fathers rather than recognize absent fathers as linked to marriage informality, Nicaraguan concepts of masculinity, and the reality of economic crisis and poverty. Nicaraguan men are caught between neo-Sandinista visions of the "new man" as both protector and nurturer, provider and partner, and enduring concepts of macho masculinity that value power over the family and especially women, assertions of virility, violence/aggression, and domination. At its best, such a masculinity translates into the patriarchal fatherfigure who provides for and protects his family. At its worst, it characterizes and values toughness, violence, and dominance as masculine behaviors. Further, these models of masculinity exist in tension with economic pressures that make it harder for men to live up to the model of husband/father as the primary provider and protector.

Economic provision is the hallmark of responsible fatherhood, a fulfillment of the traditional role of the father as breadwinner and protector. In Rio Azul, Martín viewed his role in the family in these terms:

> By nature, right? I was born, well, and you continue believing what they taught you when you were little, right? We could say that the dad, or the father of the family is the head of the household, the one who has to make an effort to take charge of everything, the whole house. What does this mean? That mama is with the children, watching them, taking care of them, and really overseeing the development that each one . . . needs a different attention. But really, if the two of us go into the street to work, or, we create this division of going so far away. To put it this way, you're left with this blemish. So all of this means to me that the father of the family has to

make an effort to earn enough to cover all the basic necessities—economic and emotional—that the family needs.

In Martín's account, the father emerged as the natural protector and provider of the family, responsible for financial well-being, while the mother guides the moral development of the children. Her role, he argues, is focused inward on the home and family, while men's role is to protect and provide for them primarily by working outside the house.

In both Costa Rica and Nicaragua, men maintained that economic provision was the most important characteristic of a father. Daniel, a migrant man who was left responsible for his young son when his partner left, said that he had never expected to be responsible for the day-to-day physical and emotional labor of caring for a child: "I wasn't born for this; I was born to be a man and have a family. [...] Like all men, I thought that I was going to have my family, my children, my woman, my wife and raise them, be a responsible father of the family, and that's it." Daniel went on to explain that popular ideas of fatherhood and machismo, in both Costa Rica and Nicaragua, made men think that men only "take charge of working, some halfway responsible ones, of bringing home provisions, and drinking."

If the role of economic provider has been key to masculine identity, the last forty years of instability in Nicaragua and broader social and economic changes in Latin America have challenged men's status as providers and their ability to meet families' needs, calling into question these masculine ideals and highlighting negative traits associated with masculinity. As men's ability to fulfill their role of breadwinner has been challenged by economic crisis, the informalization of men's work, and the large-scale incorporation of women into the workforce, so too has the basis of their masculine identity (Chant 2002). Some men, then, see migration as a way to fulfill their role as provider, even if it requires physical absence from the family.

Indeed, failure to live up to their responsibility as economic providers represented the primary way men absent themselves from families and communities in Nicaragua. Though Nicaraguan men may be physically present in homes and communities, they are understood as largely absent from families or at best, temporary members. In both Nicaragua and Costa Rica, men are present everywhere, hanging out on street corners, in bars. In Rio Azul, Diana's husband collected metal scraps from around the neighborhood and I often saw him inspecting garbage on the main road as I rode the bus to and from the community center. However, he rarely contributed to the household income, instead using his meager earnings to drink in a local cantina. Sometimes, Diana would go days without hearing from him.

When he was at home, he was often violent. In fact, community center staff warned me not to visit Diana at home because of his violent and unpredictable behavior. The one time I did visit her at home, it was because her husband was in the hospital after a fight with a neighbor, and thus we could be sure he would not arrive during our conversation.

Such violence, often compounded by alcohol use, represents another form of male absence from families, as women may seek to remove abusive partners and fathers from households or may end relationships to escape such violence. National surveys indicate that 50 percent of Nicaraguan women between the ages of fifteen and forty-nine have experienced some kind of abuse—verbal, physical, or sexual—from their partners (INIDE 2007, 2013). Aracely was a mother of two young children from Somoto, an area outside of Estelí. Even before he left her for another woman, Aracely's husband would arrive home drunk and beat her: "Yes, when he came home drunk, he'd throw us out in the street. Sometimes, my oldest son would spend the night at my neighbor's because one time [my son] was sleeping and we didn't think [my husband] was going to come home, when he arrived with a machete." Another time, after he got into an altercation at a local bar, her husband tried to climb into bed with her with a knife. Aracely pushed him out, but not before he cut her cheek so deeply she still had a scar years later. Her daughter, just two at the time, witnessed the violence and suffered from nightmares for years afterward. His abuse included emotional attacks, in which he humiliated her, often in front of his new partner. For Aracely, her husband's abuse and infidelity compounded his lack of contributions to household expenses and financial support for their two children. Eventually, she was able to move in with her mother, though her ex-partner continued to harass her.

In Nicaragua, men's infidelity has been both common and widely tolerated (Lancaster 1992, xiv). This infidelity and maintenance of multiple households is understood as a consequence of men's sexuality, with virility and sexual appetite as another hallmark of masculine identity. In talking about her ex-husband's various relationships outside their marriage, Elena argued that men were driven by their sexual needs, while women valued their children:

> I understand my ex-husband because men can't be alone. In contrast we women can. I can, and it's worth repeating that it's been almost seventeen years that I've been out of the country, and no man has pulled the rug out from under me to go rolling around with anybody. Because what mattered to me was to help my children in Nicaragua get ahead, not to come make a family here in Costa Rica.

Elena contrasted her own maternal self-sacrifice with her ex-husband's, and men's more generally, insatiable sexual appetite. Like Elena, women often experienced men's infidelity as abandonment. Given hegemonic gender roles and because custody of children from informal unions tends to stay with the mother when those unions end, the dissolution of informal marriages often results in the absence of fathers from homes where children live.

For Aracely, her husband's violence, infidelity, and lack of financial support were all linked. "At first, I had my house," she explained. "I was with my husband, my partner, and my two children, but then he fell in love with another woman, he left with another woman. Yes, that's when my life began to suffer because he abandoned my children. He didn't remember to give them anything and he was with the other woman." While some men continued to maintain two or more households, supporting children by previous partners as well as current relationships, others found it impossible to do so given low wages and unstable employment. That is, the context of marriage informality and the tolerance for men's dual households has created a contradictory situation in which men fulfill their paternal responsibility by providing economically for their family, but they may be maintaining more than one family, making it more difficult to fulfill this role or to enforce paternal obligations.

While the men I interviewed spoke little about the process of relationship breakup, they were likely to form new households with new partners (see Chant 2002; Gomáriz 1997). Most had children with multiple women, or fathered children with another woman while still married. They emphasized interpersonal conflict and jealousy as reasons for separation. Several also emphasized that decisions to dissolve a union were often the woman's choice, a process made easier by marriage informality. Digmar and Warner, security guards in our neighborhood in Costa Rica, had both separated from long-term partners several years before migrating to Costa Rica. As Digmar put it, "she switched me for another."

Men like Martín, Digmar, Warner, and Daniel were caught between contradictory and often unattainable models of masculinity. As their ability to provide for families or assert control over their romantic partners has decreased because of economic realities and new legal frameworks, they have looked for other ways to assert their masculinity. For all four, migration represented one way to fulfill what they saw as their paternal responsibilities through economic provision for families in Nicaragua. However, in practice, migration complicated these gendered expectations for family responsibilities by replacing physical presence with economic provision at a distance. This is explored further in the next chapter on transnational parenting.

Single Mothers

Mothering in Nicaragua is understood in direct contrast to these fatherly absences. Mothers assume the primary responsibility for caring for children, homes, and families. As both Costa Rican and Nicaraguan women often remarked to me in conversations about mothering, "definitively, children belong to their mothers," or in direct contrast to fathers, "las mamas damos más" ("we mothers give more"). Martín's wife, Claudia, described a mother as complementing the work of a father/husband: "Well, I think that a mamá, and this is how I am, encompasses many things. Education, protection of the children because except for the parents, children are unprotected. In the same way, I have helped my husband a lot doing the housework as well as things like keeping them in school." Claudia understood her role as providing moral guidance and overseeing her children's education as well as providing the nurturing or care work required for the household. This is a direct complement to her husband's economic provisioning. In fact, she saw her role as literally "helping" her husband, the head of the household. Both she and Martín saw mothers as the moral center of the home, contributing to discipline and watching out for the girls.

Such dedication to children and to care work is framed in terms of a feminine ideal of self-sacrifice, modeled on the religious figure of the Virgin Mary (Hidalgo Xirinachs 2016; Yarris 2017). Nicaraguan women spoke at length of the work of caring for children on a daily basis, and of the particularly taxing problems of caring for sick children. Mothers with smaller children talked about the physical demands of raising young children—the washing, feeding, and caring for little ones—that we as new mothers shared. At a workshop on care for the network of relatives of migrants in Managua, women discussed the various tasks that encompassed their labor as mothers and grandmothers. As the women complained that their work was rarely recognized or appreciated, the facilitator commented, that though care work was often denigrated as "unspecialized" or "unskilled," "who is more qualified than we girls [chiquillas] who from the time we were small have been taught to care for others?" Women explicitly described this work as physically and emotionally exhausting, a constant sacrifice requiring the giving or using up of oneself in the service of children.

Although the nurturing or care work of raising children and running households remains a mainstay of women's identity, expectations for women as mothers have shifted alongside economic crisis and transformations in masculinity in Nicaragua. Although traditional notions of motherhood reflect patriarchal values and emphasize humility, patience, obedience, and submission (Navarro 2002), as with masculinity and the traditional nuclear family more generally, this archetype of the good mother is not the only model available to Nicaraguan women. In addition to the legal reforms instituted by the Sandinistas, the Revolution provided other avenues for reshaping ideals and practices of motherhood. As in other Latin American countries, motherhood became a focal point for organizing and a justification for women's political action (Bejarano 2002; Bouvard 2002; Stephen 1995). As noted in Chapter 1, during the Sandinista Revolution, images of the "new woman" emphasized women's roles as mothers in the service of the revolution and the nation. At the same time, women faced increased economic pressures at home as they faced men's absences for compulsory military service and scarcity due to embargoes.

Since the end of the Sandinista Revolution, despite political pressure for women to resume more traditional roles as mothers and wives, Nicaraguan women have continued to combine nurturing and care work with political and community engagement and paid employment. Paid work outside the home—or from small productive activities such as selling food and drinks from the house or on the street—is particularly important in the face of relationship instability. All of the women I interviewed over the course of fieldwork had engaged in income-earning activities at some point during their lives, whether through formal employment, temporary work, or the commercialization of their domestic work (see Mannon 2006).

For example, while Martín's wife Claudia framed her mothering in terms of traditional gender roles as a complement to her husband's economic provision for the family, she and her husband worked alongside each other, sewing small-scale clothing orders for local stores in San José, Costa Rica. In 2011, she would migrate by herself to work in Spain while Martín remained in Costa Rica with their daughters. In both Costa Rica and Nicaragua, many women made and sold tortillas out of their houses. When Elena's daughter stopped studying to get married, Elena sent her money to start selling food from her house so that she would have a way to support herself, rather than waiting for her husband to provide. Like many of the women I interviewed, Elena believed that women need to be capable of fending for themselves, rather than depending on unreliable men to take care of them. As though to prove her point, a few years later, her daughter, Scarleth, and her husband separated, and Scarleth and her two young children moved back into Elena's house. Both the instability and informality of conjugal relationships mean that women are likely, at some point in their lives, to be both single mothers and sole providers for their children. This, in turn, may drive some women to migrate to be able to ensure children's well-being.

Conclusion

In Nicaragua, practices of family-making exist in the context of decades of economic crisis, political conflict, and weak state institutions as well as in the shadow of powerful images of the nuclear family, the Virgin Mary, and the Sandinista Revolution. State institutions, politicians, and religious institutions attempt to stabilize and legitimate or, conversely, pathologize, certain family forms. The language of family is used not only to blame migrants for leaving, but also to blame the poor for their irresponsibility and lack of respectability. Such language informs the discourse on the redistribution of responsibilities between the private and public sectors in neoliberal reforms.

While discourses about the ideal nuclear family may permeate Nicaraguan communities, these discourses rarely describe how people "do" or even have "done" family for generations. Nicaraguan women—young and old—draw on a variety of representational regimes to portray their experiences of motherhood which include not only nurturing or care work but also productive and political work focused on children and children's futures. Women often described their mothering in contrast to the irresponsibility and absence of men as fathers. Single motherhood, while not necessarily an ideal, is culturally acceptable, especially in the face of infidelity, violence, and men's unemployment. And single mothers are rarely expected to "go it" alone but enjoy the support of extended family, as will be explored further in Chapter 5. Men, on the other hand, found themselves caught between two unattainable models of masculinity—that of the patriarchal breadwinner or the solidary partner and nurturer. Many turned to asserting their masculine identity in other ways—whether through migration or through drinking, infidelity, and violence.

The lived experiences of Nicaraguan families point to the malleable nature of ties based on marriage and practices of care that exist within broader conditions made possible by political and historical shifts. Indeed, discourses around family breakdown obscure the ways families try to make do in conditions of extreme economic crisis, seeking ways to provide for loved ones and forge tenuous futures. The instability that pervades Nicaraguan social life and economic conditions also affects marriage and intimate relations.

Thus, transnational families draw on family arrangements already in use by Nicaraguan families and already common in Nicaraguan society. Further, marriage regimes in Costa Rica are similar, with high levels of consensual unions, divorce and separation, and single-mothers. Such configurations, if not seen as ideal, are common, particularly among the poor and working class communities where many Nicaraguan migrants live (Budowski and Bixby 2003; Mannon 2006). Focusing on the diversity and flexibility of Nicaraguan family configurations and the reality of marriage informality highlights the tenuous nature of family ties believed to be fundamental to social relations. Indeed, fatherly absences make clear that absence, separation, and physical mobility are features of Nicaraguan kinship more broadly, not simply pathologies of transnational family life.

These flexible arrangements also offer a way to rethink men's and women's participation in families. Rather than highlight how transnational families deviate from cultural and political ideals of the nuclear family, flexible care arrangements point to the ways we may see kinship as an active process (Carsten 2000, 2004) and how all family relations must be understood within historical kinship patterns and economic and political transformations. The next chapter turns to the changes migration and the Costa Rican context bring to these families and reconsiders men's participation in transnational family life.

CHAPTER 4

Reconfiguring Relationships across Borders

ONE AFTERNOON, AFTER PARTICIPATING in an event with the Network of Migrant Women in San José, I talked with Rosa about why Nicaraguan women persisted in living and working in Costa Rica despite the hardships they encountered. Rosa explained, "like the majority of women, when we migrate, we migrate thinking of our children and of our families. On improving their quality of life. We don't even think about ourselves." Rosa had lived in Costa Rica for more than ten years and had first left her two daughters back in Nicaragua when they were very young. In linking their migration to parenting and other family responsibilities, Nicaraguan migrants like Rosa build on the changing ideals and expectations for family and parenting examined in the previous chapter. They also resist discourses that blame migration and migrants for family breakdown by insisting that far from abandoning families when they migrate, they migrate for their children. For both Nicaraguan men and women, migration represents an extension of their parenting. This chapter turns to transnational families as one configuration people employ to care for one another and explores reconfigurations of parenting in the context of migration.

While accounts of breakdown may be exaggerated, migration certainly entails a remaking of family life across borders. For those Nicaraguans whose family lives are already characterized by instability and separation, migration can exacerbate tensions within families. Further, the ways migrant men and women and family members back home understand parenting from afar and family responsibilities differ. Migrants with children in both Costa Rica and Nicaragua are caught between different models and expectations of parenting. Further, for children in Nicaragua, transnational separation means a readjustment of expectations and relationships. Children of migrants also develop their own perspectives on what family should look like through their experiences of transnational family life.

Parenting from Afar

The meanings of migration and practices through which migrants parent from afar are highly gendered. As noted in Chapter 3, migration may represent an active form of fathering in the context of high unemployment that endangers Nicaraguan men's abilities to fulfill expectations as breadwinners. This creates a paradox—men may be physically absent from homes, but financially present. As Jason Pribilsky (2007) and others (see for example Haenn 2019; Hirsch 2003) have argued, some Latin American men see the key cultural markers of masculine identity—for example, land and house ownership, marriage, and the ability to support a family—as often solely accessible through the economic opportunities provided by migration. Thus, Martín, who, in the last chapter saw the role of a father as that of provider, argued that, in the context of high unemployment and low wages in Nicaragua, he could not fulfill this role without leaving Nicaragua.

However, for many women and children, men's migration is fraught with fears over physical, financial, and emotional abandonment. In Nicaragua, women often expressed such fears, but I rarely observed cases in which fathers had cut off both financial support and contact with families in Nicaragua. One such case I observed secondhand, when talking to a group of Nicaraguan women over coffee after an ASTRADOMES workshop in 2009. As I asked the women why they had come to Costa Rica, Mardelí, a woman in her forties who had migrated from Chinandega in 1997, said that she had come because her husband had left her, abandoning her and their children when he himself moved to Costa Rica: "It's difficult to face the separation of a couple. The distance affected us, but the consequences are suffered by the children. He made his life one way, and I had to remake mine another." After fourteen years of marriage and two years of separation, her husband had found a new partner in Costa Rica. Shortly after, Mardelí made her way to Costa Rica herself to support the eight children her husband had left behind.

While Mardelí's husband used migration as a way to leave the marriage and family, in most families I observed, marriage dissolution or separation preceded both men's migration and their lack of remittances. That is, the abandonment that women and children experienced was due to the kind of relationship instability, informality, and infidelity examined in the previous chapter, rather than migration itself. For example, Aracely had worked for six months in Costa Rica after her abusive partner had left her and her children for another woman. She returned to Estelí because her mother warned her that her ex-husband was threatening to go to the authorities because he claimed Aracely had "abandoned" her children. She went to the Nicaraguan Ministry of the Family to protest:

> When I left for Costa Rica, he said he was going to take the children from me because I had abandoned them. Yes, so when I returned, I went to the Ministry of the Family with my mama. And my mama signed papers. And there we talked about why I left, that it wasn't because I had abandoned them. So they made an appointment with my ex-husband and he came. Yes, he arrived, and there they told him that what he had done *was* abandonment. Yes. And that I left to work out of necessity to support my children.

Here, Aracely contrasted her own absence "out of necessity" with her ex-*compañero*'s "abandonment." While he left the family for another woman, Aracely left the country for her children. Indeed, her ex's failure to provide for them necessitated Aracely's leaving. This further highlights how both informal and official understandings of "abandonment" incorporate not only physical distance but also financial absence.

However, Aracely's situation demonstrates how migrant women often face complex decisions over leaving children and social criticism for physically "abandoning" their families because they are often single mothers before migration. In other words, when men migrate, children are left at home with their mothers, but when women migrate, there is rarely another parent present to care for them (Abrego 2009). Indeed, it is common for men to provide little or no financial support for children after divorce or separation (Poeze and Mazzucato 2013). In the case of Aracely and her ex, the local office of the Ministry of the Family supported her custody of the children because they were not formally married, there was evidence of abuse, and he had not provided financial support after leaving the family.

Like Aracely and Mardelí, many women cited separation or abandonment as the impetus for their own migration. Women contrasted their absences as a result of migration with men's perpetual absences from family life, framing their own migration as part of their mothering. One migrant activist echoed the sentiments of other Nicaraguan mothers in Costa Rica by drawing on images of maternal sacrifice to explain remittance sending: "the expression of a mother's love is to wait in line for hours to take out and send this little bit of money. To endure the sun, the rain, the lines." Framing migration as maternal sacrifice has a double effect. First, it frames material support—sending money—as a form of affective labor (a theme taken up in the chapter on remittances). Second, it reinterprets women's physical absence from households in Nicaragua as maternal sacrifice, justifying migration as part of their mothering responsibilities rather than as abandonment or irresponsibility.

But the same cultural understandings of motherhood that require mothers to be both emotional and economic providers for Nicaraguan families mean that migrant mothers are subject to harsher judgment for their decisions to migrate even as they face greater pressures from families back home to fulfill this double role of provider and nurturer while abroad. Their physical absence ensures their economic provision even as it threatens their ability to fulfill their traditional role as nurturer and caregiver. Indeed, even as Mardelí emphasized that she had left because she had no other way to support her eight children, she struggled with "losing" her children. She said that although she "came with the illusion of getting my family ahead," she had "lost my second daughter." While her seven other children had eventually joined her in Costa Rica, this daughter refused to move and had not even visited her in the last ten years. Her daughter's resentment was due to her interpretation of Mardelí's migration as abandonment: "She never understood why I had left. She said she'll never forgive me."

However, the other women in the group jumped in to criticize how Mardelí herself framed her absence as abandonment. "To fight for your children, to be looking after them while you're out of the country, that's not abandonment," her friend Sugey said. While the other women agreed with Sugey, Mardelí's anguish over the lost relationship with her daughter and the vehemence of the women's defense of mothers' migration show how women confront expectations for face-to-face caregiving that make interpreting their long-distance participation in kin relations especially problematic in transnational families. That is, despite the realities of physical mobility, separation, and women's migration, children's suffering is largely explained through reference to nuclear family ideals that emphasize not only the superiority of biological ties, but also mothers' physical proximity as key to providing adequate care for children.

Relationship instability and informality can also create further strains on transnational parenting because of custody issues. Andrea first came to Costa Rica after separating from her husband. She came temporarily with her former mother-in-law on a short trip, leaving her three children with her ex and his new partner, but she ended up staying in Costa Rica. Eventually, she married another Nicaraguan but was never able to bring her children over because her ex-husband refused to sign their passports and exit permits. When I first met Andrea in 2009, she was waiting for her youngest daughter to turn eighteen so that she could visit Costa Rica without parental permission. Andrea hoped her daughter Stephanie might decide to stay and live with her.

However, the years of enforced separation had taken their toll on their relationship. While her oldest son eventually moved to Costa Rica and lived just a few blocks from Andrea, Stephanie had never visited. When we met in Managua in 2012, Stephanie explained, "You know, I love them both, mother and father equally. But since I've grown up more with my father, I'm the only one who hasn't left the country." Although scholars have suggested that such refusal to reunite may represent a critique of migrant mothers' absences (Boehm 2012; Dreby 2010), in Stephanie's case, it had become less an expression of resentment and more a constraint of her own new family circumstances. Although she had contemplated visiting Andrea in 2011, she feared asking her own son's father to sign the child's passport and exit permit, assuming that he would refuse to let the toddler leave the country.

Further complicating transnational relationships are the differences in the day-to-day lives of migrant parents and their children in the two countries. Parents and children do not necessarily experience time in the same way; young children's lives revolve around school, extended family, and the rhythms of life in Nicaragua, while migrant parents' lives revolve around work and their legal vulnerabilities. Parents may lose track of how their children are growing and changing in their absence. For example, a number of grandmother caregivers in Nicaragua complained that migrant parents sent clothes in the wrong sizes for children, or still treated older children as though they were "babies." Further, young children often lacked a clear understanding of why their parents migrated. For example, when Lisseth's mother, Dulce, first left for Costa Rica, when Lisseth was eight, she did not understand and, much as many migrant parents feared, she saw her mother's migration as abandonment. "Before, I used to say that my mom couldn't be here because she didn't love me. That's what I thought as a little kid." During those first few years, Lisseth often refused to speak to Dulce on the phone. However, eight years later, as a sixteen-year-old, she had gained new perspective. "No, she left because she was looking to improve our lives for me and my brother. And even though I always said that she left because she wanted to, well, it wasn't like that. She left to look for a better life for us."

Children may feel parents' absences differently at different ages. Elena's daughter Scarleth said that because of her grandmother's good care she did not feel her mother's absence until many years later, as a teenager:

When she left, I was about six years old. I didn't feel her migration much because I was left in good hands—her mother's, my grandmother, and my aunt who lives nearby, they gave us a lot of affection, a lot of love. But yes, I missed my mama when I was an adolescent. I missed her in the sense that I couldn't talk about things that happened with my grandmother or my aunt because she was in classes or had her own kids. When I moved from childhood to adolescence, I missed my mother.

For Scarleth, her mother's absence was increasingly important as she grew older and felt she could no longer confide in her grandmother or aunts about her social world. When Elena moved back to Nicaragua in 2011, Scarleth said that they had developed the kind of relationship she had hoped for for years. In contrast, her older brother felt that he missed his mother most when she first left. As the oldest, he had clearer memories of her and he bristled under their grandfather's strict discipline. As he grew older, he developed a stronger relationship with his father, Elena's ex-husband, and found that he did not miss his mother as much.

While children at home often felt disconnected from migrant parents, at least during some periods of their lives, migrant parents also complained that families back home did not recognize the struggles they faced in Costa Rica. Such lack of understanding could exacerbate disconnection. Rosa, who had left her two young daughters back in Managua, explained:

> And when we migrated, back in our communities, and even now in the communities, women who migrate, are seen as *la vaga*, as prostitutes, that we came to find other men here. And they don't see the support, all the sacrifice that we have made as women here in Costa Rica. Because they don't know how we live, how we eat, and all the things we have to do to be able to be in this country.

Rosa went on to remark that she felt migrants were doubly vilified: in Costa Rica for not having their papers in order and by widespread xenophobia and in Nicaragua by their own families for leaving in the first place.

Other migrants argued that their families back home did not understand the challenges of being undocumented in Costa Rica. Hazel, the oldest daughter of Daisy, a woman I met at the community center, demonstrated this kind of disconnection from her migrant mother. Hazel, who was twenty-five and lived outside Masaya with her partner and young son, felt deep resentment toward Daisy for leaving her and her younger sister fifteen years earlier. She had not realized that her mother had sent remittances for her education and other needs. In contrast, she readily credited her father for sending money. He had lived in the US for twenty years after leaving Daisy with two young daughters. She further did not understand why her mother chose to stay in Costa Rica now that both Hazel and her sister were in their twenties and married. "I say that she's there because she wants to. Because she has a house here and everything, she doesn't need to be in some other place. To visit, sure, but she's not even working there, I don't think." Hazel went on to ask me many questions about her mother's life in Costa Rica, curious about the neighborhood where Daisy lived, whether she was really in good health, how she spent her time. She rarely spoke to her mother and her perception of her mother's migration as unnecessary informed her disinterest in pursuing a closer relationship. It would not be until late 2012, when Daisy returned to Nicaragua with her Costa Rican husband and their ten-year old daughter, that the women would begin to rebuild their relationship.

Feelings of disconnection or at least tensions among long-distance relationships may be common, but both migrant organizations and changes in technology are slowly shifting discourses of abandonment. Rosa noted, "So, it's about breaking down that mindset that if a woman migrates she's bad and if a man migrates, he's a hero. But also with our own families, we don't realize what they're thinking. At least, my family thought that I had left them, that I had abandoned them." With support from an NGO, the Network of Migrant Women began facilitating workshops with family members back in Nicaragua. Because of these workshops and the conversations they sparked, Rosa's daughter Tania realized for the first time the kinds of sacrifices her mother was making in order to provide for her and her younger sister. Lisseth, who also participated with her grandmother Marina, said she learned a new perspective on why her mother had left, and began to think about what her responsibilities as a member of a transnational family might be. In Nicaragua, the young women and grandmothers formed a parallel network of family members of migrants to raise awareness of the conditions their relatives faced abroad as well as to advocate for and support family members in Nicaragua. Such efforts do not directly challenge the ideal of the nuclear family, but instead focus on maintaining substantive transnational connections through affective labor and communication. In some ways, by emphasizing migrant mothers' sacrifices these efforts also reified women's mothering and gender roles.

Many family members in both countries noted that increasing access to technology, specifically cell phones, improved the possibilities for transnational relationships. The opening of the telecommunications sector in Costa Rica and decreasing cost of cell phones and data plans has made it easier for both migrants and those back in Nicaragua to communicate regularly. In 2005, when I first met many of the women at ASTRADOMES while on a Fulbright grant, only Costa Rican citizens and permanent residents could purchase cell phone accounts. Those in the country on just a passport or without any permanent status could not purchase or rent an account. Instead, we would buy international calling cards and either use a landline, for those lucky enough to live in a house with one, or go to a payphone to call. This meant many migrants were able to contact family for fifteen minutes every two weeks. I spent many afternoons at a pay phone in a shopping center near ASTRADOMES, several of us taking turns making our biweekly calls home. Even in 2009, in Nicaragua most families of migrants went to internet cafes or to a neighbor with a phone; very few had landlines or cell phones.

However, by 2011, prepaid cell phones were ubiquitous both in Costa Rica and among transnational family members back in Nicaragua. Indeed, cell phones and prepaid data were priority purchases for families receiving remittances. In Costa Rica, migrants, no matter their legal status, could purchase prepaid lines with just a passport, and smartphones had become popular. One afternoon as I chatted with Andrea in the ASTRADOMES office, I asked her if I could contact her daughter and son back in Nicaragua. "Oh, sure, let me see what they say," she replied, pulling out her smartphone and sending an instant message to both. She explained that she "talked" to them via messages several times a day. By 2012, they had a family WhatsApp chat through which they sent voice messages, inspirational quotes, and Bible verses throughout the day.

In Managua, Lisseth talked about how she communicated with her mother Dulce almost every day: "Well, just now in December, she brought us a computer. She has her Facebook; I have my Facebook. And that way we can chat. There, I tell her things, even though I don't connect that often, we talk. And when we don't have time to chat on Facebook, she calls my phone and we put effort into staying in contact too." Such avenues for virtual co-presence, through voice and text messaging applications, meant not only more frequent contact but a better understanding of the daily challenges and struggles both migrants and those back home faced. Her mother, Dulce, noted that when she was having a bad day in Costa Rica, all she had to do was reach out to Lisseth or Marina through Messenger. "Then, they tell me *¡ánimo!* [cheer up]." Although all agreed it was not the same as face-to-face, these digital connections helped bridge some of the emotional distance between migrant parents and children back home in ways that were not possible even a few years prior for families like Daisy and Hazel.

Parenting in Costa Rica

If migrant men and women focused efforts on parenting from afar and maintaining financial and emotional obligations to children in Nicaragua, migration also shaped the way they parented in Costa Rica. Many Nicaraguan migrants have children born in Costa Rica as well as children back in Nicaragua. In 2014, for example, 16 percent of all births in Costa Rica were to Nicaraguan mothers (INEC 2015). Further, many migrants bring Nicaraguan-born children with them when they migrate.

This binational parenting can mean reduced support for families back in Nicaragua because resources are split between households and across borders. This is especially the case for Nicaraguan men who remarry or find new partners in Costa Rica. Nestor, whose teenage daughter Jessy lived with her maternal grandmother in Managua, found himself caught between maintaining a relationship with Jessy by sending money home for her upbringing and the financial and emotional strain of his new family in Costa Rica. In 2011, he and his Costa Rican wife, Melissa, had two small boys and lived in a small rented house in Rio Azul. "It's too much stress," said Nestor. And Melissa explained:

> Because he wants to send her money, but he can't. Sometimes I get to think-ing, and I say to Nestor, "Ay, Nestor, and those people [his family in Nica-ragua], maybe, I don't know, right? They might think that you don't send money to your daughter because you don't want to." But it's not because you don't want to. They don't see how we get by here sometimes. He can't send her money sometimes because of it. Because in his job he doesn't make very much. If he was paid well, he could send her something.

Instead, most of Nestor's income went to rent, food, and baby formula for his growing Costa Rican family. He had not returned to see Jessy since 2008, before he remarried. He tried to send money when he could, like when Jessy was diagnosed with depression, and tried to maintain regular phone communication with her and her grandmothers.

However, his prolonged absence and lack of financial support led Jessy and her maternal grandmother to characterize him as having "forgotten" her. Jessy blamed Melissa. In mid 2012, when I brought her pictures of her two-year-old and six-month-old half-brothers in Costa Rica, she marveled at how blond the children were and even suggested that they weren't her father's children, insisting they looked nothing like her or her father. She insisted she did not want to meet them. "Not them, no. I just want to go to meet my aunt Gloria and my other aunt in Heredia. My cousins. But them, no. Not them or his woman." As she got up to slam doors closed against an afternoon rain shower, Mirna, Nestor's mother, explained, "He came, four years ago when he was single, he came [to visit] a lot. When he was single. But once he got married, he forgot the child, he doesn't come back anymore." Esther, Mirna's neighbor and Jessy's maternal grandmother and caregiver, went on to explain, "She has this idea that she's the *tierna*, the baby of the family, but now there's a new reality, and she doesn't accept it. She feels that that woman Melissa is to blame. That because of this woman he left her." The physical distance and his stopped visits, coupled with Jessy's jealousy over her father's remarriage, have heightened tensions between Nestor and Jessy. While Melissa and Nestor hoped to bring Jessy to live with them in Costa Rica, Jessy believed the relationship was lost. Her grandmothers, on the other hand, felt things would eventually work themselves out, "It's the law of life. Those are her brothers," said Esther. Such perceptions of inequality between older children living in Nicaragua and younger children in Costa Rica shaped children's understandings of parental absence, often exacerbating feelings of abandonment and disconnection.

For some men distance provided an opportunity to positively reshape their relationships with children back in Nicaragua. For example, Abel improved his relationship with his two older sons in Nicaragua by facilitating their relationship with his Costa Rican–born son, Omar. He often called, he said, so that his children in Nicaragua could speak with their little brother. As he explained, "I call and tell the oldest, and he says 'yes, I can help Omar with his schoolwork.'" Abel's oldest son was studying agricultural engineering, and Abel encouraged him to keep studying by reminding him he was a role model for Omar. Abel also encouraged Omar to bring his grades up by urging him to study "just like his brother." Further, although Abel admitted that the geographic distance between his two children in Nicaragua and his family in Costa Rica sometimes strained relations, the distance also relieved other tensions. It kept his own mother and ex-wife far from his current wife, Darling, with whom they did not get along.

In addition to dividing their parenting efforts between households and countries, migration to Costa Rica entails encounters with different cultural models of family, parenting, and gender. The community center in Rio Azul, for example, actively promoted companionate love and equality as foundational values within homes and encouraged children to report physical punishment and verbal abuse. This model is reinforced by the Costa Rican state. Nicaraguan parents in Rio Azul often complained that in Costa Rica, children learned quite early that they had legal rights and sometimes threatened to call protective services, known as PANI (Patronato Nacional de la Infancia), when threatened by parents with physical punishment. For example, when Marcela discovered that her fifteen-year-old daughter, Adriana, was pregnant, she reacted by slapping her:

> Because I hit her, she called PANI on me. Well, you already knew that. I've talked with the community center director about everything. Because she got mixed up with a guy as a minor. And then I went and I hit her because, *diay*, I didn't want the same thing that happened to me to happen, maybe. You know? Then she stayed with the guy and she called the PANI.

Marcela was frustrated with Adriana's repeating her own mistakes of becoming a single teenage mother and responded exactly as her own mother had to her sixteen years earlier. In Costa Rica, though, she found that the community center and schools frowned on physical punishment and supported her daughter's report. Her daughter temporarily moved in with her boyfriend's mother, with the support of PANI. However, Adriana then skirted PANI's oversight and that of her boyfriend's mother by moving back to Nicaragua to live with an aunt. Marcela felt she had little recourse to re-establish custody across borders. Fears that interactions with PANI or other government agencies could lead to deportation meant parents tried to avoid such encounters with state institutions.

Despite fears over legal status, Nicaraguan migrants also frequently remarked about the institutional and cultural differences that provided more support for low-income parents in Costa Rica. As noted in the chapter on migrant illegality, while parents hesitated to seek or found it difficult to obtain services for themselves, they found it much easier to access education and healthcare for their children, whether the children were Costa Rican citizens or not. Raquel, a young mother at the community center, summed it up, "Here, there's not as much violence as there [in Nicaragua] and the government helps more here." Or, as another mother, Noemi, put it, "Look, things are cheaper in Nicaragua, but here it's easier, there are more possibilities for work, for support than in Nicaragua." For single mothers, in particular, stricter and better enforced child-support laws, as well as social programs like the community center, provided support no matter one's legal status. In Nicaragua, Darling's daughters marveled at the free lunches and school supplies Omar received in Rio Azul's community center. The oldest, Marcelina, lamented the lack of available childcare in Nicaragua and having to choose between relying on her own grandmother and sister or not being able to complete her nursing degree.

Further, the same situational, cultural, and institutional differences that influenced shifting parenting styles also offered resources for renegotiating intimate relationships and gendered expectations for Nicaraguan men and women. For some women, migration to Costa Rica itself offered a way out of violent relationships. For Aracely, leaving for Costa Rica represented both a way to provide for her children in the absence of a responsible father and a way to establish physical distance between her abusive ex-partner and herself. Migration may give women more control over household budgeting and decision-making and more spatial mobility. It may also affect women's abilities to achieve or negotiate their ideals for marriage and family life. Certainly, the marked gendered differences between *casa* and *calle*, the private space of the house and the public space of the street, are less pronounced in Costa Rica than in Nicaragua (see Hirsch 2003). Women have more freedom to leave the house and neighborhood, especially as mothers pursuing their children's needs. Economic opportunities, less gendered organization of social space, and the enforcement of domestic violence and child support laws represented real gains for migrant women.

However, the range of migrant women's experiences demonstrate that some women are better able to take advantage of the opportunities that migration offers depending on legal immigration status, family networks, the point in family formation when they migrate, employment experience, and other characteristics. Feminist scholars have long warned of framing women's migration experiences as a dichotomy that locates liberation in host country and oppression at home, which risks reifying the sending country or society as traditional, backward, and static, while the host country is seen as modern, and progressive (Chant and Radcliffe 1992; Hirsch 2003; Pessar 1999). This dichotomy obscures how gender inequality may be changed but not necessarily erased in migration and how experiences of race and class may themselves mitigate possibilities for gender change. Migration does not automatically provide women with social and economic mobility—as those who struggled to find work, obtain documentation, and face xenophobia could attest. Nor is it always an emancipatory or empowering experience for all women vis-à-vis household power dynamics.

Indeed, violence may follow migrant women across the border. For example, Diana migrated to Costa Rica in the early 2000s with her abusive partner. Moving to Costa Rica made it more difficult for her to leave him. He had an extensive family network in Rio Azul where they lived, while Diana had no relatives nearby. Though her older son Kenneth in Nicaragua urged Diana to go to a Costa Rican police station and report her husband's abuse, she resisted reporting or leaving him for years because she feared he would call PANI and take the children from her. She also felt that she would have nowhere to go, even if she were to leave him and take the children. In some cases, undocumented women may be dependent on spouses for legal status, deepening the abuse they suffer.

Although Costa Rican laws that allow women to claim residency based on children may lessen such dependency on spouses, migrant women are less likely to report abuse to health services, call police on a partner, or leave an aggressor than Costa Rican women (Pacheco Rojas and Arguedas Molina 2011). Indeed, even once Diana achieved residency through her children in 2012, she continued to stay with her abusive partner because she feared losing custody. Besides their isolation and vulnerability as undocumented migrants, migrant women are also often unfamiliar with Costa Rican laws or legal avenues available for escaping abuse. Migration to Costa Rica may also generate other forms of violence—such as enforced separation from children in Nicaragua because of fathers' refusals to sign exit permits. For migrant mothers, this is particularly important because leaving Nicaragua may be the only way to leave an abusive partner, but it may have devastating consequences for her relationship with her children, who are often left behind. For others, as domestic workers inside people's houses, they faced exposure to sexual and other violence by employers.

Still, many Nicaraguan women with Costa Rican partners often claimed that they are able to achieve more egalitarian relationships because Costa Rican men were "less *machista*" than Nicaraguans. They characterized Costa Rican men as "more respectful" and willing to compromise than Nicaraguan men, whom they characterized as controlling and demanding. An equally important attraction of Costa Rican men, noted many Nicaraguan women, was the likelihood that they would have more stable jobs and earn higher wages than migrant men, making them regular contributors to household incomes. When they first saw my Costa Rican husband rock our infant daughter to sleep on the community center patio, several women congratulated me for marrying a Costa Rican who was, as they described him, both "responsible" and "affectionate." In contrast, a favorite caricature among the women gathered at the community center gate was that you could easily spot a woman married to a Nicaraguan because she would be walking down the street carrying the baby, the diaper bag, and all the groceries, while her husband walked empty-handed at her side.

However, such characterizations of Nicaraguan machismo are largely exaggerations. Some men felt that Costa Rica gave more scope for them to enact the kinds of solidary masculinities evoked by visions of the "New Man." Indeed the precariousness of life in urban Costa Rica often required a shifting of Nicaraguan men's behavior, resulting in more active participation in household work and childcare. While some studies suggest that in Nicaragua, men participate in 15 percent of household work (O. Montoya 2002), migrant women noted that their partners in Costa Rica often actively "helped" with housework. Since many men had migrated by themselves before meeting or being joined by their partners, they were often used to cooking and cleaning for themselves, and many women noted that they shared domestic labor more evenly in Costa Rica than they had in Nicaragua. Andrea, for example, said that she and her husband shared household responsibilities:

> Because he spends more time in the house, so he knows that he has to cook. The dishes, he washes the dishes. The only thing he doesn't wash is the laundry because where we live there's no running water. So I'm the one that does laundry because you have to wash by hand there. Or if not, then we give the laundry to a *señora*. But all the chores we share between us.

Her husband also came to the ASTRADOMES office to cook for the women on weekends. "He says that since domestic workers work every day cooking in houses, then he comes to spoil them. So he comes, and we buy the food, and he cooks for everyone."

Further, although Nicaraguan men and women described nurturing and the daily care of children as part of "mothering," many men understood responsible fathering to include emotional and affective aspects, as well as economic. Daniel, a single father in Rio Azul, joked that he was not made for this kind of work, but took on the responsibility of daily care for his son anyway. Daniel lamented the long hours, the sleepless nights, the worry when his young son was hospitalized with asthma, in short, all the concerns that migrant mothers listed as the everyday work of mothering. Still, there were limits to what men expected to do with regards to childcare and domestic responsibilities. Daniel explained:

> So, it's hard in that respect, to always try to be in that care, twenty-four hours day and night. You should see when I go to bed at eight or nine at night, I go to bed super tired—mentally and physically—because it's a job that I as a man, it's not for me. Like I always say in the [community center] meetings—joking with them—being a single mother is a job that's not for me.

While Daniel took an active role in his son's life, attending school functions, bringing him to the community center, he noted that he was the exception, not the rule. Indeed, community center staff and Daniel him-self, referred to him not as a single father, but as a *madre soltero*, that is, a masculine version of a single mother.

Rethinking Fatherly Absences

As Andrea's husband, Abel, Martín, and Daniel show, not all men follow the pattern of fatherly absence. Instead, even when separated from children's mothers—either through the dissolution of a *union de hecho* or through migration—many men remained active and involved in their children's lives. Many migrant men continued to send remittances for their children through their own mothers. For example, Digmar, who had six children by his ex-wife back in Nicaragua, had maintained contact with his children after their separation. By 2011, he no longer sent them money because the youngest was twenty and graduating from seminary, but for almost two decades, he sent money to his mother or sister to provide for the children's upbringing. Today, one of his adult daughters lives close by; he helped her find a job when she moved to Costa Rica.

Further, when ex-partners and children from previous relationships talked about paternal absence, it represented only one side of the story. That is, men's absence from households in Nicaragua allowed for their presence and participation in other families in Costa Rica and the develop-ment of new ties to children born in subsequent relationships. While this was painful for children left behind, like Jessy, who interpreted her father's remarriage as abandonment, it was also a common part of informal mar-riage patterns and family life in Nicaragua more broadly.

While scholars have often focused on men's involvement in fathering when children are very young, the experiences of migrants' adult children reveal that despite absences or perceived "abandonment" in children's early years, men take on new responsibilities and roles as children grow (see Gutmann 1996). For example, while Elena's husband had "abandoned" her and their children when she was pregnant with their youngest son, he re-entered their lives as the children grew. As a teenager, Elena's oldest son, Kobe, moved in with his father for a few years, when he became too much for his grandparents to handle. His father contributed to his school-ing and helped build part of the house Kobe and his siblings live in today. Kobe recalled, "At that time, my father began to take charge of my edu-cation, he started to take on more direct costs." Although Kobe disagreed with the way his father had treated his mother, over the months he lived with him, Kobe and his father became "thick as thieves he and I, closer."

After two years, Kobe moved out to live with his siblings and an aunt in the home his mother was building through her remittances.

A year later, when his aunt declared she could no longer care for Elena's three teenagers plus her own daughter, Elena returned and reconciled with Kobe's father, who moved into the house. Kobe remembers, "They said that it was for the kids: 'Kobe's growing up. So that he'll be a good man. Now they're all growing up and need a home where there's a father-figure.'" Although their reconciliation did not last, and Elena returned to Costa Rica, Kobe's father remained in the house. He managed to maintain a relationship with Kobe through both his financial and emotional support, even as tensions grew between him and Elena.

In contrast, Kobe's younger siblings Scarleth and Bryan both eschewed any relationship with their father. Bryan argued that he and Scarleth had never really had a relationship with their father, while Kobe still had early memories of him. Further, their father contributed to Kobe's education and other expenses, but rarely provided for the other two children. "I sometimes said to him that I wished he'd send [money] for my other two siblings, and he disliked that," explained Kobe. "But a few days later or after he scolded me, he'd send a certain amount for them. Of course, it wasn't constant, and I always had that disagreement with him, we always were at odds over that; I said to myself, now I understand why my siblings say that I'm his favorite." Both Kobe's memories of his father and his fraught attempts to maintain an active presence in their lives as teenagers, point to the shifting responsibilities and contributions of men depending on their relationships with children's mothers and with children themselves. They also highlight Kobe's role as older brother and eldest son.

Migrant men with older children expressed concern with the importance of a father figure for children during adolescence, a time during which many rebelled against their caretakers and during which parents feared they might be vulnerable to negative influences. Thus, Nestor said he regularly called Jessy back in Managua to give her advice, even when he could not afford to send remittances:

> You know how it is there [in Nicaragua] . . . If you don't tell her, if you don't advise her, well you know how, a criminal or someone who wants to harm someone will look for a way to convince her [to let them in]. So if you tell her, "Look, don't pay any attention, don't listen to them," then, she's going to have the mentality to say no.

While Nestor was explicitly speaking of protecting his daughter's physical safety in Managua, his comment also reflects the importance men placed on safeguarding their daughters' sexuality. Here, responsible fathering means protecting girls from other men. While attempting to maintain transnational connections, then, Nestor was also reinforcing traditional gender roles, including that of the authoritative, protective father and the dichotomy of passive, vulnerable women and active sexually aggressive men.

Men also created lasting relationships within transnational families, acting as providers, confidants, and disciplinarians not just as fathers, but as grandfathers, uncles, brothers, and sons. Although fathers may only be intermittently physically present in Nicaraguan households, children develop enduring relationships with various male kin. Indeed, feminist scholars have noted that looking to male relatives who have often been seen as peripheral to nuclear family organization provides new insight into men's contributions to families (Stack 1974). Grandfathers, in particular, provided important male role models and discipline as well as financial support for children. Elena's children spoke at length about the discipline that their grandfather instilled in them. Although Kobe balked at their grandfather's rules (indeed, in part this is why he left to live with his father), Scarleth understood her grandfather's discipline as reinforcing her mother's sacrifice. For example, their grandfather made the children take off their school shoes and play barefoot after classes. Scarleth explained, "Today my grandfather says, 'what I wanted was the best for you, because your mama was working.' And so it wasn't fair for us to go and destroy a pair of shoes a month. And since Kobe went through shoes quickly, my grandfather didn't like that." In households where grandfathers were present, they were employed or received pensions, meaning they could be relied on to ensure a basic level of financial security for extended-family households, even though the everyday managing of household budgets fell to grandmothers.

In other instances, brothers attempted to fill the role of "man of the house" when faced with paternal absence. Diana's son Kenneth protected and provided for his younger brother. When we interviewed him in 2012, he had a pot of beans on a small electric stovetop and was preparing the family's one meal for the day. He also asked to speak about his mother while his younger brother was at school, so as not to upset him. He had taken on the role of nurturer and protector from a young age, after witnessing the violence his mother experienced at the hands of his stepfather, including once when he was twelve and his stepfather, "came and stabbed her with a knife." Today, Kenneth not only takes care of his younger brother, he offers support and advice to his mother in Costa Rica, encouraging her to leave an abusive relationship. However, he noted the irony of the situation, "I can't make her do anything. She's big enough to make her own decisions.

She should be giving me advice! Not me giving her advice!" Kobe, too, was a powerful presence in his younger siblings' lives, but when he moved out, Scarleth says that her younger brother, Bryan, became an important source of comfort and friendship and a constant playmate.

The changing configurations of families and the myriad forms of men's absence from and participation in family life have also prompted young men to rethink what kinds of family formations are possible and desirable under such conditions. Although Daniel's active engagement in single "mothering" was motivated by circumstances outside his control, many young Nicaraguan men I met—migrant or not—were rethinking what it meant to be a father. Kenneth, for example, talked about how he would be different from his own parents. At the time, his girlfriend was four months pregnant with their first child. He framed his fathering in terms of the care he had *not* received from his father, mother, and stepfather.

> I want to give the best to my children and not have them go through what I went through. That is, to live far from them. Instead, to try to see them, see them start to walk. Well, feel close to them. To try to get along with them the way I've gotten along with my partner. To give them the best, you know. I know that when you have a baby, I know that you start to mature more because you start to think in terms of what they need, what they don't need. You worry more. And I've talked with her, with my partner that I live with. What I've told her is that, if some day, I don't know, if something happens between us and we separate, that she shouldn't worry. That I will take responsibility for the boy or girl, whatever God wants to send into the world. I will take responsibility for him or her.

Unlike his own father, who had left them, or his stepfather, who abused them, Kenneth understood his role as father as a lifelong commitment. In particular, Kenneth's understandings of fatherhood were informed not only by his father's absence, but also by what he saw as his mother's immaturity in not actively sustaining a relationship with him. "Because a mature person, I'd say, who thinks the right way, knows how to talk with her children, how to approach them, but I didn't see that in her." Kobe and Bryan also expressed their desires to be a different kind of father than either their father or grandfather. They identified trust, a willingness to listen, and participation in domestic chores and care work as key elements of the kind of fathers they wanted to be. At the time I was writing this book, Kobe had moved to the US with his wife, and they were expecting their first daughter. "There is no manual that tells you how to be a father, guide, counselor, best friend, coach, protector 24/7, life partner, tutor, confidant," he told me. But he noted, he wanted his daughter to see him treat her mother with respect and to be someone she could talk to.

Conclusion

These multiple and diverse forms of men's participation in transnational families allow us to rethink the absences engendered by migration as well as the kinds of families to which men contribute. In Nicaragua, policy changes under the Sandinistas have provided a new legal landscape for paternity and fatherhood, recognizing children born outside of wedlock as well as the status of consensual unions. But migrants point out that paternal irresponsibility is still widespread and it is easy for men to avoid the financial responsibility for children, especially when they are not legally married to the child's mother. In Costa Rica, in contrast, stronger paternity and child support laws and sanctions provide a legal landscape in which migrant men find themselves tied to Costa Rican–born children in ways not possible in Nicaragua.

Thus, if notions of motherhood have expanded to incorporate both nurturing activities and income-earning labor, notions of fatherhood are also expanding. While Nicaraguan men continue to define fatherhood principally in terms of economic provision, they also see other kinds of engagements as at least partly defining father-child relations. Further, young men's experiences with uncles, grandfathers, and brothers also shape how they understand men's involvement in family life, both in Nicaragua and across borders.

In all the families I met, men and women were working out what family meant to them, what their ideal families might look like, and what kind of mothers, fathers, children, siblings, and grandparents they wanted to be and could be given social and economic realities. For example, despite his desire to be physically present for his first child, Kenneth planned to leave for Costa Rica once the baby was born in order to pay off the medical debt he and his girlfriend had incurred.

How separation and absence are understood by children and other family members in Nicaragua, though, is not always the same. Thus, transnational family life provides insight into different and often conflicting expectations about what makes a good mother, father, wife, or husband. As these ideas, and the practices through which members of transnational families enact them, are negotiated and contested, ideas about family and gender roles are transformed or reinforced. These shifts in practices and ideas about motherhood, fatherhood, and family are linked not only to experience with family separation but also to encounters with new cultural models and institutions in Costa Rica and the multiple insecurities of life in Nicaragua. In the next chapter, I turn to the role of grandmother care-givers within transnational families to show how extended families have long represented another flexible configuration that underlies Nicaraguan family life that is transformed in the context of migration.

CHAPTER 5

Mamitas

Grandmother Caregivers and Extended Family Households

IF FAMILY CONFIGURATIONS AND gendered expectations of parenting inform transnational experiences, the ubiquity of extended family households in Nicaragua represents a key resource for ensuring care within transnational families while reinforcing the importance of women's care work. While the literature on transnational families has highlighted the important role of grandmother caregivers in particular, it has often focused on the new responsibilities and burdens such women take on when their daughters migrate and they are left to care for grandchildren (Dreby 2010; Yarris 2011, 2017).

However, in Nicaraguan families, grandmothers and mothers have long shared care responsibilities within extended households. While I do not want to suggest that grandmothers and other female kin do not take on additional burdens when parents migrate, the experiences of Nicaraguan transnational families point to the flexibility of kinship networks and the importance of intergenerational care within families prior to migration. The prevalence of extended family households may contribute to women's decisions to migrate because female kin are already present in the household. Further, practices of child circulation and fostering are common in Nicaragua and elsewhere in Latin America. In the neighborhoods where we lived in Granada, Managua, and Esteli, families often took in a cousin, a grandchild, or niece or nephew when parents were out of work, migrated within the country, or remarried. Migrant women in Costa Rica and grandmother caregivers in Nicaragua often asked why I traveled with Magda, who at the time was less than a year old: "Don't you have a mother or mother-in-law to leave her with?" Multiple mothering, child fostering, and reliance on extended family are not simply responses to transnational migration but part of a larger repertoire of family-making in Nicaragua, where the extended family has played an important role both ideologically and in practice.

This chapter examines the continued importance of grandmother care-givers within Nicaraguan family strategies and the adaptation of this role in the context of migration. As a fundamental link in the global care chain, grandmother caregivers contribute to the transnational circulation and commodification of care, even as they are often expected to provide care without remuneration. Rather than replace or substitute for mothers, grandmothers in such families serve as intermediaries between parents and children and children and the state, what Joanna Dreby (2010) has called "middlewomen." In such cases, grandmothers take on the everyday tasks of caring for children—feeding, clothing, ensuring their education and health—the same sharing of substance that builds and strengthens relat-edness. I begin by contextualizing extended family households in Nicaragua more generally. I then look at the multiple mothering that women engage in, providing care for children, grandchildren and others in the context of economic crisis and parents' relationship instability. Finally, I turn to the new arrangements and responsibilities transnational migration entails for grandmother caregivers.

Extended Family Households, Child Minding, and Fostering in Latin America

Feminist work on kinship and families has highlighted the importance of extended female-kin networks to the resilience of families in the face of poverty (Collier and Yanagisako 1987; Stack 1974; Stack and Burton 1994). While parent-child relationships are often the basis for larger kin-based networks, these relationships are not necessarily limited to "natural" or "biological" parents. Instead, grandmothers or other female kin take on pri-mary caregiver roles in many cultures. Interestingly, in biological anthro-pology, research on the "grandmother hypothesis," which seeks to explain menopause in older women, has shown a positive correlation between decreasing infant mortality and the presence of maternal grandmothers (Hawkes and Smith 2009; Jamison et al. 2002).

In Latin America, extended families and female kin represent key emotional and economic support systems in the face of poverty, racism, and economic inequality. Studies of Caribbean "child-minding" and fostering practices have seen the circulation of children between households not only as an adaptive care practice but also as an integral part of wider networks of exchange and reciprocity that strengthen kin and community bonds (Olwig 1985, 2013; Soto 1987). There is also an extensive literature on child circulation and adoption in Latin America, especially in the Andes, where race, class, and indigeneity intersect in the circulation of children between rural homes and urban adoptive families (Leinaweaver 2008; Van Vleet 2009; Weismantel 1995). At play in accounts of child circulation among Andean families are tensions between abandonment and care, connection and disconnection linked to movement, distance, and the state. As Jessaca Leinaweaver (2007, 2008) points out, such circulation operates on the margins of or outside state agencies and institutions. State authorities often equate such informal care arrangements with abandonment. However, such informal practices represent a way for poor rural families to deal with poverty, violence, and insecurity, while reinforcing social connections to other households and networks. Such arrangements may have variable durations—some more, some less permanent. Child keeping operates both within and against legal systems and social agencies, creating lasting bonds between caregivers and children.

Similarly, extended family households, which include members beyond the nuclear family, represent a key arrangement for sharing resources and reinforcing kinship bonds. As noted in Chapter 1, Nicaragua has one of the highest rates of extended family households in Latin America. In particular, scholars have noted the growth of extended family households in Nicaragua in the 1990s as part of an "accordion effect," in which households expand to pool resources in times of need and contract when resources allow members to separate (Agurto and Guido 2001). However, in Nicaragua, such households appear to be less a temporary reaction to economic conditions than a long-term strategy for survival. The only families interviewed in Nicaragua that lived in nuclear family households lived on the same property or next door to other kin. The lasting bonds created through child fostering and extended family households may be built upon blood ties, but they are shaped by sharing and preparing meals, providing shelter and clothing, and ensuring children's health and education (Walmsley 2008; see also Carsten 2000). As noted in previous chapters, the provision of care in Nicaragua—healthcare, education, childcare—has long depended on the unpaid work of women. Women feed children, care for elderly, cook, and clean. In both transnational families and extended family households throughout Nicaragua, grandmother caregivers do much of this "work" of kinship (Carsten 2004; Franklin and McKinnon 2001; Weston 2001).

Mamitas: Multiple Mothering in Nicaragua

In Nicaragua, the instability of marriages and changing partners throws into sharp relief the importance of grandmother caregivers and other female kin who engage in multiple mothering relationships over the course of their lives. Julie Cupples (2001) notes that in Nicaragua, it has been widely accepted that other people carry out the actual physical care of children, especially while biological mothers work outside the home or in a different town. Today, women are more likely to find work in Costa Rica than in a neighboring city or nearby town. It is common for children to live with grandmothers, either with their parents in extended family households or after being informally fostered or adopted by grandmothers. Indeed, according to a national survey, over 9 percent of children under the age of fifteen do not live with either of their parents (INIDE 2007, 2014). Over 26 percent live with their mother, but not their father, and often those with single mothers live in multigenerational homes with grandmothers and other female kin (INIDE 2014).

Such patterns have remained consistent since the 1990s but stretch back generations, evidencing the long-term economic instability of Nicaraguan family life. Our neighbor in Granada, don Eloy, who liked to tell stories about Nicaragua before the Contra War, explained:

> I was ten years old in 1945. The country's economy was pretty messed up. My parents left for Costa Rica. They were traders. They left for Limón. They didn't go to cut sugar cane. They went to buy and sell for three or four years while we were in my grandmother's house. My mother's mother. We divided up—here's the philosophy you were asking about—I went with my grandmother, another brother with my aunt, another with my other grandmother.

Don Eloy referred to such child fostering as a "philosophy," a principle that guides behavior. He related that his was not the only family to *repartir* or distribute children to various relatives so that parents could work within Nicaragua or beyond. As he shared in Chapter 1, Eloy remembered Nicaragua at this time as a place of abundance. However, migration still represented an important economic activity for many families.

Such practices also reflect the political instabilities of the past decades. Esther, in Managua, explained that in the 1980s she informally adopted her first grandchild, when her oldest son, David, returned from military training with a baby. David, who was about fifteen, had gone into the mountains for military training with the Sandinistas: "The Sandinistas took my son. He was young, maybe between fourteen and fifteen years old. And there in that mountain, he met a *campesina*, and she got pregnant and had a boy. She stayed there, but he brought back the child. She gave him the little boy, you see." When David returned to Managua, he gave the child to Esther, whose youngest child at that point was only three or four years old. Esther raised the baby as her son, counting him as one of the four children from her second marriage. "And that child stayed with me. So I didn't have three anymore, I had four with this child." Today, this (grand)son, who is in his thirties, lives a few streets away from Esther with his own partner and children. Of course, when I met her, Esther was raising her teenage granddaughter Jessy and Jessy's two half siblings, each of whom had also been left with her as babies. Thus, even when parents have not migrated, grandmothers buffer other kinds of parental absence—including that produced by lack of financial support, parental irresponsibility, and relationship instability. When parents are young, unable, or even unwilling to assume responsibility for children, grandparents, who may not yet be done raising their own children, may be called upon to raise grandchildren temporarily or even permanently.

In the context of relationship informality, grandmothers' caregiving represents a way to protect children from parents' new relationships. Jasmina, a neighbor in Granada, had six children, three by a previous partner and three by her current partner. Her six-month-old daughter was just a few days younger than Magda and they came by often to play. When she first moved in with her current partner, Jasmina worried that he would not care for her children from her previous marriage as much as his own. Jasmina's mother offered to keep her three older children:

> My mother wants them with her because the guy I'm with is their stepfather. She's always said that she doesn't want my children to be with a stepfather because there've been cases . . . But no, my husband is a good man, but she says no, even more because my daughter is a young lady, my mother doesn't want her in my house, and she wants to have them in her house.

Implied in her assertion that "there've been cases" is the widespread prevalence of sexual and physical abuse of children in Nicaragua. The majority of sexual abuse against children and adolescents is committed by family members, especially fathers and stepfathers (Olsson et al. 2000; UNICEF 2019). Of course, the most famous case, which continues to resonate with Nicaraguan mothers, is that of Zoilamérica Narvaez, Daniel

Ortega's stepdaughter, who in 1998 accused him of sexual abuse over the course of nineteen years (Narváez 2002). The repudiation by the first lady, her mother, Rosario Murillo, of Zoilamérica's accusations continues to haunt the nation and the first family, which has done little to address either her accusations or the widespread physical and sexual abuse of children (Bateson 2017; Gago 2007; López Vigil 2001).

When she first remarried, Jasmina had left only her oldest and taken the two younger children with her to her new mother-in-law's house, but "I also have this problem, that my mother-in-law doesn't love them, because they aren't children of her children. The ones she loves are these three because they are her son's children." Here, we see the importance of blood ties between fathers and children as well as grandmothers and grandchildren, and the significance of the absence of such ties between stepfathers and children, as a way of limiting who has a claim on men's resources in the context of marriage informality. If sharing resources/substance can create or strengthen relatedness, the refusal to provide or resentment over providing for stepchildren is aimed at limiting those connections and kin bonds. Child keeping or fostering builds on these blood ties, reinforcing children's social identities through their incorporation in extended maternal family networks and ensuring they will be well cared for physically and emotionally. That is, care work that builds relatedness functions in tandem with traditional ideas about kinship to delineate with whom and to whom children belong.

Children are both provided for and provide support for grandmothers in these households. They provide emotional support and company as well as participate in the smooth running of the household. As in other accounts of fostered children, they are "seen as a vital cog in the everyday functioning of the home" (Walmsley 2008, 179). Through completing daily chores, running errands, and relaying messages among related households, children mediate communication and the sharing of substance within extended families. Jasmina said she slept easier knowing her children were with her mother not only because of her concerns over the treatment they would receive from her mother-in-law, but because they helped care for their aging grandmother. "Since they've grown up with her, and right now she's alone, with [my] sister who works. She doesn't have anyone to run errands, [because] the other children my sister has are small." Jasmina worried that her mother would be lonely, since Jasmina's sister, who lived with her, worked all day. Thus, Jasmina's children provided company as well as help around the house. When they lived with Jasmina and her husband, "my mom missed them, she didn't have anyone to do things for her, she told me to send them again, to have them come back to me just to sleep or for me to take food to them. That she felt lonely because my sister who lives with her works all day and doesn't get home until seven at night." Jasmina's older children ran errands for their grandmother, who had trouble walking into town to the market. They also served as an alarm system, running to Jasmina's house a few streets over for help if their grandmother was injured or unwell. Children serve not as passive recipients of care, but as active participants in the work of creating and maintaining kin networks and extended-family households.

Such situations—whether the result of economic necessity or new relationships—make clear the ways multiple mothering, as an intergenerational activity, provides stability within families faced with relationship informality and poverty. Care and reproductive labor circulate within multigenerational households, ensuring both the old and the young are cared and provided for in the context of marriage dissolution, remarriage, and economic deprivation. Although fostering—or the circulation of children—took place primarily among blood relatives, the multiple mothering relationships children established with various caregivers highlights the active processes through which kinship ties are made durable and meaningful. Although a child may have one mother, he may call a number of women *mama*, indicating affection, care responsibilities, and intergenerational linkages. Migration scholars have largely seen this practice of calling a grandmother caregiver *mother* as a sign of disconnection between migrant mothers and children left behind (Yarris 2017). For example, Joanna Dreby (2007) finds that, in Mexico, the children of migrants often use the term *mama*, but that this use of the term is emotionally fraught for migrant mothers, as children's use of the term with grandmothers challenges mothers' roles in their children's lives. However, in many places in Latin America, *mother* or *mama* are employed to describe relationships with various female kin (Nieto 2000; Walmsley 2008).

In Nicaragua, children use the term *mama* interchangeably for mothers and grandmothers or sometimes other female kin who raise them. Nevertheless, there is a difference in emphasis. When referring to mothers, children use *mamá* with the accent on the last syllable. In speaking of grandmothers, they usually employ *máma*, with the emphasis on the first syllable, or the diminutive *mamita*. Elena's son Jefferson, for example, recounted the years he had spent living with his grandmother, an elderly woman I had met a few days earlier at a Mothers' Day celebration. When I asked him about the term, which he was using to refer both to the grandmother who had raised him and his biological mother Elena, he explained:

> I always, I mean, I was always closer with my *abuelita* because I was always with her, you know? I called her *máma*. But over time, you know that when

you grow up with your *abuelita*, with your aunt, you always become fond of her, you call her mama. *Máma*, to your grandmothers or some close relative that is always with you or is taking care of you or is always watching out for you.

In calling grandmothers *mama*, Nicaraguan children may not be pointing to the interchangeability of mothers and grandmothers, or even suggesting that grandmothers may take migrant mothers' places. Rather, the term emphasizes the ways multiple women actively "mother" children by engaging in the everyday work of kin and care. This use of *mama* to refer to multiple women caregivers also reinforces the gendered nature of care work in Nicaraguan families, where cooking, cleaning, and child-rearing are synonymous with mothering and women's work. Hence, as I mentioned in the chapter on parenting, Daniel, the single father, referred to himself as a *madre soltero*, a masculine form of a single mother.

Grandmothers are key caregivers for children because their own marital and family lives tend to be more stable. Indeed, all of the grandmothers I interviewed were in long-term marriages or had been widowed or divorced for a number of years, an observation supported by household survey data (INIDE 2014). Further, though grandparents themselves often lived in the same conditions of poverty as their children and grandchildren, they protected grandchildren from the effects of poverty by creating a focal point for pooling family income and resources. For example, in Chapter 1, I discussed how Marina's family pooled resources from adult children who were working in Managua and remittances sent by Marina's daughter in Costa Rica. Similarly, Rosa had been living with her mother in Managua before she migrated in the 1990s. Before migrating, living with her mother had allowed her to work and to pool resources with her mother (who took on small odd jobs in addition to taking care of the girls) and a sister who lived nearby.

Leaving children in the care of grandmothers lessens the disruption for children of parents' migration. When Elena first left, she and her children had been living in her parents' house close to the city center. For many children, then, their parents' leaving did not require a change in household, though it might have been a change of rules and routines. For example, as noted in the last chapter, his grandfather's discipline was especially hard for Kobe to adapt to in Elena's absence. Although Elena's children moved into the new house under construction while she was abroad, it was not until almost ten years after she left. Most children I talked to in Nicaragua did not move at all. Rather, they had already, at least in the time immediately preceding their parents' migration, lived with their grandmothers in multigenerational extended households.

Rosa's three daughters continued to live with her mother when she left for Costa Rica:

> For example, my kids. My mom has lived with us forever. Back then, I used to work in Nicaragua. So, the majority of the time, my kids, most of the time, all the time they had to enjoy, they enjoyed it with my mama because I always, since I was a single mother, I always had to work. So all this time [their childhood] they lived it with my mama. Yes, they were already adapted because she, my mama is their mama. They don't call my mama *abuela*, she's their *mama*. Yes, so, I think the majority of Nicaraguans live almost always with their mama. So, there isn't this big blow when you leave them [to migrate].

Similarly, for Esther, who had already raised the grandson brought home to her from the war, raising her teenage granddaughter Jessy and Jessy's two half siblings was not so different. Their mother left them as babies, and they had always lived with Esther in her tiny home in Managua. Thus, when Jessy's father, Nestor, left for Costa Rica in 2003, what changed was the frequency and duration of his visits, not Jessy's home or her primary caregiver. Nestor explained that "when I was there [in Nicaragua], well, her *abuela* had her. [. . .] I would go to Esther's house and take my daughter to [visit] my mother's house." He gave Esther money for Jessy's upbringing—food and clothes and other necessities. Jessy's siblings, who have a different father, had much the same arrangement. Esther attributes these arrangements to her daughter's "irresponsibility," that is her lack of both emotional and financial support. But such informal care arrangements can also be tied to parents' relationship, job instability, and migration, as well as the legacies of decades of political and social instabilities in the country, as in the case of her adopted (grand)son.

Mothering in the Meantime

Still, for Nicaraguan grandmothers, the shifting responsibilities and expectations they face as caregivers in the context of migration represent new responsibilities within extended family networks. In particular, their day-to-day caring activities are compounded by new responsibilities to explain and manage parental absence. Given the context of multiple mothering, the distinctions between grandmother caregivers and mothers may be more difficult to maintain especially for small children. In such situations, grandmothers walk a fine line between providing care and taking a mother's place. As noted earlier, when Elena first left for Costa Rica twenty years ago, her youngest son Jefferson, began to call his grandmother "mama."

> So, when she [my mother] came [back] for the first time to Nicaragua, that is after her trip, when she came, she said that she was my mother, *pues*. But I said, no. So then, she told me that, yes, and that I had to be with her, but I said, no, because, well, with the time that had passed, she was . . . a stranger to me. Even though she was my mother, but to me she was a stranger.

After two years without seeing her, five-year old Jefferson had few memories of his mother. Though at first she had to "bribe" Jefferson with candies and treats to get him to call her mama, years later her frequent return visits and his grandmother's explanations helped him understand her absence.

Managing the emotional impacts of absence may be particularly difficult on emotionally charged days like birthdays or Mothers' Day. At such events, grandmothers' presences both emphasize that children are loved and cared for and make more apparent parents' absence. Elena's daughter, for example, recalled:

> For graduations, since my mama couldn't ever be there, for Jefferson's graduations, our grandmother took him from preschool, sixth grade, and fifth year. The only graduations that mamá [Elena] was there for were for mine from fifth year, and Kobe's too. But we had already thought that if she didn't come, if her employer didn't give her permission, that it was going to be my *abuelita* who would accompany us and most of the time it's *abuelita* who's been present.

Similarly, in León, where Darling's daughters lived, the walls were covered in photographs from school graduations. In each one, Darling's daughters appeared accompanied by their grandmother or a maternal aunt.

When grandmothers addressed children's expectations and framed parents' absences as being for their children, they reinforced parent-child bonds and shaped children's understandings of transnational family life. When Elena migrated, her own mother continued to reinforce with Jefferson, Scarleth, and Kobe why she had to leave. Their grandmother's explanations—and the consistency between her and Elena's explanations—helped Jefferson perceive Elena's absence as a maternal sacrifice for his own well-being. "Our grandmother always told us why she'd left the country," said Jefferson. "Or rather, today she [our mother] tells us the same. That it was to improve our quality of life." Kobe remembered the first time his grandmother took his siblings and him to see the lot their mother had bought. Their uncle drove them all to an empty lot next to an auto-repair shop. "They told us three, 'This is the land that your mama bought. This is the house your mama is building for you. This is her objective, and, when she finishes making the house, she'll come back.' When they told us this, obviously I was filled with happiness." By reinforcing parents' absence as part of their responsible parenting, by tying their efforts to the material goods that sustain children (houses, food, clothing, tuition), grandparents reinforced children's bonds to absent parents. In turn, children saw their parents' migration as positive and important for their family, even if difficult.

Further, grandmothers shape how children understand their own responsibilities in the face of parental sacrifice. For example, Lisseth began to learn about the conditions migrants faced in Costa Rica from the network of migrant family members in Managua. Her grandmother, Marina, reinforced this perspective, explaining that after these workshops she began emphasizing what her daughter Dulce faced in Costa Rica and how all the members of the family were making sacrifices for their well-being. In particular, she emphasized to Lisseth's younger brother that he should bring up his grades because of Dulce's sacrifices:

> So, I tell him, look, remember where your mother is, in a different country, with different people, who have different customs and ways of life. And all of that is a sacrifice for her. Don't you think she misses you? Her, a woman all alone, that doesn't have any family there. She's a woman far away from her family. [. . .] She doesn't have anyone. She gets up, she bathes, she goes to work. Who's going to say to her, 'Adios, mama! Take care of yourself'? Who's going to say those things to her? No one. All of this is a big sacrifice for her.

In this framing, both migration and living daily life without migrant family members are sacrifices made for the good of the family, with children playing a key role in fulfilling absent parents' expectations and making their sacrifices "worth it."

On the other hand, when relatives do not frame parents' absence as sacrifice for family, children are less likely to see their parents' migration in a positive light. Esther, for example, encouraged her granddaughter Jessy to maintain a relationship with her father in Costa Rica. In talking about Nestor's lack of visits since he remarried in Costa Rica three years earlier, Esther both acknowledged Jessy's hurt feelings and encouraged communication between Jessy and her father. When I mentioned that Jessy's stepmother was anxious to meet her and wanted to have a good relationship with her, Esther used it as fodder for her campaign to talk Jessy into moving to Costa Rica with her and reuniting with her father. However, Jessy's uncle and his wife undermined such efforts by referring to her father's absence as abandonment. As we sat and talked in Esther's house, even Esther moved from saying that Jessy needed to be more open to her father to asserting that he had forgotten about her:

AUNT: He's abandoned her. [To Jessy] Tell the truth.

ESTHER: Yes, he's abandoned her.

JESSY: Yes, he's abandoned me because he has his wife, he has his sons.

UNCLE: He's married now.

JESSY: He's married now and he forgot that he has a daughter here in Nicaragua.

AUNT: First, it was because of the economic situation. Now he has a family.

JESSY: But now I understand how things are. First, he left because of the economic situation. Then he got married. He made his life there.

ESTHER: Yes, he forgot.

Throughout our conversation, Jessy employed the phrases of her aunt and uncle to describe her father's absence and remarriage in Costa Rica. Interestingly, no one in the family used the word abandonment to describe her mother's leaving her with Esther when she was two. Such negative explanations, or even a lack of explanation at all, can affect children's long-term relationships with migrant parents and the likelihood of future reunification. Jessy, for example, refused to consider moving to Costa Rica, though her father had written and called asking her to come.

Further, as Jessy's experience shows, relatives other than grandparents may be less likely to reinforce parent-child bonds (Dreby 2010). Or, as Esther implied to me on a later visit when I asked about the aunt and uncle, they may be resentful themselves at not benefiting from remittances. Joanna Dreby (2010) has noted in the context of Mexican transnational families, grandparents often represent more willing caregivers for children, while other caregivers often provide care out of pity or for a cut of remittances. Indeed, grandmothers mediate children's relationships with their parents primarily through the medium of remittances. Such management of remittances includes financial and emotional management, as will be examined more in depth in the next chapter.

Further, other family members may be seen as less desirable caregivers in part because they may not be able to provide the kind of economic and emotional stability that grandparents can. For example, when Elena began to build her own house on a lot outside of town, her children moved out of their grandparents' house and into the new house with an aunt. However, when the three hit their teenage years, their aunt could not provide the kind of care and oversight they needed. As Scarleth explained, "Well, you know that when you're a teenager, you're very rebellious. That's when my aunt couldn't do it alone, with her kids. She only had a daughter, but she was taking care of her and us. She always took care of us, but we did whatever we wanted." Relatives other than grandparents were often seen as having other responsibilities or priorities, and not willing or able to create as strong a bond with children as grandparents. In the case of Elena's children, their aunt's lack of a steady partner meant the family felt she could not provide the kind of discipline three teenagers required.

Grandmothers' attempts to mediate on behalf of their grandchildren were often complicated by the precarious legal standing of their relationships. Most grandmother caregivers assumed care for children without formal legal custody. These informal arrangements may create vulnerability for children and grandmother caregivers and enforce parent-child separation. For example, without legal custody, grandmothers were limited in how they could intercede for children in state agencies, schools, and clinics. They were vulnerable to threats from children's noncustodial fathers, some of whom threatened to remove them from the grandmother's home or attempted to access remittance money sent for children's care (Yarris 2017). For example, Aracely returned from Costa Rica after just six months because her abusive ex-husband was threatening to take her children from her mother. Similarly, Esther did not have legal custody of Jessy or her other grandchildren, limiting her ability to make decisions regarding their care and upbringing. While she has had physical custody of her since she was little, has enrolled her in school, takes her to the doctor, and other activities, Esther cannot take Jessy out of Nicaragua, even to visit Jessy's father. Without legal custody, Ester could not sign for Jessy's passport or exit permit. In July 2012, Esther was trying to save up money to pay a lawyer and gain permanent legal custody of Jessy, which would then allow her to get Jessy a passport and exit permit so she could travel to Costa Rica and meet her younger siblings and her stepmother. Of course, such a legal petition would require a formal recognition of both Jessy's mother's and Nestor's "abandonment" of Jessy, further complicating the relationship between them.

In addition to managing migrants' absences for grandchildren, grandmother caregivers also deal with their own emotional distress. For Kristin Yarris (2011), who worked with Nicaraguan grandmother caregivers and children of migrant mothers, the stress of caregiving contributes to embodied stress and distress, characterized by physical ailments and particularly *dolor de cerebro* (brain-ache). Despite this, grandmothers mediate the emotional separations between children and parents, reinforcing children's bonds with absent parents. At the same time, they must manage their own feelings about separation from adult children. Such emotion work has important consequences for caregivers' health and well-being (Yarris 2011). For Esther, who felt she lost her "best friend," when her own daughter Gloria left for Costa Rica, Jessy became her constant companion. She worried about how she would feel if Jessy decided to stay in Costa Rica with her father and stepmother. Similarly, Marina missed her daughter Dulce. When I asked her who she talked to about all the stress of life, she said, "Who, me? Nobody!" She felt she could not talk to her husband, because he would come home from work as a long-haul truck driver exhausted, nor to her younger daughter, who had her own financial and relationship problems. Marina felt she could sometimes talk to another daughter about the difficulties of raising her grandchildren or making ends meet, but she felt alone with her feelings of loss at Dulce's absence.

Conclusion

Although a child may have one mother, they may call a number of women *mama*, indicating affection, recognizing care responsibilities, and reflecting intergenerational kinship networks. Indeed, the use of *mama* to refer to multiple women caregivers reinforces the gendered nature of care work in Nicaraguan families, where cooking, cleaning, and child-rearing are synonymous with mothering and with women's work. Understanding the cross-generational sharing of child-rearing, informal childcare and fostering arrangements, and the importance above all of female extended kin helps us rethink the kinds of family reconfigurations migration to Costa Rica entails for Nicaraguan families. The existence and availability of grandmothers, aunts, and others willing and (mostly) able to care for children informs parents' decisions to migrate as well as children's understandings of migration and parental absence.

However, grandmother caregiving may also reinforce traditional gender roles and expectations, because when female relatives take up the work of raising, feeding, and caring for children, fathers or other male relatives rarely pick up the slack (Parreñas 2005). The flexibility of female kin networks can perpetuate gender inequality and men's lack of responsibility toward care work. When fostering or caring for grandchildren becomes absorbed as part of mothering, at least in practice, if not in ideology, it reinforces mothering as a key element of women's labor throughout their lives.

Yet, both grandmother caregivers and migrant parents see migration and these care arrangements as temporary. As such, they avoid official, legal channels of custody or adoption and seek to reinforce parent-child bonds. In reinforcing those bonds, accounting for how remittances are spent, and otherwise managing the emotional consequences of parents' migration, grandmothers set up the conditions for grandchildren to leave them. They, like children themselves, expect parents to return to Nicaragua or families to be reunited in Costa Rica. However, as parents' time in Costa Rica extends because of continual expenses and demands for remittances in Nicaragua or because of legal insecurity in Costa Rica, such temporary arrangements often become more permanent and durable.

CHAPTER 6

"I Eat All My Money Here"

Remittances in Transnational Family Life

LESTER WORKED IN A furniture workshop near Atenas, in the mountains outside Alajuela. His cousin Jimmy, in Achuapa, suggested I meet him. As we sat in a shady corner of the open-air workshop, with sawdust tickling my nose, Lester talked about how his trips back to Achuapa had become less and less frequent. He had lived in Costa Rica for ten years, and returned to Nicaragua every six months for the first few years. He first migrated as a young man to join his older brother, and other family members had since followed—three other siblings, and, in 2008, his parents. He had two daughters in Nicaragua, by two different women. He sent money every two weeks to his sister, who divided the money between his daughters, and as time went by continued to visit several times a year. However, in 2009, he had not been back to Achuapa in two years. He hoped to return permanently to Nicaragua, but noted,

> You want to stay. You arrive home with a little bit of money, but then when you don't have any more, you leave again. Money doesn't last there. You arrive with $1500, with $2000, but how long can it last? Things are so expensive. We migrants leave Costa Rica happy, but when we see the little pot of beans that they eat all week, the tiny bit of rice—things that you don't see here in Costa Rica—when we see the poverty there in Nicaragua, we can't stay. My money—over there I eat it all.

Lester's statement, that money does not last in Nicaragua, that it gets eaten up by hungry families, echoed the sentiments of many migrants I met in Costa Rica and points to larger tensions around remittances within transnational families. In Nicaragua, the majority of remittances, that is the money and goods migrants send to households back "home," contribute to basic household consumption, paying for food, housing, and other critical expenses (Chaves et al. 2011; Martínez Franzoni and Voorend 2012). Up to forty percent of Nicaraguan households receive remittances from relatives in the United States, Costa Rica, and Europe (Monge-González, Céspedes-Torres, and Vargas-Aguilar 2011). However, those who send and receive remittances, parents and children, men and women, often understand the meanings and significance of remittances differently.

The last three chapters have looked at configurations of family in the transnational context—marriage, parenting, and grandparenting. This chapter turns to remittance-sending, a particular practice of transnational family life, to understand how money as well as gifts such as food and clothes mediate these forms of transnational relatedness. Remittances and the things they buy shape transnational intimacy, sustaining family ties even as they point to transformations in those relationships. They provide an important lens for understanding what is at stake in transnational family projects and the negotiations, struggles, and tensions among various household and family members, including parents, grandparents, children, siblings, and others.

At the same time, remittances tie migrants not only to families, but to communities and nations. Focusing only on what remittances mean to family risks ignoring the role the state plays in remittances and migration. In communities of origin, migrants are often subjected to heavy criticism, not just for their perceived "abandonment" of families, but for their abandonment of social and cultural heritage and values. Sending communities have become linked to the global economy not only through economic restructuring but also through remittances that have redefined local ideas of wealth and status (Pribilsky 2007). Remittances are often blamed for changing expectations for consumption and spending among the younger generation, for young people's dissatisfaction with traditional ways of life, and with perpetuating migration. House construction, for example, both represents an individual and status-building endeavor and indexes changing ideals about socio-economic class and community development (Melly 2010; Pellow 2003). While some see such investments as encouraging conspicuous consumption or indexing middle-class aspirations, migrants often emphasize the social relations imbricated in such material investments.

Indeed, reliance on remittances has allowed many families to weather economic and social policies that have made life more difficult for them.

Monthly per capita remittances to Nicaragua represent nearly double annual per capita social spending and are the largest source of national income, accounting for almost 13 percent of GDP and 38 percent of exports (Martínez Franzoni and Voorend 2012; Programa Estado de la Nación-Region 2008). Yet despite its high level of emigration and the significance of remittances as a percent of GDP, Nicaragua has done little to formally capture migrants' loyalty or remittances. Nevertheless, moral discourses around national solidarity are employed to leverage migrants' sense of responsibility toward their communities of origin. At the community and national levels, remittances are the subject of debates over solidarity, national development, and belonging.

Love, Care, and Remembering through Remittances

By moving to Costa Rica, migrants invest in the possibility of work, the opportunity to care for family members "back home" through remittances, and in education, healthcare, and futures for their children in both countries. Indeed, as Menjívar and Abrego (2009, 32) note, remittances are "the currency of transnational love." They represent a kind of emotional labor and are part of the work that produces long distance intimacy (Mckay 2007). Indeed, scholars have emphasized how migrants understand remittance-sending as part of their parenting responsibilities, love, and care, even as family members resist directly equating love and money (Abrego 2009; Boehm 2012; Dreby 2010). Migrant men and women discussed sending remittances—not only in cash, but in the form of rice, beans, and school uniforms—as a moment of "caring" in which parents or children "remember" and think of their children or elderly parents by picking out, buying, and sending food and clothing. Thus, material exchanges intended to contribute to household food security entail an affective component linked to love and gendered notions of sacrifice. Rather than focus on the binary of love versus money, we can see remittances as part of the substance of relatedness. Through the process of providing food and other materials for subsistence, migrant parents stake claims to belonging in their households of origin. Through remittances, migrants invest in an active and dynamic process of relating, through feeding, clothing, and other everyday domestic practices of caring enacted from a distance (Borneman 2001; Carsten 2000, 2004; Zharkevich 2019).

As with other kinning practices, the emotional labor and financial burden of sending remittances is highly gendered. Women frequently drew on notions of motherly sacrifice to describe their efforts, framing economic support as part of the work of mothering. Rosa explained, "All the humiliations, everything one has to go through with the employers. That when we get sick and it's between going to a doctor and sending a remittance, we prefer to send that remittance. We send all our salaries, and we are left with the littlest part." For men, too, remittances were often key to sustaining transnational emotional connections. Fulfilling their role as breadwinner provided men with the authority to act as a father in other ways. When remittances failed to materialize, though, many men also lost touch with their children. Darling, for example, was constantly reminding her husband, Abel, to call his sons back in Nicaragua, even though he had not sent them anything lately. In contrast, her own teenage daughters back in Nicaragua noted that close communication and remittances from their mother helped them maintain a strong relationship while Darling was in Costa Rica: "the six years she was there, and she never stopped calling or sending us money," explained her older daughter, Marcelina.

Migrants sent remittances both through formal channels like banks, Western Union or other money sending services, and through informal channels. Formal channels, while seen by migrants as more reliable, were also more expensive, charging anywhere from 5 percent to 20 percent fees. The streets around the Parque de la Merced, an area of San José frequented by Nicaraguan migrants, are home to many money-sending agencies. On paydays, the lines at these agencies often wrapped around the block as migrants lined up to send money to family in Nicaragua. Others bought sacks of rice, beans, and other basic goods that cost more in Nicaragua and sent them with an intermediary, someone who may have a formal courier to transport remittances in kind. For example, Warner, a security guard, regularly sent about $50 a month to his adult daughter and young grandson, but every few months also sent a large bag of clothes and shoes for them, his elderly parents, and other relatives who lived on the same property in a rural area outside Carazo. He sent the bags with doña Mirna, who worked out of a small stand near the Merced Park. While doña Mirna had a storefront, many other intermediaries were simply acquaintances from the same hometown, or cousins who were returning to Nicaragua for some other reason. Such packages are often sent for special occasions or at the end of the year in time for the new school year in Nicaragua.

Much more commonly, migrants sent small amounts more frequently. Like Warner, many men sent roughly US$50 monthly. Warner's colleague and friend Digmar explained:

> I send $50, when I can more, or sometimes less. It's just that $50 in Nicaragua is almost the monthly wages of a domestic worker, around 1200 *córdobas*. For example, my mama, I send her $50 and she can buy provisions

for the month. The other money that [my siblings] send her is to buy her things. Between this and the fruit she grows on the farm that she sells at the market, and the livestock she keeps, and, between us all, we help my parents because they are getting older.

Digmar's mother, doña Teresa, was in her seventies and lived on the family farm just outside Chinandega, en route to the port. Including Digmar, five of her thirteen children lived outside the country. Digmar and one sister were in Costa Rica, while three other sisters lived in Spain.

One afternoon in 2012, as Chris, Magda, and I descended from a taxi to walk up a narrow dirt path to the farm, past six small but brightly painted houses, I remembered Digmar had told us, "all my siblings have houses right in a row." The fresh construction, new electric and water hookups, and a new motorcycle parked outside one house stood testament to remittances sent from Costa Rica and Spain. At the end of the dirt lane sat Teresa's green house, surrounded by fruit trees, with a large patio and an outdoor kitchen. We were greeted by Teresa, her husband Justino, and four granddaughters, two of whom had parents abroad in Spain.

Despite the electric wires running overhead, Teresa preferred to cook on her outdoor wood stove, "I have a gas stove, I have a microwave, but when I make a lot of food, I do it here outside." At her comment, her granddaughter Nidia rolled her eyes and the three others giggled. Nidia, a fourteen-year-old whose mother was in Spain, pointed inside the house and explained, "She has a machine to make sandwiches, a coffeemaker, a pizzamaker! But she doesn't use them!" The girls took me on a tour of their grandmother's *chunches*, which included kitchen gadgets, a washing machine, and panini and waffle makers all stacked on shelves in a dark room with only one electrical outlet. Although impractical, Teresa kept them all—gifts for Mothers' Day or Christmas from her children abroad. At the same time, she wished her daughters in Spain would be more practical like Digmar and send money. Explaining the huge number of gadgets, she said, "They send them, they bring them back when they visit. But I tell them, what do I want all this for? Someday I'll die and you'll all fight over it. It's better to give me money. From there I could eat. *Los reales me los como.*" Her last statement, literally, "Coins, I eat them," both echoes and inverts Lester's assertion about eating money. Here cash would be preferable to small appliances precisely because Teresa and her family could use the money to buy food and other basic necessities. For those back home, the whole point of remittances is that they can be eaten—or at least used to buy things to eat.

However, Teresa's daughters may have hesitated to send cash. There is often a tension between whether emotional or economic connections take precedence in transnational relationships, and family members resist defining their relationship in purely economic or transactional terms. Yet, for Teresa, who must figure out how to make ends meet while raising several granddaughters, the cash or bags of clothes Digmar sends from Costa Rica could be employed immediately in practical ways to improve life for those living on the farm. In contrast, her daughters' gifts of panini presses were appreciated for their symbolic worth, indexing the senders' "remembering" those at home, but lacked the practical utility of cash.

Many Nicaraguan transnational family members expressed this link between remittances and care through idioms of remembering and forgetting. Alfonso, a Nicaraguan man in his sixties from Achuapa, had three adult daughters who live in Europe. Though they had not visited home in years, he noted, "They don't forget about us. They send us Euros." Another young woman whose father had been in Costa Rica for over five years explained, "Look how much my father loves me, he never forgets to send money for school and other things I need." In such cases, remittances strengthen ties back home by both mitigating parents' absences from the lives of children in particular and materially demonstrating that they remember and care. This linking of remittances to care and love is particularly important in countering discourses of abandonment.

However, migrants often interpreted expectations to maintain connection as pressure to send remittances and gifts, even when they were struggling to make ends meet in Costa Rica. Marlen, a domestic worker in San José, said she only returned to her home in Achuapa once a year, despite having two vacations, because "How awful to arrive empty-handed!" Like Lester in the opening vignette of this chapter, Marlen and other migrants felt that their remittances were not only expected, but used or "eaten" too quickly. The constant expectations for continual remittances frustrated and stressed migrants who were often living in conditions of poverty, unstable work, and uncertain legal status in Costa Rica.

In Nicaragua, family members often interpreted migrants' not sending remittances as a failure to maintain emotional connections. For example, in Managua, Esther and Jessy interpreted Nestor's lack of remittance-sending as abandonment. Esther depended almost entirely on Nestor's remittances for Jessy's care. When Jessy began to suffer chronic headaches in 2011, Esther was unable to afford the expensive medical tests doctors recommended for her. With Nestor's growing family and unsteady employment in Costa Rica, he had been unable to send much in the way of remittances and had not visited in more than a year. In fact, when I visited him in Costa Rica, he admitted to not having sent anything in at least six months. And though Esther carefully explained Jessy's medical condition to my husband

and me, it was clear that Nestor was unaware of the extent of the tests that the doctors in Nicaragua had urged for his daughter. It was his failure to send remittances, coupled with not visiting, that compelled Jessy and her relatives in Nicaragua to declare that Nestor had abandoned her. In contrast, no one expected her mother to financially support her, because she had already given up custody and any kin connection with the child.

Similarly, Diana's son Kenneth expressed deep disappointment in his mother because of what he saw as her double failures as a mother. When she left for Costa Rica with her new husband, Diana failed both to remain connected emotionally with her two children in Nicaragua and to support them financially; she neither called nor "sent." When several years later she returned to Nicaragua to reconnect, Kenneth felt it was too little, too late: "She was my mother, and even though she didn't raise me, I love her a lot, like I love my dad, like I love my brother. But she didn't approach us in the way I thought she was going to talk to me. Lovingly." Key to Diana's disconnect from Kenneth was her new husband's refusal to contribute financially to the children from her previous relationship.

The entanglement of the material and emotional dimensions of remittances creates tensions within transnational families. Although parents envision money and gifts as bridging the distance between them and their children, remittances are double-edged. They demonstrate that a migrant parent is *pendiente*, looking out for them and responsible, but they are also a constant reminder of a loved one's absence. They represent at once love and abandonment, both absence and presence.

Managing Remittances: The Role of Middlewomen

Managing remittances is also complicated by this entanglement of the emotional and economic aspects. In remittance-receiving countries in the global South, the context of migration blurs some of the stark differences between the kinds of care organized through payment and those mediated through kinship relations as families rely on remittances for social provisioning (Kofman and Raghuram 2009). Grandmother caregivers, who as we have seen, are key middlewomen within transnational families, take on the complicated job of managing both money and expectations around family separation. In all the families I worked with, migrants sent remittances to women within their own families, usually a mother or sister, whom they considered more trustworthy than other relatives and in-laws. So for example, men who were no longer in a relationship with children's mothers sent money to their own mothers to distribute to their children, rather than to their ex-partner. Indeed, Nestor doubted that the money he sent to Esther for Jessy's care was used for her benefit. So when Esther asked for more money for medical tests, Nestor was unconvinced that the doctor's bills could be that high.

For many migrants, their own mothers are the most trustworthy recipients of remittances, because of their connection—they are seen as having both their children's and grandchildren's best interests at heart. For grandmothers this meant not only making ends meet, sometimes with inconsistent remittances, but also managing the emotional aspects of family separation. Many grandmothers talked about how difficult it was to stretch remittances, especially in the face of unpredictable expenses for children. Many grandmothers paid for private schooling for grandchildren, and almost all the families I talked to used private clinics, at least for serious illnesses. When remittances did not "measure up," they did not make up for parents' absences, did not supply the income needed to care for children left behind, and disappointed both children's and caregivers' expectations (Yarris 2017). Even when parents sent money regularly, it was often not enough to cover children's expenses. For example, even with the $100 a month that Dulce sent, Marina often found it hard to make ends meet:

> I have two of her children. And I pay the schools, because I have them in private schools. And [Lisseth's] school, I pay for her because I have her in computer class, she's going to complete a year-and-a-half-long computer course. That's another school I pay. And I say, their expenses, the food, when they get sick, I have to take them to the doctor, the medicine, shoes, I mean, their clothes.

Similarly, Elena's daughter recalled that her grandmother sometimes drew from her own money when Elena's children needed something, rather than bother Elena in Costa Rica. "When she saw that we were missing something, she spent her own money so as not to bother my mama. Because she would say, 'How could we bother her because she had her own expenses too.'" Both Marina and Elena's mother tried to avoid upsetting their migrant daughters with the reality of how thinly stretched their household budgets were.

In addition to making do with meager budgets and often pooling remittances with other sources of income to care for multiple family members, grandmother caregivers provided their migrant children with a careful accounting of how they spent remittances. Marina, for example, kept a large envelope with all the receipts and notes on how she spent Dulce's remittance money. Lisseth had recently been ill and gone to a private clinic, as Marina explained:

> Well, now she got sick again, just two weeks ago. Last week she saw the doctor. I have all the receipts there. How much I had to pay. Because I save all of that for her mama. Because you know that even though she's my daughter, but you always have to move forward and never back. She tells me, "Mami," she says, "that costs you more than it does me." That I'm going to drive myself crazy giving explanations and accounts, she says. But it's so that it's clear that I'm spending the money on her children and how much I've spent.

Marina preferred to maintain careful records rather than perhaps face recriminations or doubts from her daughter about where the money she sent was going. Again, if remittances are a key substance of relatedness in transnational families, the responsible use of that money represents a form of care for the relationships they maintain.

Indeed, although Dulce felt her mother was going overboard by saving every little receipt, she felt confident in her mother's good management of the money, and said she would not hesitate to send extra to cover emergencies, because she knew exactly where the money was going. As Marina pointed out, "Raising them has not been easy for me. Even though my daughter sends the money, it's the one who's at home who knows how to make that money last. So, all of this I have to think about, it's always my responsibility." By providing a careful accounting of and judicial use of the remittances, grandmothers like Marina demonstrated to migrant parents that families back home had not squandered or frivolously "eaten" all the money. Careful accounting contributes not only to the responsible financial management of remittances, but to the mitigation of tensions between distant family members. At the same time, careful accounting and responsible remittance-management is part of the development of responsible neoliberal subjects, as grandmothers take on the responsibility for rational use of remittance-money as well as the welfare of family members.

Grandmothers also manage children's expectations around remittances and migrant parents' absences. In doing so, grandmothers emphasize the sacrifice and effort migrants make to send remittances. In this way, they reinforce children's bonds with absent parents while also managing their own feelings about separation from adult children—as in the cases of Elena and her children Kobe, Scarleth, and Jefferson. However, when grandmothers do not emphasize the economic support of migrant parents, children have a very different understanding of their relationship to absent parents. For example, Daisy's adult daughter Hazel felt disconnected from her mother and did not understand why she had moved to Costa Rica more than ten years earlier. Although she had graduated from college, was married, and had a young son, she expressed fresh resentment when asked about why her mother had left. Though Daisy had told me that she regularly sent remittances home for more than a decade when her daughters were younger, Hazel claimed that she knew nothing about the money and felt that her mother had left "on a whim." When I asked her what her grandmother told her about their mother's absence, she said they never talked about it.

When grandmothers and other caregivers make clear that new clothes, school supplies, and other goods come from remittances sent by an absent parent, they reinforce the parent-child bond, but when they fail to make explicit these connections, they may contribute to resentment and feelings of abandonment. When migrants do not live up to expectations for regular communication and remittances, as we see in the case of Nestor, Jessy, and Esther, it creates both financial and emotional burdens for caregivers and generates tensions that can spark or deepen a sense of disconnection between migrant and non-migrant kin.

Community and Consumption

Walking down the streets of Estelí, it is clear how migration and remittances have reshaped the physical infrastructure of neighborhoods. Houses built or renovated with remittances have stucco walls, brightly painted facades, bars on windows and doors, and solid roofs. Yet on the same street, one also sees houses made of local bricks or cinder block, with zinc roofs—often provided by the local government—and dirt floors.

Take, for example, the home of doña Esmeralda, Claudia's mother. When I first met her in 2009, she lived in a small brick house with no electricity and dirt floors. Nearly transparent curtains fluttered through windows that had no glass or anything to keep out the mosquitos and flies. The only furniture in the living room was a handful of rocking chairs, some wooden, others made from plastic cable. Doña Esmeralda, who is partially deaf, was dressed in a well-worn house dress. Agnes was visiting from Costa Rica and explained that four of her aunts lived in Spain. All of the daughters sent home money, to support both doña Esmeralda and the six grandchildren she cared for.

Three years later, in 2012, I returned to visit doña Esmeralda. Despite having spent time in the neighborhood before, and Agnes's detailed directions, I had to call her cousin Luisa to help us find the address. I stood on the corner where I thought she lived, but did not recognize any of the houses. As Luisa stepped out of a smartly painted house with a tile stoop and glass windows, my jaw dropped. She laughed as we went inside and I did a double take at the new façade, tile floors, new couch, phone, and electric lights in the living room. Her mother and aunts, Luisa explained, had helped renovate the house and Luisa had moved in to help care for her grandmother. Shortly after, doña Esmeralda returned home from church. She was dressed in a brightly printed dress, with a new hat and polished shoes. She seemed full of energy and, with the help of her new hearing aid, was excited to receive updates about Claudia and her granddaughters.

In neighborhoods around Estelí and other cities, houses like doña Esmeralda's are being constructed and renovated through remittances. House construction represents an individual and status-building endeavor tied to consumption (Melly 2010; Pellow 2003). However, homes anchor migrants not only to their own families but to the wider community and nation by indexing changing ideas about development, lifestyles, and belonging. While families may see remittances as emotionally fraught but key to family advancement and survival, community leaders often see such reliance on remittances as a danger to traditional ways of life by promoting lifestyles based on conspicuous consumption. At the community level, tensions over migration emerge in discourses not only about homes but also more broadly around land and consumption and the possible impacts of remittances on development.

The scholarship on remittances and development has swung back and forth between being optimistic about remittances' potential and being critical of the economic dependency remittances may create. Some have praised remittances for contributing to an improvement in living standards and nutrition indicators of receiving families, or increased resources for housing and consumer good purchases (Castles, de Haas, and Miller 2013), or higher productivity in the labor force, especially agriculture and rural industry (de Haas 2006). Remittances may induce investment (de Haas 2012; Woodruff and Zenteno 2007) or be used as a livelihood strategy or "insurance policy" that reduces vulnerability to negative shocks to income (de Haas 2012). The initial fervor of the so-called remittance mantra, the appealing idea that remittances can be channeled into economic investments that lead to development, has given way to more nuanced assessments of the potential impacts of remittances (Castles, de Haas, and Miller 2013; Kapur 2004). Remittances may increase inequality between families that receive them and those that do not (Hujo and Piper 2010; Lopez, Fajnzylber, and Acosta 2007). They may also increase prices for lands or consumer goods and other scarce resources, and may create a higher economic dependency on host countries and transnational companies (Rocha

2011). That is, remittances do not automatically lead to sustainable or equitable economic and social development.

Rather than engage with these debates about the economic impact of remittances, I want to emphasize how these tensions are understood within transnational communities. Even among families and communities that rely heavily on remittances, there are deep ambivalences over how remittances have redefined ideas about wealth, status, and well-being. For example, don Alfonso, a farmer in the small town of Achuapa in the León Department, has achieved economic security because two of his daughters regularly sent money from Europe. When he was hospitalized with liver problems, his daughters "wouldn't let me sell the plot of land to pay medical expenses. They helped." Indeed, in a context in which crop prices fluctuate, climate change makes harvests more unpredictable, and there is little access to insurance markets, remittances provide a kind of insurance against unforeseen costs that could otherwise force families to sell land or face deep poverty. Many landowners in the community migrate temporarily to El Salvador in between planting and harvesting, using money earned there to insure against poor harvests, invest in new farm equipment, or pay for special family expenses like weddings or quinceañeras. As Alfonso noted, "my children are my great capital."

At the same time, Alfonso was critical of the changes migration and remittances had brought to Achuapa and to Nicaragua. Like others, he expressed this through a critique of the kinds of consumption and dependency that remittances foster. In Achuapa, where local leaders claimed up to 30 percent of the community participated in some form of international migration, Alfonso and others critiqued young people's migration, contrasting it with the kinds of temporary migration that many small farmers employed as a form of self-insurance.

Local leaders argued that the emigration of young people to Costa Rica was leading to new expectations of consumption and an abandonment of *campesino* livelihoods. For example, Nelson, a fifty-four-year-old man who had traveled to Costa Rica six times between 2001 and 2009, and who defined himself as an *hombre de campo*, argued that his migrations strengthened his ties to the community because they allowed him to maintain his land. By paying off his loan from the cooperative in a timely manner, despite a poor harvest, his migration allowed him to maintain his status as a cooperative member in good standing. That is, migration strengthened his relationship to both the land and community.

Nelson contrasted this with "the young person of today," including his own son, who "isn't like us. He doesn't want to work the land." Indeed, local leaders were so concerned with the lure of migration on Achuapa's young people that one leader called migration Achuapa's "greatest development problem." He explained, "All the young people have gone or they don't want to work the land. Only the old people, the adults, are left. They're not going to move forward much." Physical absence was compounded by young people's lack of interest in traditional agricultural livelihoods, as their lifestyle expectations changed.

Alfonso pointed to how migrants returned from Costa Rica dissatisfied not just with farming but also with rural life more generally. According to him, young men "come back and as soon as the clothes they brought from Costa Rica are old and ugly, they leave again." Further, their remittances and gifts increased expectations of consumption among those "left behind." Again, here material goods are consumed, used up, "eaten," creating a reliance on migrant remittances to maintain certain levels of a consumer lifestyle. Alfonso described this process as "losing love for the land," echoing discourses of nationalism and solidarity at the national level (Fouratt 2017). Leaders blamed migration for this loss of interest in agricultural livelihoods rather than economic restructuring or national policies that made farming less profitable, urban areas more attractive, and higher education more attainable for many young people.

Similarly, Rosa explained that when the Network of Migrant Women held a workshop with their family members back home,

> in this meeting, we discovered that our children were consumers. Because the malls became popular. All these malls opening, and the Nicaraguan economy doing so well, but who was shopping in these malls? Our remittances were being left in the malls. Our children no longer used any shoes, they had to be brand name, brand name backpacks, the latest cell phone. And since I had migrated, since I had "abandoned" my child, then I had to buy this for my child.

In the relationships Rosa describes, remittances may be the vehicle through which irresponsible consumption is made possible, but children's looking to material goods can be traced to parental migration and "abandonment." In this case, remittances are a poor substitute for a mother's love, but function as a kind of blackmail within parent-child relationships. Through the Network of Women Relatives of Migrants, many families have transformed these narratives about financial support and emotional abandonment, but discourses about migrants as ultimately responsible for conspicuous consumption and the loss of traditional lifestyles still persist.

Further, narratives about responsible use of remittances, like the temporary migration of farmers, versus irresponsible use of remittances for consumption tie remittance sending and receiving to neoliberal subjectivity. Indeed, many families who relied on remittances saw them as a way to achieve autonomy and control over their familial well-being. For example, a young woman I met in Estelí discussed how her sisters had worked abroad and invested in housing and education for their children. "I want to go to Spain to work. To buy my little plot to build my house for my children. Here you don't earn enough to do that, just enough to eat." Debates about both remittances' development potential and individuals' use of them for investment in education or enterprise fall along a binary of consumption/dependency and productivity/autonomy (Hernandez and Coutin 2006). In focusing on the responsibility of migrants and their families to employ remittances in productive and responsible ways, such discourses obscure the larger economic and social policies that make migration and remittances necessary for survival for a large segment of the population.

Remittances, Solidarity, and the State

Whether interpreting them as an act of love or as driving abandonment of national and local values, discourses around remittances that focus on individual migrants and their choices obscure the role of remittances at the national level and particularly the role the state plays in remittance-sending and spending. In Nicaragua, remittances represented the largest source of national income, accounting for somewhere between 10 and 18 percent of GDP and 38 percent of exports (Banco Central de Nicaragua 2015; Martínez Franzoni and Voorend 2012; Orozco 2009; Programa Estado de la Nación-Region 2008). While remittances decreased with the global financial crisis after 2008, Nicaragua did not suffer as large a loss in remittance growth as other remittance-receiving countries in Latin America, and remittances rebounded more quickly, in part because of the diversity of destinations of Nicaraguan migrants (Orozco 2009; Monge-González, Céspedes-Torres, and Vargas-Aguilar 2011). The money sent by migrants is particularly important in ensuring healthcare, education, and other needs for children in Nicaragua.

Not far from don Alfonso's house in Achuapa, I met four sisters whose parents were in Costa Rica. The oldest, Dalia, explained that their parents had gone to Costa Rica "to buy medicine" for her youngest sister, a teenager at that time, who had a chronic heart condition. *Buying medicine*, I soon learned, was a euphemism for the more than two years their parents had spent working in Costa Rica, sending home money for the vital but expensive medication that the Nicaraguan public healthcare system did not cover. While some medications are available free or at low cost through the Nicaraguan healthcare system, many, particularly for serious chronic conditions, are not covered, and patients must pay out of pocket.

Many Nicaraguan families turn to the private sector for healthcare, using remittances to afford clinic appointments, medications, and diagnostic tests. In Managua, Marina explained that when her grandchildren were sick, she almost always took them to a private clinic:

> When they get sick, I take them . . . especially since they don't have insurance here. So, I take them to a doctor. If you take them to a health center, right? A public one, and they don't take care of them, then you have to take them to a paid doctor. [. . .] I have to take them to a private doctor so that they pay more attention to the illness.

Indeed, Marina explained that she took them to private clinics because when Lisseth was young she almost died from a secondary infection after her appendix was removed in a public hospital. Dissatisfaction with public healthcare services in Nicaragua was widespread, and migration and the remittances it provides offered a way for families to sidestep state sponsored services and purchase care in the private sector (Fouratt and Voorend 2018). Remittances also paid for private school or classes to supplement the public schooling in Nicaragua, like Lisseth's computer and English classes. Migrant parents hoped that such investments would lead to better job and university opportunities for their children. At the time of this writing, Lisseth was studying business at a university in Managua. Elena's two sons had graduated college, as had both of Darling's daughters and two of Andrea's three children.

However, when migrants were unable to send remittances, it significantly affected children's access to healthcare and other services. For example, Ester reported frustration that the father of her granddaughter, Jessy, had not sent money recently, even though Jessy had been suffering from recurring headaches and needed diagnostic tests outside the public hospital:

> I don't know. It looks like things are going badly for him economically. That's what I feel. Because Jessy has been very sick, she was in the hospital, and his help has been minimal, almost absent. The difference a CT scan would make. But that costs almost $200. And he couldn't send that. So we haven't been able to get the scan for her.

A lack of remittances, then, may translate into not only familial disconnection, but also a lack of access to healthcare, especially for children. Key here is that grandmothers take on these additional responsibilities of managing remittances and accessing care for children in the absence of stable financial resources.

While families struggled to send and manage remittances, they often contrasted the care embodied by family remittances with the neglect of the state. In this sense, remittances are key to notions of the "community of care" as they highlight the state's lack of responsiveness to the people. Elena's son Kobe, for example, contrasted the reliability of his mother's remittances, which has financed the house he and his siblings lived in in Granada, with the frivolous spending of the Ortega administration. His mother, he argued, had built the house "cinder block by cinder block" even though she did so at great sacrifice and from a distance. In contrast, he pointed to his experiences as an intern in the Nicaraguan First Lady's office where he learned firsthand about the polarization of local and national politics and began to complain to me about the pointless expenditures on beautification campaigns as mentioned in Chapter 1. He, and others, argued that only those who proved themselves "good Sandinistas" were able to access housing funds or roofing materials provided by the government.

When families use remittances to access services in the private sector, to bypass formal banks to finance house construction, or to contribute to local projects like schools, clinics, or hospitals, they are participating in the privatization of public services (Hernandez and Coutin 2006). Martínez Franzoni and Voorend (2011) calculate that monthly per capita remittances received by Nicaraguans represent 50 to 100 percent of the state's annual per capita social spending. Though not all remittances are spent on social provisioning, some regional studies suggest close to half goes to housing, education, and healthcare (Martínez Franzoni and Voorend 2011; Chaves et al. 2011). Like discourses of family breakdown, discourses around self-responsibility serve to mold migrants and transnational families into responsible subjects while distracting from state policies that make remittances necessary in the first place.

Many migrant-sending states rely on migration and remittances as part of economic growth. The costs of remittances, from transfer fees to exploitative labor conditions, "illegal" status, family separation, and emotional hardship are ignored or erased in national accounting practices of these countries. Esther Hernandez and Susan Coutin (2006, 201) have called this the "purification" of remittances, a process by which central banks in receiving countries are able to figure remittances as cost-free donations to the national economy. Through this process, remittances become the ideal neoliberal currency as official accounts figure them as the result of hard work and individual success, ignoring the very real costs to trans-national families or the economic and political structures that undergird remittances.

These "developmental migration states" (Adamson and Tsourapas 2020) often create policies that encourage both labor migration and remittance sending. The Philippines, for example, has organized the export of workers abroad through government agencies as a way to encourage temporary migration, stem unemployment, and secure foreign exchange (Sassen 2000). In Mexico, the government has encouraged local trans-national connections by encouraging and supporting Hometown Associations (Orozco 2004). In all these cases, remittances—even when destined for individual households—represent links between migrants and sending nations and communities. El Salvador and Peru have both capitalized on their citizens abroad, encouraging return migration of successful and entrepreneurial migrants and promoting remittance sending (Coutin 2007; DeLugan 2012; Gammage 2006; Berg 2010). Migrant-sending countries not only try to claim "migra-dollars" but also migrants' loyalties to encourage their continued remitting. For example, in El Salvador, remitting is figured as a moral act despite the fact that it requires illegal actions, such as migrating without authorization. National discourses of migration and remittance sending as patriotic sacrifices scale up the emotional and financial imbrications of remittances from individual families to the national level.

Yet the Nicaraguan government has done little to capture the loyalty of migrants, despite the power of discourses of solidarity and nationalism. Instead, the lack of public and political support for migrants meant that they felt criticized for leaving while their financial contributions to households and the national economy were ignored. Juana, for example, described the relationship between migrants and the Nicaraguan government in familial terms, "like when a mother or father abandons you. Because we feel alone here, emotionally. We feel not only everything we left behind there in Nicaragua, but we also come here to this country and there isn't anyone, on our government's part, who looks out for the Nicaraguan emigrant here." Juana turns the discourses critiquing migrants for abandonment on their head, using the framework of family breakdown to condemn the Nicaraguan government for not taking care of its citizens abroad. She went on to cite the case of Natividad Canda, the young man killed by Rottweilers, as another example of how migrants are abandoned by the Nicaraguan state: "Who are we going to cry to, 'look, this and this and this is happening to me'? The dog that ate a Nicaraguan—that was tremendous xenophobia. Who were we going to go crying to? Who could

we go to in the government that would say that they were on our side?"
For Juana, though, the blame lay with both the Nicaraguan and Costa
Rican governments. Both take advantage of the labor and financial contributions of migrants without recognizing or reciprocating their efforts.
She emphasized, "I've noticed how much Nicaragua gains through family
remittances migrants send from here to there. And I also think of how
much the Caja here, the Caja Costarricense gains with Nicaraguans paying into it." Yet, when migrants return to Nicaragua, they lose any social
security they may have paid in Costa Rica and receive no benefits from
Nicaragua.

Rosa explained that such abandonment by the state was part of why
the Network of Migrant Women was formed originally, so that migrants
would not be forgotten by the Nicaraguan government, "and so we won't
be only a symbol of remittances, but that they will really think about us.
Because in our country of origin, they remember us for the remittances
but they don't remember any policy that will make life easier for us." Here,
Rosa's use of *remembering* echoes the way members of transnational families employ the term to discuss remittance sending—that is, as encom-
passing both financial support and emotional connection. In arguing that
the government, and sometimes their own families, think only of remittances and not of the sacrifices and costs migrants face in Costa Rica, Rosa
is critiquing their lack of solidarity. She criticized Nicaragua for "closing
doors" for migrants. For example, in 2012, Costa Rica implemented a series
of temporary measures to allow undocumented migrants to regularize
their status. While the program itself had many flaws, it represented an
important opportunity for regularization, but, as Rosa noted, "Costa Rica
had the good will to apply a *transitorio* to regularize people and the only
obstacle was in Nicaragua," which refused to make getting the necessary
documents easier.

Lack of public recognition of their sacrifices also creates an emotional
disconnection between migrants and the nation-state. For migrants like
Juana and Rosa, it is an official erasure of their experiences with illegality,
labor exploitation, and family separation. If remittance-sending is figured
as a moral act, a contribution to the nation, then migrants still "count" in
nation-building projects of solidarity and development. However, when
migrant experiences and family remittances are discounted as individual
economic or lifestyle choices, as matters of conspicuous consumption
rather than necessities born of state absences, migrants have no way to
participate in discourses of solidarity that require connection to and love
for family, community, and nation.

Conclusion

Remittances, even as they represent important income sources for families to access healthcare, education, and better housing, reinforce the state's continued reliance on families to generate and sustain fragile levels of social provisioning at the national level. For both migrants and their families back in Nicaragua, exclusion from public services drives them to develop informal strategies for ensuring access to services like healthcare, especially for children. Such informal strategies rely, at least in part, on the flexibility of transnational kin and care. It is female caregivers who take on new responsibilities when transnational families bypass the state. It is migrant mothers who delay or forgo caring for their own health needs to ensure care for children, who deal with xenophobic clinic staff, and consistently send money home. It is grandmothers, who take children to appointments, figure out how to stretch meager budgets to cover tests and specialists, and provide emotional support to sick children. Further, the blurred distinctions between paid and unpaid care serves to naturalize women's roles in social provisioning and devalue paid care work. Gendered strategies of remittance sending and management allow public discourses of solidarity and equality to resonate in the national imaginary despite deep inequality and poverty. Transnational family members' understandings of remittances and the affective meanings associated with them are, in part, a reflection of state discourse, building on and reinforcing these discourses of solidarity, even as migrants may feel themselves ignored or unrecognized by the state.

CHAPTER 7

Returns and Reunions

ONE AFTERNOON IN THE ASTRADOMES office in early 2012, I remarked that I had not seen Elena lately. "Oh, she went back to Nicaragua," Andrea told me, as she bounced Magda on her knee. "She had some issue with her children and her house, so she went back." A few months later, I tracked Elena down in Granada, Nicaragua. At first glance, her house, financed through her remittances, with its breezy open living space and modern appliances, represented the successful end of her migration story. It had taken more than fifteen years, but she owned her own house, was working on an advocacy program for domestic workers in Nicaragua, and was building her own business selling popsicles and cold drinks from her deep freezer. Her two sons were poised to finish university, and she doted on her two grandchildren.

It would be easy to hear Elena's story and view family reunification or migrants' return to their country of origin as the ultimate goal. However, the mobility of Nicaraguan family members points to the multiple movements and migrations and, ultimately, shifting goals, expectations, and unexpected outcomes for transnational family members. Migration for Nicaraguans is not a one-time, permanent decision, but a repeated, temporarily permanent strategy for getting by or getting ahead. The proximity of Nicaragua and Costa Rica, relatively lax border enforcement, and continuous structural demand for migrant labor in Costa Rica have reinforced these high levels of mobility and the use of migration in family welfare strategies.

As I have noted throughout this book, it is important to take into account the changing geographic locations, relationship statuses, and shifting perspectives of family members. Elena's return home was just one more return to Nicaragua in what had been years of back and forth movements. For example, in 2009, she had returned to Nicaragua to deal with a family situation and intended to stay, but in September 2011, I found her once again at the ASTRADOMES office in Costa Rica. However, just months later, Andrea would tell me about her return to Nicaragua. And in mid-2012, in Granada Elena would tell me she was thinking of leaving for Costa Rica again. As of the time of writing, Elena was still in Granada, but feeling isolated and frustrated. A series of family situations with her elderly mother, her youngest son, and her own siblings had led to her losing touch with her friends in Costa Rica.

Like Elena's first migration to Costa Rica, many migrants go to Costa Rica intending to return to Nicaragua within a year or two. However, continuing needs back home—schooling, housing, or health needs—delay such dreams for return. Those that return find, like Elena or Lester in the previous chapter, that they cannot stay. While I only followed these families for a few years, the frequency with which family members moved back and forth between Costa Rica, Nicaragua, and even beyond, was striking.

This chapter traces the hoped for and real returns and reunions between migrants and their families. Returns should not be seen as the final chapter of families' migration stories, but rather part of the flexible arrangements of kin and care through which Nicaraguans forge meaningful family relationships. I begin by looking at how migrants' dreams for returns are often delayed or deferred. The chapter then turns to what happens when migrants do return to Nicaragua and the importance of family circumstances in determining returns. I also look at how migrant parents' returns, sometimes after more than a decade, create new family tensions as adult children and migrant parents renegotiate living together. Further, migrant mothers' returns are often tied to intergenerational responsibilities that make possible their own daughters' migrations. Finally, while many migrants want to return to Nicaragua or reunite with family, some prefer to cut ties. For many, cutting ties with relatives in Nicaragua also means cutting ties to the nation-state where they are unable to envision a future for themselves or their families.

Longings for Return

As we have seen, many Nicaraguans envision their migration to Costa Rica as temporary and migrate initially with goals for building houses, paying for school, or otherwise supporting their families back home. However, their plans for return are often delayed by a number of factors. For some, the demands their families place on them increase the pressure to achieve financial success in Costa Rica before returning to Nicaragua. For example, Mardelí, who worked as an assistant in a shop in San José and had a daughter back in Achuapa, Nicaragua, wanted to return permanently and open a small store. When she first left her small town for Costa Rica, she envisioned that she would only stay for a year or two, so that she could be back in Nicaragua "to be able to advise my daughter in adolescence." However, when I interviewed her in 2009, she had already been in Costa Rica for twelve years. She would return only for vacations throughout the time I was conducting fieldwork. Indeed, even for vacation, she went home less frequently than she could have because she felt ashamed and frustrated that she could not provide more for her daughter and family back home. Low wages, the high cost of living in Costa Rica, and her undocumented status made it nearly impossible to get ahead.

In the previous chapter, I noted that migrants faced expectations to send remittances and support families back home. Over time, these expectations shifted, as children grew and new financial needs arose within families. Elena had originally migrated to earn enough to build a house for her children and to pay their school and other expenses. However, over the course of ten years, her children's needs changed. Money for house construction was diverted to schooling, clothes, and emergencies. Although she returned frequently, and sometimes for up to a year, she ultimately continued working in Costa Rica to afford university tuition for them. As she told me in 2009, "At first I sent money just for my children to eat. Then for their studies. I've stayed here so long to give them opportunities that I never had." However, in December 2009, when she returned to Granada for Christmas, she found out that Kobe had been skipping classes and spending the tuition money she sent on drinking and drugs. She had thought he was less than a year away from graduating, and instead he had dropped out. In this case, her return felt less than triumphant, and it would prove less than permanent when she returned to Costa Rica a year later to continue working.

With constantly changing goals, objectives, and circumstances, what counts as success for returning migrants? For many, it was returning with the financial security to enact future plans. As Rosa explained:

Most of us, we don't think about staying in Costa Rica. We're making plans. Sometimes those plans fall apart, but yes, each of us has a project for the future, to return to Nicaragua. And sometimes we say, "That's it! This year we're going." But something unexpected happens and the dream gets postponed, but yes, yes . . . We all want to return and see what we can do there [in Nicaragua].

Rosa left Nicaragua when her daughters were young children to pay for their basic needs, but over the years, her plans had changed. When I met her oldest daughter, Tania, she was finishing her degree at a top Nicaraguan university. And though she worked part time, it was Rosa's remittances that paid tuition and most of the family's living expenses.

Rosa was also working toward a future with her daughters in Nicaragua. Tania explained, "We have a life plan that is to build an eatery in Ometepe. My mom would take out a loan to build the house in Ometepe, then return to Nicaragua and get started with the business, whether a restaurant or a little hotel." However, that dream too had been delayed. Tania's father was going to sign a plot of family land over to her, but other expenses prevented the women from taking the final steps to start the new project on the tourist destination of the island of Ometepe in Lake Cocibolca:

> Right now all that's left is for me to go to Ometepe so that my father will sign the transfer, but since this year I finish university, there are the costs of my thesis, all that, it's about $1,000. So my mama is in the middle of that right now. She says that we should finish paying the expenses for my degree, the $1,000 that she has to come up with, and that you can't just pull from nowhere. And then after we'll take out a loan to build the house and we'll move there to Ometepe.

While Rosa also talked about the project, she expressed joy and commitment to her work as an activist in Costa Rica. Returning to Nicaragua would mean leaving behind the women she had worked with for more than a decade and stepping back from her advocacy and activist work in Costa Rica. Given her opposition to the Ortega regime and her political commitments to sheltering the opposition in exile, in 2020 she had once again delayed her plans to return.

Recurring Returns

Although for many migrants permanent returns seem out of reach, the proximity of the two countries means that migrants return for vacation or longer stays with relative frequency. Like Elena, many migrants return annually for Christmas or Holy Week. Indeed, every year, around seventy thousand Nicaraguans cross the border during Holy Week, taking advantage of vacations to visit family and bring home money, supplies, and gifts. Others return for longer periods of time, often hoping their homecomings will be permanent. Such returns are often tied to family responsibilities. For example, I had first interviewed Juana at the house she shared with three other migrant women in Curridabat, the town where I lived outside San José. Although at the time, she shared no plans to return to Nicaragua any time soon, as I followed up with one of her roommates, she noted that Juana had returned suddenly to Nicaragua because her father had died. A few weeks later, as I sat in Juana's house in Jinotepe, she explained that she had actually returned because her twenty-six-year-old son had suffered a traumatic brain injury. While he was recovering, her father passed away, leaving her mother suffering emotionally and financially. Her sister, who had also been in Costa Rica, returned for their father's funeral and found her own teenage son unmanageable, and so both Juana and her sister decided to stay in Jinotepe, at least for the foreseeable future.

Elena, too, had returned in 2004 for a few years when her children entered that "sensitive" age of adolescence and she reconciled with her husband. Her daughter, Scarleth, explained that the three children became too much first for their elderly grandmother, then for their aunt who took over their care. Elena and her husband discussed the situation and, as Kobe remembered, "He suddenly came to the house, talked to my mom. And it seems like they said that 'for the children, now Kobe is growing up, so that he'll be a good man, now all of them are growing up and need a home where there's a father figure.' And my mom put it that way, and returned home and they started to make projects together to finish the house." Elena explained that while she was visiting for Christmas, her estranged husband approached her:

> He had pursued me before, every time I returned, but this time was different. We hadn't divorced, well we still haven't. So in 2004, I tell him that yes, we can get back together, but only if we renew our vows in church because we had been separated for so long. Only my oldest son was in favor of it, the other two, no. [. . .] Also, my sister turned all three children over to me, saying that she couldn't take care of them anymore. So I go and look for their dad. And that's when I said, yes, we'll get back together, renew our vows.

Elena set up a small *venta*, selling sodas and snacks and other items to nearby construction and autoshop workers. However, the small store never made enough and eventually Elena returned to Costa Rica. This cycle was repeated several times over the course of more than a decade, with Elena going to Costa Rica after splitting from her husband again, when her young adult children were out of work, and, eventually, to pay for their university tuition.

Like Elena, many returned migrants find that, after the higher wages they earned in Costa Rica, they cannot afford to stay in Nicaragua, where they earn barely enough to eat. Juana hoped to return to Costa Rica as soon as her son's injury improved. "I'm thinking about going back at the beginning of January," she said in May 2012, "I have to work four months here [in Nicaragua] to be able to earn what I earned in one month in Costa Rica. There I earned $400. Here I earn $100." Besides her father's funeral expenses, it appeared her son would need long-term physical and occupational therapy, which would be too expensive on her Nicaraguan salary. Thus, even returns envisioned as permanent may become temporary. As Rosa noted, "Those are the plans. Because those experiences are ugly too, right, that maybe here in Costa Rica the women have this dream to improve their house in Nicaragua. And when they get there, everything is in disarray, the families have spent the money; they didn't invest it in what they should have. So those are the blows and setbacks too."

Reunions and Re-adaptations

As migration extends longer and longer, some migrant parents try to bring children to live with them in Costa Rica. These family reunifications are fraught with tension and difficulties for all those involved. In particular, when children migrate to Costa Rica to rejoin parents, it can represent a second separation for grandmother caregivers. Separated from their children, grandmothers must also sacrifice the companionship of the grandchildren they care for in the name of parent-child bonds (Yarris 2017). However, among the families I worked with, no reunions between migrant parents and children brought children to Costa Rica until they were adults. Reunification in Costa Rica is often uncertain as migrant illegality and remarriage may prevent parents from bringing their children abroad. In many families, the noncustodial parent refused to sign children's passports or exit permits to allow them to leave the country and reunite with migrant parents.

Instead, as happened with Elena, Juana, and others, migrants may return home after years in Costa Rica. When such reunions mean living together with children they have not lived with for more than holidays or vacations for more than a decade, reunions require negotiation and flexibility. For Elena's children, each return over the years, no matter how temporary, required new adjustments and adaptations. Kobe explained, "It was pretty hard because each time things came up, like with changes, it was really hard to begin to adapt, especially when you're little." The children would face different rules and expectations when Elena was present than when their aunt or grandparents cared for them.

The situation was similar when Elena returned in 2012, with all three adult children and Scarleth's two small children living at home. The youngest, Jefferson, noted:

> Well, because she brings an atmosphere from there of domestic work. That everything should be done when she says, how she says. So, sometimes there are conflicts in that aspect. She was used to getting up at 4 a.m. or getting ready at 3:30 a.m. I had never had that, you see. But those aren't serious things, just things she's used to from Costa Rica.

However, for Kobe, who had chafed under the strict rules of his grandfather growing up, adapting to life with his mother was more difficult. Scarleth often played mediator between Elena and Kobe because she felt she and her mother had strengthened their own relationship. Scarleth explained:

> Thank God I've known how to understand her. Because I know sometimes she feels frustrated. Like I say to her, if I've felt bad, how must she have felt with her problems and frustrations, that sometimes, we're the ones that create problems for her. Now I'm patient with the woman, and sometimes she gives me advice, and sometimes I give her advice, most of the time. We had a disagreement last Saturday, it was horrible, because I yelled at her, but when things calmed down, I apologized to her for yelling.

She tried to adapt to her mother's expectations and early morning schedule, which she admitted was probably easier for her than for her brothers because she had two young children. But in the back of her mind, she felt a lot of pressure to keep the peace at home: "I try to do things perfectly the way she wants them done so she'll be happy. The last thing I want is to see her angry and see that she'll decide to leave again." However, at the same time, they expected Elena to adapt to their form of doing things. "We tell her that it's not that she has to accept the way we want to live, but she has to adapt. And if she's going to say something to us, that she not say it in a way that perhaps we think is bad," argued Scarleth. Their mother's criticism of Kobe's social life, in particular, was a sore point that sparked many disagreements and tensions within the house.

Yet when I talked to Kobe, just days after another blow up with his mother, he emphasized that he appreciated the sacrifices she had made, first to help him get clean in 2010 and then to finish his degree. "My mama came back and left her job to take care of me, even though she knew I was probably beyond all hope. Because when you get into drugs, it's very hard to try to get out of that." Despite their conflicts, Elena also hired him to help with a project she was working on advocating for domestic worker rights in Nicaragua. "We've had conflicts because there are things I don't like, but she's the boss and I have to do them. But that has helped me a lot to become more mature in a professional sense," he explained.

For many migrant women, the decision to remain in Costa Rica or return to Nicaragua is part of their intergenerational care responsibilities. For Elena, her latest stints in Costa Rica have been in the context of her children's unemployment and needing to provide for her two grandchildren. When Elena returned to Granada in 2012, she began to take on more responsibilities for caring for her own aging mother. She also began to provide care to Scarleth's two children so that Scarleth could look for work. When she could not find a job, Elena helped her set up shop selling food out of the house. In Costa Rica, many migrant women considered returning to Nicaragua to care for grandchildren so that their own daughters could work. They fully expected to take on care responsibilities for their own grandchildren, just as they once left their children in grandparents' care to migrate to Costa Rica. For example, in León, Darling's daughter Marcelina was trying to convince her mother to return to León so that she could care for Marcelina's daughter once she graduated from nursing school and started working. In 2019, however, Marcelina and her partner would join Darling in Costa Rica.

Disconnections

Reunions with loved ones in Nicaragua also meant separation from loved ones in Costa Rica. Martha, for example, a good friend and roommate of Juana's, explained how every trip home meant separation from the people she most depended on day-to-day, and how much she missed her friend when Juana moved back to Carazo:

> It's difficult because we don't all go back at the same time. And you get used to being here [in Costa Rica] together. And maybe someone couldn't go back, and maybe some are happy [in Nicaragua] with their families, but we're thinking of the others. We see each other as family; I don't consider them friends anymore, that woman [Juana] in particular. If she doesn't have something, I do, we've always been like that, that we don't see ourselves as friends but rather as family.

Thus, returning to Nicaragua meant another family separation, from the family of friends, colleagues, and neighbors that migrants have built in Costa Rica, often through the shared struggles and obstacles of migrant life.

The women of ASTRADOMES and the Network of Migrant Women came together not only over advocacy efforts or in search of support for their labor rights. Just as important as this public-facing political work were the afternoons spent trading gossip, sharing meals, and lending support in the face of loneliness, financial concerns, and worries about loved ones in Nicaragua. This same work of relating that strengthened kin ties within transnational families produced enduring bonds among Nicaraguan women in Costa Rica. Leaving behind these networks of support was difficult, and left returning migrants feeling displaced even when they resettled in family homes in Nicaragua. Elena, in particular, felt isolated in Granada despite what appeared to be her successful return. When we talked in 2019, she said she especially missed Andrea and the support of her colleagues at ASTRADOMES, with whom she had worked and even lived far more closely than her own children for close to two decades.

For migrants who had children in Costa Rica, returning to Nicaragua also represented a displacement for them. Many young children at the community center and in other families we interviewed moved back and forth—like Darling's son Omar, who was born in Costa Rica but lived in Nicaragua until he was five, or Claudia's middle daughter, Agnes, who we had first met in Estelí visiting her grandmother. Such movements may be during school vacations or may disrupt schooling for children, who also have trouble adapting to life in another country, even if they had visited during vacations. Years earlier, Agnes's younger sister Yessica had returned to Nicaragua for a year. Although all three of Claudia's daughters had highly positive if not idealized views of life in Nicaragua and complained about the restrictions of life in Costa Rica as being "locked up," the girls all returned to Costa Rica. Yessica and Agnes both talked about being close to their parents, sisters, and Costa Rican friends, better school systems and job prospects, and the difficulties of getting used to their grandmother's rules and the extreme poverty of life in Estelí.

In 2012, Daisy returned to Masaya with her Costa Rican–born daughter and her Costa Rican husband. Her return allowed her to begin rebuilding her relationship with her adult daughters and her grandson. However, ten-year-old, Costa Rican–born Estefany struggled to adjust to life in Nicaragua. While she liked having chickens in the yard and having her older sisters nearby, she complained about the constant heat, missed her friends, and did not like the local public school she attended. Daisy's husband found it nearly impossible to find a job as a Costa Rican in Nicaragua, and was considering moving back to Costa Rica. In this sense, even when migrants return to Nicaragua, they are caught between two countries and two lives. As transnational migrants rooted in both countries, permanently settling in one place uproots them from the other. Many find it impossible or unthinkable to cut those roots in either country.

Elephant Graveyards: Envisioning Non-futures in Nicaragua

Despite migrants' plans, changing family dynamics and shifting political and social contexts mean that many migrants never return to Nicaragua permanently. For some, this does mean cutting ties to Nicaragua or at least letting them fade over time. Such instances of family disconnection are important because they point us to the moments in which economic crisis, migration, care, and longing converge to produce both connection and disconnection. Thus, while most of the families I have introduced in this book mobilized family relations to provide care for a large network of loved ones, others found that cutting ties was the best way to care for themselves. Migration represents a key way to sever or at least weaken connections, as distance and time may weaken the demands family back in Nicaragua can place on those in Costa Rica. Given cultural understandings of marriage and gender that limit the durability of marriage bonds, encourage men to maintain more than one household, and put the burden of raising children on women, Nicaraguan men find it easier than women to cut ties to families and households.

Others cut ties not necessarily to disconnect from families but rather because they could not envision futures for themselves in Nicaragua. Like Lester who "eats all his money" there, many migrants saw no viable way to return to Nicaragua. I always ended interviews asking folks about the future—their own future, the future of Nicaragua, of Costa Rica. And almost every single interviewee, whether a migrant in Costa Rica or a family member back in Nicaragua, expressed deep pessimism about Nicaragua's future. When asked if they wanted to return to Nicaragua, migrants like Andrea, Gloria, Dulce, and Claudia answered with some version of "if the situation there gets better" or "if the country improves." However, given their critiques of the Ortega administration, such a possibility seemed far-fetched.

Even if many migrants saw no future in Nicaragua, they did eventually return, though often in less than ideal circumstances. Elena, for example, noted the lack of legal status or access to pensions and other labor benefits in Costa Rica limited possibilities for retirement in Nicaragua: "What we take with us when we leave this country, Caty, is only old age, sickness, and bones. Nothing else." Elena counted off on her fingers the women she knew who had returned to Nicaragua without savings and with serious health problems. "I've known *compañeras* that well, one of them, the sister of my friend, was here for three years and after three years she left. She left with a kidney semi-paralyzed. And in Nicaragua the other went. She only went to die in Nicaragua, and she was a young woman, but she died because of all of the demands on her, all of the abuse." The lack of future for migrant women is as much about the abuse they suffer in Costa Rica as about conditions in Nicaragua. Rosa compared such returns to the myth of elephant graveyards: "Sometimes people laugh when I say we're like elephants. That when we're sick, we go back to our place of origin." When I asked her to explain what she meant, she said,

> An elephant can wander and wander and wander, right? But when he feels sick and that he's going to die, he goes back where he was born. And he dies there. Yes, so that's what we are like. When we feel sick, well, sometimes we go back with terminal illnesses, because since we don't have a health system that will take care of us here in Costa Rica, or when we finally get the employers to insure us and we go to the doctor, we already have terminal illnesses. We have six *compañeras* who have died of cancer because they didn't have access to healthcare, or at least timely access. And so, most of them decide to go back to Nicaragua. To die there in their country.

For many migrants, dreams of new houses, children's education, and a better future clash with the realities of low wages, lack of legal status, and few labor protections, as well as with continued poverty and the increasing unresponsiveness of the Ortega administration. At the same time, they are caught up in a chaotic present that requires moving back and forth across the border, piecing together livelihoods from remittances and the pooling of family resources, and always, the unpaid labor of generations of women.

Building a Transnational Community of Care

While this chapter has attempted to provide an end to this book, it is clear that returns and reunions are not the end of families' migration stories, as people return to Costa Rica, go further afield to Panama, Spain, or other destinations, or help their adult children migrate. Migration continues to be an intergenerational strategy for care both for families and, in the context of the current national crisis, the "pueblo" or nation.

On April 19, 2018, I woke up to messages from Nicaraguan friends and colleagues sharing stories of police attacking student protestors in Managua. Ongoing protests over the mishandling of a wildfire on the Indio Maíz Biological Reserve were joined by public outcry over pension reforms. The combined protests gained momentum as students joined pensioners and human rights and environmental activists in protests that quickly expanded to encompass calls for Ortega's resignation. The police responded to protestors with live ammunition. Andrea sent videos from her nephew who had been chased inside a church by Sandinista youth, the militant youth arm of the Sandinista party. "Caty," she wrote, "he wrote his ID number on his arm, in case they come in and kill them all. Please, spread this so the world knows what's happening in Nicaragua."

Given the intense dissatisfaction and disillusionment of so many of the families I worked with, it was not surprising to learn that so many young adult children of migrants had joined the protests. For Nicaraguan transnational families who participated from afar in supporting and talking about the protests and ensuing violence, or in helping asylum seekers cross the border to Costa Rica, the same strategies of transnational connection used to maintain family relations across borders served to unify the opposition both in Nicaragua and Costa Rica. As protests spread and the Nicaraguan government suspended news channels, migrants found themselves viewing the conflict through social media and messages from family and friends back home. Like Andrea, many expressed a sense of helplessness and frustration at being simultaneously connected to loved ones and too far to help as their elderly parents and adult children faced violence and repression.

At the same time, my interlocutors, and protestors more generally, framed the opposition's struggle within epic narratives of the Sandinista Revolution—with Ortega cast as dictator and protestors as liberators. Commenting on a video sent by her son of police shooting and looting in her neighborhood, Andrea claimed, "It's just like the war." Indeed, the opposition staged some protests and barricades in the same places and on the anniversaries of major Sandinista victories to topple the Somoza regime, reclaiming and reinscribing Sandinista memories that had been evacuated of meaning by the Ortega administration (Chamorro 2018).

Many of those who had planned to return to Nicaragua were instead joined by loved ones in Costa Rica. By the end of 2018, more than fifty thousand Nicaraguans would flee to neighboring Costa Rica. Their sense of the possibilities for a future are even more dire than before. University students, many the children of migrants, have been hard hit: a number of students were detained or killed by government or paramilitary forces and universities were closed; students who participated in the protests were expelled, and they now find themselves in Costa Rica with uncertain legal status and no way to complete their degrees. These young people's precarious situations represent more dreams delayed for them and their migrant parents.

Migrants in Costa Rica struggle to find a way forward in the midst of this newest crisis, with both returns to Nicaragua and their status in Costa Rica more uncertain than ever. As they have in the past, they continue to draw on gendered kin networks and configurations and avoid official, legal channels to enact intimate solidarities. For example, Rosa no longer works only with the Network of Migrant Women protecting migrant women from domestic violence; she also helps organize safe houses for LGBTQI+ refugees fleeing the Ortega regime. Others have taken in relatives or neighbors persecuted or detained by Nicaraguan police or paramilitary groups. Drawing on their experiences as migrants in Costa Rica, they employ a range of strategies to develop a provisional sense of security, ensure care for others, and access needed services. In providing the kinds of solidarities long enacted through transnational families and migrant networks, Nicaraguan migrants are enacting provisional kinds of solidarity that point to the kinds of intimate and political futures they want. Such solidarity is enacted through sharing meals and space in homes in informal settlements around San José where poverty, xenophobia, and precarious legal status threaten the flexibility and durability of kinship networks.

Reconfigurations of family are often temporary, their outcomes uncertain. Making sense, then, of the creative ways people make do in situations of not only family separation but also forced migration requires recognizing the limits of family and of solidarity. To romanticize such efforts to care and connect on the part of both men and women is to expect herculean tasks of care and commitment that may not be possible or even desirable in the contexts in which people struggle to live and love. Rather, instances of failure or disconnection in transnational families as well as the nation highlight the tension points, moments when economic crisis, migration, solidarity, and care converge to produce both connection and disconnection. In these extraordinary contexts, ordinary people—Nicaraguan migrants and their loved ones—respond to and are responsible for caring for others as they attempt to build transnational communities of care.

REFERENCES

Abrego, Leisy. 2009. "Economic Well-Being in Salvadoran Transnational Families: How Gender Affects Remittance Practices." *Journal of Marriage and Families* 71, no. 4: 1070–85.

———. 2014. *Sacrificing Families: Navigating Laws, Labor, and Love across Borders.* Stanford, CA: Stanford University Press.

Acuña, Guillermo, and Edith Olivares. 2000. *La población migrante nicaraguense en Costa Rica: Realidades y respuestas.* San José, Costa Rica: Fundación Arias para la Paz y el Progreso Humano, Centro Recursos para el Desarrollo Sostenible de los Asentamientos Humanos (CERCA).

Adamson, Fiona B., and Gerasimos Tsourapas. 2020. "The Migration State in the Global South: Nationalizing, Developmental, and Neoliberal Models of Migration Management." *International Migration Review* 54, no. 3: 853–82. https://doi.org/10.1177/0197918319879057.

Agurto, Sonia, and Alejandra Guido. 2001. *Mujeres, Pilares Fundamentales de La Economía Nicaragüense.* Managua: Fundación Internacional para el Desafío Económico Global. Alvarado, Nikolai A. 2020. "Migrant Politics in the Urban Global South: The Political Work of Nicaraguan Migrants to Acquire Urban Rights in Costa Rica." *Geopolitics*, June 17, 2020. https://doi.org/10.1080/14650045.2020.1777399.

Alvarenga, Patricia. 2004. "Passing: Nicaraguans in Costa Rica." In *The Costa Rica Reader: History, Culture, Politics*, edited by Steven Palmer and Iván Molina, 257–63. Durham, NC: Duke University Press.

Babb, Florence E. 1996. "After the Revolution: Neoliberal Policy and Gender in Nicaragua." *Latin American Perspectives* 23, no. 1: 27–48. https://doi.org/10.1177/0094582X9602300103.

———. 1998. "From Cooperatives to Microenterprises: The Neoliberal Turn in Postrevolutionary Nicaragua." In *The Third Wave of Modernization in Latin America: Cultural Perspectives on Neoliberalism*, edited by Lynne Phillips, 109–22. Wilmington, DE: Scholarly Resources.

————. 2001. *After Revolution: Mapping Gender and Cultural Politics in Neoliberal Nicaragua*. Austin, TX: University of Texas Press.

Baldassar, Loretta. 2008. "Missing Kin and Longing to Be Together: Emotions and the Construction of Co-Presence in Transnational Relationships." *Journal of Intercultural Studies* 29, no. 3: 247–66. https://doi.org/10.1080/07256860802169196.

Baldassar, Loretta, and Laura Merla. 2013. "Locating Transnational Care Circulation in Migration and Family Studies." In *Transnational Families, Migration and the Circulation of Care: Understanding Mobility and Absence in Family Life*, edited by Loretta Baldassar and Laura Merla, 25–58. New York: Routledge.

Banco Central de Nicaragua. 2015. "Informe de remesas familiares. II Trimestre 2015." Managua: Banco Central de Nicaragua (BCN), División Económica. https://www.bcn.gob.ni/system/files_force/documentos/Remesas_II_trim_2015.pdf.

Bateson, Ian. 2017. "'Justice Is Afraid of the Priest's Robe': Rape and Power in Nicaragua." *World Policy Journal* 34, no. 3: 36–40. https://doi.org/10.1215/07402775-4280148.

Bejarano, Cynthia L. 2002. "Las Super Madres de Latino America: Transforming Motherhood by Challenging Violence in Mexico, Argentina, and El Salvador." *Frontiers: A Journal of Women Studies* 23, no. 1: 126–50.

Belli, Gioconda. 1982. "La ternura de los pueblos." In *Truenos y arco iris*. Managua, Nicaragua: Editorial Nueva Nicaragua.

Berg, Ulla D. 2010. "El Quinto Suyo: Contemporary Nation Building and the Political Economy of Emigration in Peru." *Latin American Perspectives* 37 (5): 121–37.

————. 2017. *Mobile Selves: Race, Migration, and Belonging in Peru and the U.S.* New York: New York University Press.

Biehl, João. 2005. *Vita: Life in a Zone of Social Abandonment*. Berkeley: University of California Press.

Boehm, Deborah A. 2012. *Intimate Migrations: Gender, Family, and Illegality Among Transnational Mexicans*. New York: New York University Press.

————. 2019. "Un/Making Family: Relatedness, Migration, and Displacement in a Global Age." In *The Cambridge Handbook of Kinship*, edited by Sandra C. Bamford, 432–50. Cambridge, UK: Cambridge University Press.

Borneman, John. 2001. "Caring and Being Cared For: Displacing Marriage, Kinship, Gender, and Sexuality." In *The Ethics of Kinship*, edited by James Faubion, 29–46. Lanham, MD: Roman and Littlefield.

Bouvard, Marguerite Guzman. 2002. *Revolutionizing Motherhood: The Mothers of the Plaza de Mayo*. Lanham, MD: Rowman and Littlefield.

Budowski, Monica, and Luis Rosario Bixby. 2003. "Fatherless Costa Rica: Child Acknowledgment and Support Among Lone Mothers." *Journal of Comparative Family Studies* 34, no. 2: 229–54.

Burrell, Jennifer L., and Ellen Moodie. 2013. *Central America in the New Millennium: Living Transition and Reimagining Democracy*. New York: Berghahn Books.

Bustos Mora, Giselle. 2000. *Objeciones a una novia nica*. Documentary video. San José: Universidad de Costa Rica.

Caamaño Morúa, Carmen. 2011. *Entre "arriba" y "abajo": La experiencia transnacional de la migración de costarricenses hacia Estados Unidos*. San José: Editorial Universidad de Costa Rica.

Cabrera, Martha. 2002. "Living and Surviving in a Multiply Wounded Country." *Revista Envío*, no. 257 (Dec. 2002). https://www.envio.org.ni/articulo/1629.

Calavita, Kitty. 2005. *Immigrants at the Margins: Law, Race, and Exclusion in Southern Europe*. Cambridge, UK: Cambridge University Press.

Cardoso, Ruth C. L. 1984. "Creating Kinship: The Fostering of Children in *Favela* Families in Brazil." In *Kinship Ideology and Practice in Latin America*, edited by Raymond Thomas Smith, translated by Elizabeth Hansen, 196–203. Chapel Hill: University of North Carolina Press.

Carsten, Janet. 2000. "Introduction: Cultures of Relatedness." In *Cultures of Relatedness: New Approaches to the Study of Kinship*, edited by Janet Carsten, 1–36. Cambridge, UK: Cambridge University Press.

———. 2004. *After Kinship*. Cambridge, UK: Cambridge University Press.

Carte, Lindsey. 2014. "Everyday Restriction: Central American Women and the State in the Mexico-Guatemala Border City of Tapachula." *International Migration Review* 48, no. 1: 113–43. https://doi.org/10.1111/imre.12072.

Castles, Stephen, Hein de Haas, and Mark J. Miller. 2013. *The Age of Migration: International Population Movements in the Modern World*. New York: Palgrave Macmillan.

Castro, Arachu, and Virginia Savage. 2019. "Obstetric Violence as Reproductive Governance in the Dominican Republic." *Medical Anthropology* 38, no. 2: 123–36. https://doi.org/10.1080/01459740.2018.1512984.

Castro Martín, Teresa. 2002. "Consensual Unions in Latin America: Persistence of a Dual Nuptiality System." *Journal of Comparative Family Studies* 33, no. 1: 35–55.

Castro Valverde, Carlos. 2007. "Dimensión cuantitativa de la inmigración nicaragüense en Costa Rica: Del mito a la realidad." In *El mito roto: Inmigración y emigración en Costa Rica*, edited by Carlos Sandoval G., 25–50. San José: Editorial Universidad de Costa Rica.

Cerrutti, Marcela, and Emilio Parrado. 2015. "Intraregional Migration in South America: Trends and a Research Agenda." *Annual Review of Sociology* 41: 399–421.

Chamorro, Luciana. 2018. "'Love Is Stronger than Hate': Managing Revolutionary Passions in Neo-Sandinista Nicaragua." Paper Presented at the American Anthropological Association Annual Meeting, San Jose, CA, Nov. 14–18, 2018.

Chant, Sylvia. 2002. "Researching Gender, Families and Households in Latin America: From the 20th into the 21st Century." *Bulletin of Latin American Research* 21, no. 4: 545–75.

———. 2003. "Gender, Families and Households." In *Gender in Latin America*, edited by Sylvia Chant and Nikki Craske, 161–93. London: Latin American Bureau.

Chant, Sylvia, and Sarah A. Radcliffe. 1992. "Migration and Development: The Importance of Gender." In *Gender and Migration in Developing Countries*, edited by Sylvia Chant, 1–29. London: Belhaven Press.

Chaves, Erika, Priscilla Barrantes, Evelyn Hernández, Yuliana Muñoz, and Walia Valverde. 2011. "Investigación de campo: 'Aspectos socioeconómicos de las remesas familiares en Costa Rica' 2010." San José: Banco Central de Costa Rica, División Económica. https://www.bccr.fi.cr/publicaciones/DocPolitica CambiariaSectorExterno/Remesas_2010.pdf.

Chavez, Leo. 1992. *Shadowed Lives: Undocumented Immigrants in American Society.* 2nd ed. Ft. Worth, TX: Harcourt Brace and Jovanovich College.

———. 2008. *The Latino Threat: Constructing Immigrants, Citizens and the Nation.* Stanford, CA: Stanford University Press.

Chen Mok, Mario, Luis Rosero Bixby, Gilbert Brenes Camacho, Miriam León Solis, María Isabel González Lutz, and Juan Carlos Vanegas Pissa. 2001. *Salud reproductiva y migración nicaragüense en Costa Rica 1999–2000: Resultados de una encuesta nacional de salud reproductiva.* San José: Universidad de Costa Rica.

Chinchilla, Norma Stoltz. 1990. "Revolutionary Popular Feminism in Nicaragua: Articulating Class, Gender, and National Sovereignty." *Gender & Society* 4, no. 3: 370–97.

Close, David. 2016. *Nicaragua: Navigating the Politics of Democracy.* Boulder, CO: Lynne Rienner Publishers.

Close, David, and Salvador Martí i Puig. 2011. "The Sandinistas and Nicaragua Since 1979." In *The Sandinistas and Nicaragua since 1979,* edited by David Close, Salvador Martí i Puig, and Shelley A. McConnell, 1–19. Boulder, CO: Lynne Rienner Publishers.

Coe, Cati, Rachel R. Reynolds, Deborah A. Boehm, Julia Meredith Hess, and Heather Rae-Espinoza. 2011. *Everyday Ruptures: Children, Youth, and Migration in Global Perspective.* Nashville, TN: Vanderbilt University Press.

Collier, Jane, and Sylvia Yanagisako. 1987. *Gender and Kinship: Essays toward a Unified Analysis.* Stanford, CA: Stanford University Press.

Collier, Ruth Berins, and David Collier. 2002. *Shaping the Political Arena: Critical Junctures, the Labor Movement, and Regime Dynamics in Latin America.* Notre Dame, IN: University of Notre Dame Press.

Collombon, Maya, and Dennis Rodgers. 2018. "Introduction. Sandinismo 2.0: Reconfigurations autoritaires du politique, nouvel ordre économique et conflit social." *Cahiers des Amériques latines,* no. 87 (September): 13–36. https://doi.org/10.4000/cal.8475.

Contreras Castro, Fernando. 1993. *Única mirando al mar.* San José, Costa Rica: Editorial Legado.

Coronil, Fernando. 2011. "The Future in Question: History and Utopia in Latin America (1989–2010)." In *Business as Usual: The Roots of the Global Financial Meltdown,* edited by Craig Calhoun and Georgi M. Derluguian, 231–64. New York: New York University Press.

Coutin, Susan Bibler. 2005. "Being en Route." *American Anthropologist* 107, no. 2: 195–206. https://doi.org/10.1525/aa.2005.107.2.195.

———. 2007. *Nations of Emigrants: Shifting Boundaries of Citizenship in El Salvador and the United States.* Ithaca, NY: Cornell University Press.

Cupples, Julie. 2001. "Flexible Mothering: Articulating Rights and Negotiating Ideologies in Nicaragua." *Development* 44, no. 2: 23–27.

De Genova, Nicholas. 2002. "Migrant" Illegality" and Deportability in Everyday Life." *Annual Review of Anthropology* 31, no. 1: 419–47.

De Genova, Nicholas, and Nathalie Peutz. 2010. *The Deportation Regime: Sovereignty, Space, and the Freedom of Movement.* Durham, NC: Duke University Press.

De Haas, Hein. 2006. "Migration, Remittances and Regional Development in Southern Morocco." *Geoforum* 37 (4): 565–80.

———. 2012. "The Migration and Development Pendulum: A Critical View on Research and Policy." *International Migration* 50 (3): 8–25.

De Lombaerde, Philippe, Fei Guo, and Helion Póvoa Neto. 2014. "Introduction to the Special Collection." *International Migration Review* 48 (1): 103–12. https://doi.org/10.1111/imre.12083.

Delgado Jiménez, Francisco. 2013. "el empleo informal en Costa Rica: Características de los ocupados y sus puestos de trabajo." *Revista de Ciencias Económicas* 31, no. 2: 35–51.

DeLugan, Robin Maria. 2012. *Reimagining National Belonging: Post-Civil War El Salvador in a Global Context*. Tucson: University of Arizona Press.

DGME, Dirección General de Migración y Extranjería. 2012. "Migración e Integración En Costa Rica: Informe Nacional 2012." San José, Costa Rica: Dirección General de Migración y Extranjería.

Dixon, Lydia Zacher. 2020. *Delivering Health: Midwifery and Development in Mexico*. Nashville, TN: Vanderbilt University Press.

Dore, Elizabeth. 1997. "The Holy Family: Imagined Households in Latin American History." In *Gender Politics in Latin America: Debates in Theory and Practice*, edited by Elizabeth Dore, 101–17. New York: New York University Press.

Dosal, Paul J. 2009. "Natural Disaster, Political Earthquake: The 1972 Destruction of Managua and the Somoza Dynasty." In *Aftershocks: Earthquakes and Popular Politics in Latin America*, edited by Jürgen Buchenau and Lyman L. Johnson, 129–55. Albuquerque: University of New Mexico Press.

Dreby, Joanna. 2007. "Children and Power in Mexican Transnational Families." *Journal of Marriage and Family* 69, no. 4: 1050–64. https://doi.org/10.1111/j.1741-3737.2007.00430.x

———. 2010. *Divided by Borders: Mexican Migrants and Their Children*. Berkeley: University of California Press.

Drotbohm, Heike. 2009. "Horizons of Long-Distance Intimacies: Reciprocity, Contribution and Disjuncture in Cape Verde." *History of the Family* 14 (2): 132–49.

Duryea, Suzanne, Analía Olgiati, and Leslie Stone. 2006. "Working Paper: The Under-Registration of Births in Latin America." IDB Working Paper No. 458. Inter-American Development Bank, Research Department. https://ssrn.com/abstract=1820031.

ECLAC, Economic Commission for Latin America and the Caribbean. 2013. *Social Panorama of Latin America 2012*. Santiago, Chile: United Nations. https://www.cepal.org/sites/default/files/publication/files/1248/S2012960_en.pdf.

European Union Election Expert Mission. 2010. "Republic of Nicaragua—Regional Elections, 7 March 2010. Final Report." Brussels: European Union Election Expert Mission. http://eeas.europa.eu/eueom/pdf/missions/eueoem_finalreport.pdf.

Fitzgerald, David. 2006. "Towards a Theoretical Ethnography of Migration." *Qualitative Sociology* 29, no. 1: 1–24.

Fouratt, Caitlin E. 2014. "'Those Who Come to Do Harm': The Framing of Immigration Problems in Costa Rican Immigration Law." *International Migration Review* 48, no. 1: 144–80.

———. 2016. "Temporary Measures: The Production of Illegality in Costa Rican Immigration Law." *PoLAR: Political and Legal Anthropology Review* 39, no. 1: 144–60.

———. 2017. "Love for the Land: Remittances and Care in a Nicaraguan Transnational Community." *Latin American Research Review* 52, no. 5: 792–806. https://doi.org/10.25222/larr.248.

Fouratt, Caitlin E., and Koen Voorend. 2018. "Sidestepping the State: Practices of Social Service Commodification among Nicaraguans in Costa Rica and Nicaragua." *Journal of Latin American Studies* 50, no. 2, 441–68. doi:10.1017/S0022216X17001195.

Franklin, Sarah, and Susan McKinnon. 2001. *Relative Values: Reconfiguring Kinship Studies*. Durham, NC: Duke University Press.

Gago, Verónica. 2007. "Dangerous Liaisons: Latin American Feminists and the Left." *NACLA Report on the Americas* 40, no. 2: 17–19. https://doi.org/10.1080/10714839.2007.11722310.

Gallo, Ester, and Francesca Scrinzi. 2016. *Migration, Masculinities and Reproductive Labour*. London: Springer.

Gammage, Sarah. 2006. "Exporting People and Recruiting Remittances A Development Strategy for El Salvador?" *Latin American Perspectives* 33, no. 6: 75–100.

Garth, Jose, and Ericka Gertsch R. 2010. "La miliciana de Waswalito." *Magazine— La Prensa Nicaragua*, March 2, 2010. https://www.laprensa.com.ni/magazine/reportaje/la-miliciana-de-waswalito.

Gobat, Michel. 2018. *Empire by Invitation: William Walker and Manifest Destiny in Central America*. Cambridge, MA: Harvard University Press.

Goldade, Kate. 2009. "'Health Is Hard Here' or 'Health for All'?" *Medical Anthropology Quarterly* 23, no. 4: 483–503.

———. 2011. "Babies and Belonging: Reproduction, Citizenship, and Undocumented Nicaraguan Labor Migrant Women in Costa Rica." *Medical Anthropology* 30, no. 5: 545–68. https://doi.org/10.1080/01459740.2011.577043.

Gomáriz, Enrique. 1997. *Introducción a los estudios sobre masculinidad*. San José, Costa Rica: Centro Nacional para el Desarrollo de la Mujer y la Familia.

Gonzales, Roberto G., and Leo R. Chavez. 2012. "'Awakening to a Nightmare': Abjectivity and Illegality in the Lives of Undocumented 1.5 Generation Latino Immigrants in the United States." *Current Anthropology* 53, no. 3: 255–81.

González Briones, Heydi Jose. 2013. "Perfil migratorio de Nicaragua 2012." Managua, Nicaragua: Organizacion Internacional para las Migraciones (OIM).

González de la Rocha, Mercedes. 1994. *The Resources of Poverty: Women and Survival in a Mexican City*. Oxford, UK: Blackwell.

Gutmann, Matthew C. 1996. *The Meanings of Macho: Being a Man in Mexico City*. Berkeley: University of California Press.

Haenn, Nora. 2019. *Marriage after Migration: An Ethnography of Money, Romance, and Gender in Globalizing Mexico*. New York: Oxford University Press.

Hage, Ghassan. 2009. *Waiting*. Melbourne, Aus.: Melbourne University Publishing.

———. 2012. *White Nation: Fantasies of White Supremacy in a Multicultural Society*. New York: Routledge.

Han, Clara. 2012. *Life in Debt: Times of Care and Violence in Neoliberal Chile*. Berkeley: University of California Press.

Haraway, Donna. 1988. "Situated Knowledges: The Science Question in Feminism and the Privilege of Partial Perspective." *Feminist Studies* 14, no. 3: 575–99.

Harvey, David. 2005. *A Brief History of Neoliberalism*. New York: Oxford University Press.

Hawkes, Kristen, and Ken R. Smith. 2009. "Brief Communication: Evaluating Grandmother Effects." *American Journal of Physical Anthropology* 140, no. 1: 173–76. https://doi.org/10.1002/ajpa.21061.

Hayden, Bridget A. 2003. *Salvadorans in Costa Rica: Displaced Lives*. Tucson: University of Arizona Press.

Heidbrink, Lauren. 2014. *Migrant Youth, Transnational Families, and the State: Care and Contested Interests*. Philadelphia: University of Pennsylvania Press.

———. 2020. *Migranthood: Youth in a New Era of Deportation*. Stanford, CA: Stanford University Press.

Hernandez, Ester, and Susan Bibler Coutin. 2006. "Remitting Subjects: Migrants, Money and States." *Economy and Society* 35 (2): 185–208.

Heyman, Josiah. 2012. "Capitalism and US Policy at the Mexican Border." *Dialectical Anthropology* 36, no. 3-4: 263–77.

Hidalgo Xirinachs, Roxana. 2016. *Mujeres de las fronteras: Subjetividad, migración y trabajo doméstico*. San José: Editorial Universidad de Costa Rica.

Higgins, Michael James, and Tanya Leigh Coen. 1992. *Óigame! Óigame!: Struggle and Social Change in a Nicaraguan Urban Community*. Boulder, CO: Westview Press.

Hirsch, Jennifer S. 2003. *A Courtship after Marriage: Sexuality and Love in Mexican Transnational Families*. Berkeley: University of California Press.

———. 2007. "'Love Makes a Family': Globalization, Companionate Marriage, and the Modernization of Gender Inequality." In *Love and Globalization: Transformations of Intimacy in the Contemporary World*, edited by Mark B. Padilla, Jennifer S. Hirsch, Miguel Muñoz-Laboy, Robert E. Sember, and Richard G. Parker, 93–106. Nashville, TN: Vanderbilt University Press.

Hochschild, Arlie Russell. 2000. "Global Care Chains and Emotional Surplus Value." In *On the Edge: Living with Global Capitalism*, edited by Will Hutton and Anthony Giddens, 130–46. London: Jonathan Cape.

Horton, Sarah B. 2020. "Introduction. Paper Trails: Migrants, Bureaucratic Inscription, and Legal Recognition." In *Paper Trails: Migrants, Documents, and Legal Insecurity*, 1–26. Durham, NC: Duke University Press.

Hujo, Katja, and Nicola Piper. 2010. *South-South Migration: Implications for Social Policy and Development*. London, UK: Springer.

IDESPO, UNFPA, and Foro Permanente sobre Población Migrante. 2000. "Memoria final, mesa redonda: La población migrante en Costa Rica y su tratamiento en los medios de comunicación." San José, Costa Rica: IDESPO.

Idiáquez, Marcos Membreño. 2001. "Cincuenta Años de Migraciones Internas y Externas En Nicaragua (1950-2000)." *Encuentro* 33, no. 59: 92–112.

Inda, Jonathan Xavier. 2006. *Targeting Immigrants: Government, Technology, and Ethics*. Oxford, UK: Blackwell.

INEC, Instituto Nacional de Estadísticas y Censos. 2011. *X Censo nacional de población y VI de vivienda 2011 resultados generales*. San José, Costa Rica: INEC.

———. 2015. "2014. Total de nacimientos por nacionalidad de la madre, según país de origen de la madre." San José, Costa Rica: INEC. http://www.inec.go.cr/poblacion/nacimientos.

INIDE, Instituto Nacional de Informacion de Desarrollo. 2007. "Encuesta Nicaraguense de Demografia y Salud 2006/2007." Managua: INIDE.

———. 2013. "Encuesta Nacional de Demografia y Salud 2011/2012: Informe Preliminar." Managua: INIDE.

———. 2014. "Encuesta Nacional de Demografia y Salud 2011/2012: Informe Final." Managua: INIDE.

IIS, Instituto de Investigaciones Sociales, Centro de Investigación en Cultura y Desarrollo, Programa radiofónico Casa Abierta 870 UCR, and Servicio Jesuita para Migrantes Costa Rica. 2012. "Conferencia de prensa. La ley de migración en Costa Rica: A dos años de su entrada en vigencia. Promesas, realidades y desafíos." *Nueva prensa*, March 28, 2012. http://www.lanuevaprensacr.com/la-ley-de-migracion-en-costa-rica-a-dos-anos-de-su-entrada-en-vigencia-promesas-realidades-y-des.

Jacobsen, Christine M., Marry-Anne Karlsen, and Shahram Khosravi. 2020. *Waiting and the Temporalities of Irregular Migration*. London: Taylor and Francis.

Jamison, Cheryl Sorenson, Laurel L. Cornell, Paul L. Jamison, and Hideki Nakazato. 2002. "Are All Grandmothers Equal? A Review and a Preliminary Test of the 'Grandmother Hypothesis' in Tokugawa Japan." *American Journal of Physical Anthropology* 119, no. 1: 67–76. https://doi.org/10.1002/ajpa.10070.

Jiménez, Juanita. 2015. "El Código de La Familia Es El Último Eslabón de Un Proyecto de Control Social." *Revista Envío*, no. 398: 12–18.

Kampwirth, Karen. 1996. "The Mother of the Nicaraguans: Doña Violeta and the UNO's Gender Agenda." *Latin American Perspectives* 23, no. 1: 67–86.

———. 1998. "Legislating Personal Politics in Sandinista Nicaragua, 1979–1992." *Women's Studies International Forum* 21(1): 53–64.

———. 2008. "Abortion, Antifeminism, and the Return of Daniel Ortega in Nicaragua, Leftist Politics?" *Latin American Perspectives* 35, no. 6: 122–36.

Kapur, Devesh. 2004. "Remittances: The New Development Mantra?" G-24 Discussion Paper Series. New York: United Nations Conference on Trade and Development (UNCTAD). http://g24.org/wp-content/uploads/2014/03/Kapur-1.pdf.

Khan, M. Adil, and Munshi Israil Hossain. 2017. "The Emerging Phenomenon of Post-Globalized, South-South Migration: In Search of a Theoretical Framework." In *South-South Migration: Emerging Patterns, Opportunities and Risks*, edited by Patricia Short, Moazzem Hossain, and M. Adil Khan, 11–33. New York: Taylor and Francis.

Kilkey, Majella. 2010. "Men and Domestic Labor: A Missing Link in the Global Care Chain." *Men and Masculinities* 13, no. 1: 126–49.

Kofman, Eleonore, and Parvati Raghuram. 2009. "The Implications of Migration for Gender and Care Regimes in the South." Social Policy and Development Programme Papers. Geneva: United Nations Research Institute for Social Development.

Kubal, Agnieszka. 2013. "Conceptualizing Semi-Legality in Migration Research." *Law and Society Review* 47, no. 3: 555–87. https://doi.org/10.1111/lasr.12031.

Kuznesof, Elizabeth, and Robert Oppenheimer. 1985. "The Family and Society in Nineteenth-Century Latin America: An Historiographical Introduction." *Journal of Family History* 10, no. 3: 215–34.

Lancaster, Roger N. 1992. *Life Is Hard: Machismo, Danger, and the Intimacy of Power in Nicaragua*. Berkeley: University of California Press.

Laplante, Benoît, Teresa Castro-Martín, Clara Cortina, and Teresa Martín-García. 2015. "Childbearing within Marriage and Consensual Union in Latin America, 1980–2010." *Population and Development Review* 41, no. 1: 85–108.

Leinaweaver, Jessaca B. 2007. "On Moving Children: The Social Implications of Andean Child Circulation." *American Ethnologist* 34, no. 1: 163–80. https://doi.org/10.1525/ae.2007.34.1.163.

———. 2008. *The Circulation of Children: Kinship, Adoption, and Morality in Andean Peru*. Durham, NC: Duke University Press.

Leon Segura, Gabriela. 2012. "Caso: Costa Rica." In *Migraciones y derechos laborales en Centroamerica: Caracteristicas de las personas migrantes y de los mercados de trabajo*, 127–217. San José, Costa Rica: FLACSO.

Levine, Rebecca. 2015. "Victims of Obstetric Violence in Costa Rica." *Human Rights Brief* (blog), October 24, 2015. http://hrbrief.org/hearings/victims-of-obstetric-violence-in-costa-rica.

Loebach, Peter, and Kim Korinek. 2019. "Disaster Vulnerability, Displacement, and Infectious Disease: Nicaragua and Hurricane Mitch." *Population and Environment* 40, no. 4: 434–55. https://doi.org/10.1007/s11111-019-00319-4.

Lopez, J. Humberto, Pablo Fajnzylber, and Pablo Acosta. 2007. *The Impact of Remittances on Poverty and Human Capital: Evidence from Latin American Household Surveys*. Washington, DC: The World Bank.

López Vigil, Maria. 2001. "The Wounds of Sexual Abuse." *Revista Envío*, no. 242 (September). https://www.envio.org.ni/articulo/1531.

Luibheid, Eithne. 2013. *Pregnant on Arrival: Making the Illegal Immigrant*. Minneapolis: University of Minnesota Press.

Mannon, Susan E. 2006. "Love in the Time of Neo-Liberalism: Gender, Work, and Power in a Costa Rican Marriage." *Gender and Society* 20, no. 4: 511–30.

Mantoo, Shabia. 2020. "COVID-19 Driving Nicaraguan Refugees to Hunger and Desperation." *United Nations High Commissioner for Refugees, Press Briefing* (blog), August 28, 2020. https://www.unhcr.org/news/briefing/2020/8/5f44c56d4/covid-19-driving-nicaraguan-refugees-hunger-desperation.html.

Marcus, George. 1995. "Ethnography in/of the World System: The Emergence of Multi-Sited Ethnography." *Annual Review of Anthropology* 24: 95–117.

Martínez Franzoni, Juliana. 2008. *Domesticar la incertidumbre en América Latina. Mercado laboral, política social y familias*. San José: Editorial Universidad de Costa Rica.

Martínez Franzoni, Juliana, and Koen Voorend. 2011. "Who Cares in Nicaragua? A Care Regime in an Exclusionary Social Policy Context." *Development and Change* 42, no. 4: 995–1022.

———. 2012. "The Limits of Family and Community Care: Challenges for Public Policy in Nicaragua." In *Global Variations in the Political and Social Economy of Care: Worlds Apart*, edited by Shahra Razavi and Silke Staab, 122–40. Routledge/UNRISD Research in Gender and Development 8. London: Routledge.

May, Robert E. 2002. *Manifest Destiny's Underworld: Filibustering in Antebellum America*. Chapel Hill: University of North Carolina Press.

Mckay, Deirdre. 2007. "'Sending Dollars Shows Feeling': Emotions and Economies in Filipino Migration." *Mobilities* 2, no. 2: 175–94.

McKenzie, Sean, and Cecilia Menjívar. 2011. "The Meanings of Migration, Remittances and Gifts: Views of Honduran Women Who Stay." *Global Networks* 11, no. 1: 63–81.

Melly, Caroline. 2010. "Inside-out Houses: Urban Belonging and Imagined Futures in Dakar, Senegal." *Comparative Studies in Society and History* 52, no. 01: 37–65. https://doi.org/10.1017/S0010417509990326.

Mendoza, José. 2005. "Ticos Temen Rebelión de Nicaragüenses." *Nuevo Diario*, November 26, 2005. http://archivo.elnuevodiario.com.ni/nacional/168154-ticos-temen-rebelion-nicaraguenses.

Menjívar, Cecilia. 2002. "Living in Two Worlds? Guatemalan-Origin Children in the United States and Emerging Transnationalism." *Journal of Ethnic and Migration Studies* 28, no. 3: 531–52.

———. 2014. "Immigration Law beyond Borders: Externalizing and Internalizing Border Controls in an Era of Securitization." *Annual Review of Law and Social Science* 10, no.1: 353–69.

Menjívar, Cecilia, and Daniel Kanstroom. 2013. *Constructing Immigrant "Illegality": Critiques, Experiences, and Responses.* New York: Cambridge University Press.

Menjívar, Cecilia, and Leisy J. Abrego. 2009. "Parents and Children Across Borders: Legal Instability and Intergenerational Relations in Guatemalan and Salvadoran Families." In *Across Generations: Immigrant Families in America*, edited by Nancy Foner, 160–89. New York: New York University Press.

Metoyer, Cynthia Chavez. 2000. *Women and the State in Post-Sandinista Nicaragua.* Boulder, CO: Lynne Rienner Publishers.

Miranda Aburto, Wilfredo. 2013. "De los CPC a los Gabinetes de la familia." *Confidencial*, February 23, 2013. https://archivo.confidencial.com.ni/articulo/10408/de-los-cpc-a-los-gabinetes-de-la-familia.

Molyneux, Maxine. 1985a. "Family Reform in Socialist States: The Hidden Agenda." *Feminist Review*, no. 21: 47–64. https://doi.org/10.2307/1394839.

———. 1985b. "Mobilization without Emancipation? Women's Interests, the State, and Revolution in Nicaragua." *Feminist Studies* 11, no. 2: 227–54.

Monge-González, Ricardo, Oswald Céspedes-Torres, and Juan Carlos Vargas-Aguilar. 2011. "South-South Remittances: The Costa Rica Nicaragua Corridor." San José, Costa Rica: Inter-American Development Bank. http://publications.iadb.org/handle/11319/5430.

Montoya, Oswaldo. 2002. "Nicaragua: Educación reproductiva y paternidad responsable." In *Educación reproductiva y paternidad responsable en el Istmo Centroamericano*, edited by Comisión Económica para América Latina y el Caribe, 357–401. México, DF: CEPAL. https://repositorio.cepal.org//handle/11362/2741.

Montoya, Rosario. 2003. "House, Street, Collective: Revolutionary Geographies and Gender Transformation in Nicaragua, 1979–99." *Latin American Research Review* 38, no. 2: 61–93. https://doi.org/10.1353/lar.2003.0021.

———. 2013. "Contradiction and Struggle under the Leftist Phoenix: Rural Nicaragua at the Thirtieth Anniversary of the Revolution." In *Central America in the New Millennium: Living Transition and Reimagining Democracy*, edited by Jennifer L. Burrell and Ellen Moodie, 33–48. New York: Berghahn Books.

Moodie, Ellen. 2011. *El Salvador in the Aftermath of Peace: Crime, Uncertainty, and the Transition to Democracy.* Philadelphia: Univ of Pennsylvania Press.

———. 2013. "Democracy, Disenchantment, and the Future in El Salvador." In *Central America in the New Millennium: Living Transition and Reimagining Democracy*, edited by Jennifer L. Burrell and Ellen Moodie, 96–112. New York: Berghahn Books.

Morales, Abelardo, and Carlos Castro. 1999. *Inmigración laboral nicaragüense en Costa Rica.* San José, Costa Rica: FLACSO, Fundación Friedrich Ebert, Instituto Interamericano de Derechos Humanos, Defensoría de los Habitantes.

Narváez, Antonio Brenes, and Freddy Cruz Rivera. 2016. "Determinantes de la informalidad en Nicaragua." *Revista de Economía y Finanzas BCN* 3: 11–152.

Narváez, Zoilamérica. 2002. "Case 12,230: Zoilamérica Narváez vs. the Nicaraguan State." *Revista Envío, no.* 248 (March). https://www.envio.org.ni/articulo. php?id=1567.

Navarete, Orlando. 2011. "Sin fusil y con casa." *La Prensa*, La Prensa Domingo, July 31, 2011. https://www.laprensa.com.ni/2011/07/31/suplemento/la-prensa-domingo/1111550–5651.

Navarro, Marysa. 2002. "Against Marianismo." In *Gender's Place: Feminist Anthropologies of Latin America*, edited by Rosario Montoya, Lessie Jo Frazier, and Janise Hurtig, 257–72. Houndmills, UK: Palgrave Macmillan.

Nieto, Sonia. 2000. *Puerto Rican Students in U.S. Schools*. Mahwah, NJ: Routledge.

Nowalski, Jorge. 2002. *Asimetrías económicas, laborales y sociales en Centroamérica: Desafíos y oportunidades*. San José, Costa Rica: FLACSO.

Nowalski, Jorge, and Manuel Barahona. 2003. *Asimetrías económicas, sociales y políticas en Costa Rica: Hacia una calidad ve vida digna*. San José, Costa Rica: PNUD; Centro Internacional para el Desarrollo Humano (CIDH).

Oliveira, Gabrielle. 2018. *Motherhood across Borders: Immigrants and Their Children in Mexico and New York*. New York: New York University Press.

———. 2019. "'Here and There': Children and Youth's Perspectives of Borders in Mexico–United States Migration." *Children & Society* 33 (6): 540–55.

Olsson, Ann, Mary Ellsberg, Staffan Berglund, Andrés Herrera, Elmer Zelaya, Rodolfo Peña, Felix Zelaya, and Lars-Åke Persson. 2000. "Sexual Abuse during Childhood and Adolescence among Nicaraguan Men and Women: A Population-Based Anonymous Survey." *Child Abuse and Neglect* 24, no. 1: 1579–89.

Olwig, Karen Fog. 1985. *Cultural Adaptation and Resistance on St. John: Three Centuries of Afro-Caribbean Life*. Gainesville, FL: University of Florida Press.

———. 2013. "Migration and Care: Intimately Related Aspects of Caribbean Family and Kinship." In *Transnational Families, Migration and the Circulation of Care: Understanding Mobility and Absence in Family Life*, edited by Loretta Baldassar and Laura Merla, 133–48. New York: Routledge.

Orozco, Manuel. 2004. "Mexican Hometown Associations and Development Opportunities." *Journal of International Affairs* 57, no. 2: 31–51.

———. 2009. *Migration and Remittances in Times of Recession: Effects on Latin American Economies*. Washington, DC: Inter-American Dialogue. http://www.oecd.org/dev/americas/42753222.pdf.

Pacheco Rojas, Mariela, and Mercedes Arguedas Molina. 2011. *Responder a las mujeres II. Monitoreo participativo de la aplicación de las leyes sobre violencia contra las mujeres: Resultados en Alajuelita, Los Guido y Guarari*. Proyecto Mujeres Migrantes Frente a La Violencia. San José, Costa Rica: Proyecto Mujeres Migrantes frente a la Violencia, CEFEMINA.

Padilla, Mark B., Jennifer S. Hirsch, Miguel Muñoz-Laboy, Robert E. Sember, and Richard G. Parker. 2007. "Introduction: Cross-Cultural Reflections on an Intimate Intersection." In *Love and Globalization: Transformations of Intimacy in the Contemporary World*, edited by Mark B. Padilla, Jennifer S. Hirsch, Miguel Muñoz-Laboy, Robert E. Sember, and Richard G. Parker, ix–xxxi. Nashville, TN: Vanderbilt University Press.

Parreñas, Rhacel Salazar. 2005. *Children of Global Migration: Transnational Families and Gendered Woes*. Stanford, CA: Stanford University Press.

Pastor Gómez, María Luisa. 2018. "Nicaragua En La Encrucijada: Del Síndrome de Hybris a La Convulsión Que No Cesa." *Instituto Espanol de Estudios Estrategicos*, no. 10: 248–60.

Pellow, Deborah. 2003. "New Spaces in Accra: Transnational Houses." *City & Society* 15, no. 1: 59–86. https://doi.org/10.1525/city.2003.15.1.59.

Pérez D'Gregorio, Rogelio. 2010. "Obstetric Violence: A New Legal Term Introduced in Venezuela." *International Journal of Gynecology & Obstetrics* 111, no. 3: 201–2. https://doi.org/10.1016/j.ijgo.2010.09.002.

Pérez-Alemán, Paola. 1992. "Economic Crisis and Women in Nicaragua." In *Unequal Burden: Economic Crises, Persistent Poverty, and Women's Work*, edited by Lourdes Benería and Shelley Feldman, 239–58. Boulder, CO: Westview Press.

Pessar, Patricia R. 1999. "Engendering Migration Studies: The Case of New Immigrants in the United States." *American Behavioral Scientist* 42, no. 4: 577–600.

Poeze, Miranda, and Valentina Mazzucato. 2013. "Ghanaian Children in Transnational Families: Understanding the Experiences of Left-Behind Children through Local Parenting Norms." In *Transnational Families, Migration and the Circulation of Care: Understanding Mobility and Absence in Family Life*, edited by Loretta Baldassar and Laura Merla, 149–69. New York: Routledge.

Prado, Silvio. 2007. "The Mettle of Our Civil Society Is Going to Be Put to the Test." *Revista Envio* 307 (February). https://www.envio.org.ni/articulo/3461.

Pribilsky, Jason. 2007. *La chulla vida: Gender, Migration, and the Family in Andean Ecuador and New York City*. Syracuse, NY: Syracuse University Press.

Programa Estado de la Nación. 2001. *Estudio binacional: Situación migratoria entre Costa Rica y Nicaragua. Análisis del impacto económico y social para ambos países*. San José, Costa Rica: Organización Internacional para las Migraciones.

Programa Estado de la Nación. 2016. "Capitulo dos: Equidad e integracion social." In *Vigesimosegundo informe estado de la nación en desarrollo humano sostenible*, 85–136. San José, Costa Rica: PEN-CONARE. https://estadonacion.or.cr/informes.

Programa Estado de la Nación-Region. 2008. "Estado de La Región En Desarrollo Humano Sostenible: Un Informe Desde Centroamérica y Para Centroamérica." San José, Costa Rica: Programa Estado de la Nación-Region.

Punch, Samantha. 2012. "Studying Transnational Children: A Multi-Sited, Longitudinal, Ethnographic Approach." *Journal of Ethnic and Migration Studies* 38 (6): 1007–23.

Quesada, James. 1998. "Suffering Child: An Embodiment of War and Its Aftermath in Post-Sandinista Nicaragua." *Medical Anthropology Quarterly* 12, no. 1: 51–73.

———. 2009. "The Vicissitudes of Structural Violence: Nicaragua at the Turn of the Twenty-First Century." In *Global Health in a Time of Violence*, edited by Paul Farmer, Linda Whiteford, and Barbara Ryko-Bauer, 157–80. Santa Fe, NM: School of American Research.

Randall, Margaret. 1994. *Sandino's Daughters Revisited: Feminism in Nicaragua*. New Brunswick, NJ: Rutgers University Press.

Rapp, Rayna. 1987. "Toward a Nuclear Freeze? The Gender Politics of Euro-American Kinship Analysis." In *Gender and Kinship: Essays toward a Unified Analysis*, edited by Jane Fishburne Collier and Sylvia Junko Yanagisako, 119–31. Stanford, CA: Stanford University Press.

Ratha, Dilip, and William Shaw. 2007. "South-South Migration and Remittances." World Bank Working Paper 102. Washington, DC: World Bank.

Renda, Mary A. 2001. "'Sentiments of a Private Nature': A Comment on Ann Laura Stoler's 'Tense and Tender Ties.'" *Journal of American History* 88, no. 3: 882–87.

Rivers-Moore, Megan. 2007. "No Artificial Ingredients? Gender, Race and Nation in Costa Rica's International Tourism Campaign." *Journal of Latin American Cultural Studies* 16, no. 3: 341–57.

Rocha, José Luis. 2011. "Remittances in Central America: Whose Money Is It Anyway?" *Journal of World-Systems Research* 17, no. 2: 463–81.

Rodgers, Dennis. 2004. "'Disembedding' the City: Crime, Insecurity and Spatial Organization in Managua, Nicaragua." *Environment & Urbanization* 16, no. 2: 113–23.

———. 2007. "'Each to Their Own': Ethnographic Notes on the Economic Organisation of Poor Households in Urban Nicaragua." *Journal of Development Studies* 43, no. 3: 391–419. https://doi.org/10.1080/00220380701204240.

———. 2008. "Un Síntoma Llamado Managua." *New Left Review*, no. 49: 107–23.

———. 2012. "Haussmannization in the Tropics: Abject Urbanism and Infrastructural Violence in Nicaragua." *Ethnography* 13, no. 4: 413–38. https://doi.org/10.1177/1466138111435740.

Rubenstein, Hymie. 1983. "Caribbean Family and Household Organization: Some Conceptual Clarifications." *Journal of Comparative Family Studies* 14, no. 3: 283–98.

Ruiz Guevara, Paula. 2013. "Multa Para Quienes Empleen Inmigrantes Se Reduciría En 85%." *Prensa Libre*, October 15, 2013. http://www.prensalibre.cr/lpl/nacional/92160-multa-para-quienes-empleen-inmigrantes-se-reduciria-en-85.html.

Sadiq, Kamal. 2009. *Paper Citizens: How Illegal Immigrants Acquire Citizenship in Developing Countries*. Oxford, UK: Oxford University Press.

Sadler, Michelle, Mário JDS Santos, Dolores Ruiz-Berdún, Gonzalo Leiva Rojas, Elena Skoko, Patricia Gillen, and Jette A. Clausen. 2016. "Moving beyond Disrespect and Abuse: Addressing the Structural Dimensions of Obstetric Violence." *Reproductive Health Matters* 24, no. 47: 47–55. https://doi.org/10.1016/j.rhm.2016.04.002.

Safa, Helen I. 1995. "Economic Restructuring and Gender Subordination." *Latin American Perspectives* 22, no. 2: 32–50.

Sandoval García, Carlos. 2002. *Otros amenazantes. Los nicaragüenses y la formación de identidades nacionales en Costa Rica*. San José: Editorial de la Universidad de Costa Rica.

———. 2004. "Contested Discourses on National Identity: Representing Nicaraguan Immigration to Costa Rica." *Bulletin of Latin American Research* 23, no. 4: 434–45.

———. 2013. "To Whom and to What Is Research on Migration a Contribution." *Ethnic and Racial Studies* 36, no. 9: 1429–45. https://doi.org/10.1080/01419870.2013.800218.

———. 2015. "Nicaraguan Immigration to Costa Rica: Tendencies, Policies, and Politics." *LASA Forum* xlvi, no. 4: 7–10.

Sassen, Saskia. 2000. "Women's Burden: Countergeographies of Globalization and the Feminization of Survival." *Journal of International Affairs* 53, no. 2: 503–24.

Schneider, David M. 1984. *A Critique of the Study of Kinship*. Ann Arbor: University of Michigan Press.

Sharma, Nandita. 2006. "Global Apartheid and Nation-Statehood: Instituting Border Regimes." In *Nationalism and Global Solidarities: Alternative Projections to Neoliberal Globalisation*, edited by James Goodman and Paul James, 81–100. New York: Routledge.

Sharman, Russell Leigh. 2001. "The Caribbean Carretera: Race, Space and Social Liminality in Costa Rica." *Bulletin of Latin American Research* 20, no. 1: 46–62.

Silber, Irina Carlota. 2004. "Mothers/Fighters/Citizens: Violence and Disillusionment in Post-War El Salvador." *Gender & History* 16, no. 3: 561–87. https://doi.org/10.1111/j.0953-5233.2004.00356.x.

———. 2011. *Everyday Revolutionaries: Gender, Violence, and Disillusionment in Postwar El Salvador*. New Brunswick, NJ: Rutgers University Press.

Smith, Raymond T. 1984. *Kinship Ideology and Practice in Latin America*. Chapel Hill: University of North Carolina Press.

———. 1987. "Hierarchy and the Dual Marriage System in West Indian Society." In *Gender and Kinship: Essays toward a Unified Analysis*, edited by Jane Collier and Sylvia Yanagisako, 163–96. Stanford, CA: Stanford University Press.

Solano, Hugo. 2013. "Más de 70.000 Cruzarán La Frontera de Peñas Blancas Para Semana Santa." *La Nación*, March 19, 2013. http://www.nacion.com/archivo/mas-de-70-000-cruzaran-la-frontera-de-penas-blancas-para-semana-santa/IR3DA2P7ZVERRMJ734PEWESBYY/story.

Soto, Isa Maria. 1987. "West Indian Child Fostering: Its Role in Migrant Exchanges." In *Caribbean Life in New York City: Sociocultural Dimensions*, edited by Constance R. Sutton and Elsa Chaney, 121–37. New York: Center for Migration Studies of New York.

Spener, David. 2011. "Global Apartheid, Coyotaje, and the Discourse of Clandestine Migration." *Global Human Smuggling: Comparative Perspectives*, edited by David Kyle and Rey Koslowski, 157–85. Baltimore, MD: Johns Hopkins University Press.

Spesny Dos Santos, Sara Leon. 2015. "Undeserving Mothers? Shifting Rationalities in the Maternal Healthcare of Undocumented Nicaraguan Migrants in Costa Rica." *Anthropology & Medicine* 22, no. 2: 191–201.

Stack, Carol B. 1974. *All Our Kin: Strategies for Survival in a Black Community*. New York: Harper and Row.

Stack, Carol B., and Linda M. Burton. 1994. "Kinscripts: Reflections on Family, Generation, and Culture." In *Mothering: Ideology, Experience, and Agency*, edited by Evelyn Nakano Glenn, Grace Chang, and Linda Rennie Forcey, 33–44. New York: Routledge.

Stephen, Lynn. 1995. "Women's Rights Are Human Rights: The Merging of Feminine and Feminist Interests among El Salvador's Mothers of the Disappeared (CO-MADRES)." *American Ethnologist* 22, no. 4: 807–27.

———. 2018. "Creating Preemptive Suspects: National Security, Border Defense, and Immigration Policy, 1980–Present." *Latin American Perspectives* 45, no. 6: 7–25. https://doi.org/10.1177/0094582X17699907.

Stephens, Beth. 1988. "Changes in the Laws Governing the Parent-Child Relationship in Post-Revolutionary Nicaragua." *Hastings International and Comparative Law Review*. 12(1): 137–71.

Stoler, Ann Laura. 2001. "Tense and Tender Ties: The Politics of Comparison in North American History and (Post) Colonial Studies." *Journal of American History* 88, no. 3: 829–65.

Strathern, Marilyn. 2005a. *Kinship, Law and the Unexpected: Relatives Are Always a Surprise*. Cambridge, UK: Cambridge University Press.

———. 2005b. *Partial Connections*. Lanham, MD: Rowman Altamira.

Thompson, Charis. 2002. "Strategic Naturalizing: Kinship in an Infertility Clinic." In *Relative Values: Reconfiguring Kinship Studies*, edited by Sarah Franklin and Susan McKinnon, 175–202. Durham, NC: Duke University Press.

UNICEF / Instituto de Medicina Legal. 2019. "Estudio sobre Violencia física, sexual y psicologica en contra de Niñas, Niños y Adolescentes en Nicaragua." Managua, Nicaragua: Instituto de Medicina Legal / Fondo de las Naciones Unidas para la Infancia. https://www.unicef.org/nicaragua/informes/estudio-sobre-violencia-en-contra-de-ni%C3%B1as-ni%C3%B1os-y-adolescentes-en-nicaragua.

Van Vleet, Krista E. 2009. "'We Had Already Come to Love Her': Adoption at the Margins of the Bolivian State." *Journal of Latin American and Caribbean Anthropology* 14, no. 1: 20–43.

Vergara, William Grigsby. 2014. "35 Aniversario de La Revolución: Mis preguntas para el 19 de Julio." *Envío: Publicación mensual del instituto histórico centroamericano* 33, no. 388: 23–28.

Vogt, Wendy A. 2018. *Lives in Transit: Violence and Intimacy on the Migrant Journey*. Berkeley: University of California Press.

Voorend, Koen. 2014. "'Shifting in' State Sovereignty: Social Policy and Migration Control in Costa Rica." *Transnational Social Review* 4, no. 2–3: 207–25.

———. 2016. "A Welfare Magnet in the South?: Migration and Social Policy in Costa Rica." PhD diss., International Institute of Social Studies of Erasmus University Rotterdam. http://hdl.handle.net/1765/94392.

Voorend, Koen, and Karla Venegas B. 2014. "Tras de cuernos, palos: Percepciones sobre Costa Rica como imán de bienestar en la crisis del seguro social." *Revista de ciencias sociales*, no. 145: 13–33.

Walmsley, Emily. 2008. "Raised by Another Mother: Informal Fostering." *Journal of Latin American Anthropology* 13, no. 1: 168–95.

Weegels, Julienne. 2018. "Inside Out: Confinement, Revolt and Repression in Nicaragua." *Association for Political and Legal Anthropology* (blog), October 3, 2018. https://politicalandlegalanthro.org/2018/10/03/inside-out-confinement-revolt-and-repression-in-nicaragua.

Weismantel, Mary. 1995. "Making Kin: Kinship Theory and Zumbagua Adoptions." *American Ethnologist* 22, no. 4: 685–704.

Weston, Kath. 2001. "Kinship, Controversy, and the Sharing of Substance: The Race/Class Politics of Blood Transfusion." In *Relative Values: Reconfiguring Kinship Studies*, edited by Sarah Franklin and Susan McKinnon, 147–74. Durham, NC: Duke University Press.

Willen, Sarah S. 2007. "Toward a Critical Phenomenology of 'Illegality': State, Power, Criminalization, and Abjectivity among Undocumented Migrant Workers in Tel Aviv, Israel." *International Migration* 45, no. 3: 8–38.

Williams, Caitlin R., Celeste Jerez, Karen Klein, Malena Correa, Jose Belizan, and Gabriela Cormick. 2018. "Obstetric Violence: A Latin American Legal Response to Mistreatment during Childbirth." *BJOG: An International Journal of Obstetrics & Gynaecology* 125, no. 10: 1208–11. https://doi.org/10.1111/1471-0528.15270.

Wilson, Ara. 2015. "The Infrastructure of Intimacy." *Signs: Journal of Women in Culture and Society* 41, no. 2: 247–80. https://doi.org/10.1086/682919.

Woodruff, Christopher, and Rene Zenteno. 2007. "Migration Networks and Microenterprises in Mexico." *Journal of Development Economics* 82 (2): 509–28.

World Bank. 2017. "Nicaragua—Systematic Country Diagnostic." Washington, DC: World Bank Group. http://documents.worldbank.org/curated/en/365991498843795990/Nicaragua-Systematic-Country-Diagnostic.

———. 2021. "GDP per Capita (current US$)." *World Development Indicators*. The World Bank Group, https://data.worldbank.org/indicator/NY.GDP.PCAP.CD

Yanagisako, Sylvia Junko, and Jane Fishburne Collier. 1987. "Toward a Unified Analysis of Gender and Kinship." In *Gender and Kinship: Essays toward a Unified Analysis*, edited by Jane Fishburne Collier and Sylvia Junko Yanagisako, 14–50. Stanford, CA: Stanford University Press.

Yarris, Kristin E. 2011. "The Pain of 'Thinking Too Much': Dolor de Cerebro and the Embodiment of Social Hardship among Nicaraguan Women." *Ethos* 39, no. 2: 226–48.

———. 2017. *Care across Generations: Solidarity and Sacrifice in Transnational Families*. Stanford, CA: Stanford University Press.

Yeates, Nicola. 2009. *Globalizing Care Economies and Migrant Workers: Explorations in Global Care Chains*. Houndmills, UK: Palgrave Macmillan.

Zentgraf, Kristine M., and Norma Stoltz Chinchilla. 2012. "Transnational Family Separation: A Framework for Analysis." *Journal of Ethnic and Migration Studies* 38, no. 2: 345–66.

Zharkevich, Ina. 2019. "Money and Blood: Remittances as a Substance of Relatedness in Transnational Families in Nepal." *American Anthropologist* 121, no. 4: 884–96. https://doi.org/10.1111/aman.13316.

Zilberg, Elana. 2011. *Space of Detention: The Making of a Transnational Gang Crisis between Los Angeles and San Salvador*. Durham, NC: Duke University Press.

———. 2018. "Transnational Securityscapes." In *Panic, Transnational Cultural Studies, and the Affective Contours of Power*, edited by Micol Seigel, 199–220. New York: Routledge.

INDEX